WHAT W

CW00326387

'Assagioli's work, a fruitful marriage of spirit and psychology, is
faithfully and clearly presented in this volume. The pragmatic
simplicity of the writing reflects Piero Ferrucci's deep
understanding of the method as student and practitioner.'

— *Ram Dass*

'A most illuminating and important book.'

— *Yehudi Menuhin*

WHAT WE MAY BE

The Vision and Techniques
of Psychosynthesis

PIERO FERRUCCI
Foreword by Laura Huxley

Mandala
An Imprint of HarperCollinsPublishers

Mandala
An Imprint of Grafton Books
A Division of HarperCollins*Publishers*
77-85 Fulham Palace Road,
Hammersmith, London W6 8JB

Published by Mandala 1990
First published by Turnstone Press 1982

3   5   7   9   10   8   6   4   2

Copyright © Piero Ferrucci 1982

Piero Ferrucci asserts the moral right to
be identified as the author of this work.

British Library Cataloguing in Publication Data

Ferrucci, Piero
What we may be: the vision and techniques
of psychosynthesis.
1. Self-realization
I. Title
158'.1

ISBN 0-85274-053-1

Printed in Great Britain by
Mackays of Chatham, Kent

CONTENTS

LISTING OF EXERCISES

Epigraph

Lord, we know what we are, but know not what we may be.

William Shakespeare

The Tragedy of Hamlet, Prince of Denmark
Act IV, Scene V

FOREWORD

My first contact with psychosynthesis took place in Florence in 1954. I met there an elderly gentleman, Mr. P., who was interested in psychological and spiritual studies. We exchanged some information, and he became interested in my work. He then asked me to give him a session. (As early as 1950 I had started to develop the techniques which I later described in my books.)

I was living in a respectable and old-fashioned pension where they call you for the evening meal with a little bell, reminiscent of the Holy Mass. Mr. P. came at five o'clock. He had a deep session, eliciting a powerful reaction accompanied by tears and sobs. As this subsided, and we were proceeding on a lighter and more pleasurable note toward what I thought was the end of the session, suddenly Mr. P. found himself in Heaven: "Light, light everywhere," he kept repeating.

This was twenty-seven years ago, before I had ever heard of mystical experiences, psychedelics, and the like. But the expression on Mr. P.'s face was so beatific, and his words so beautiful, that I knew I should not disturb whatever was going on. On the other hand, it was seven-thirty, and I heard the little bell in the corridor. What was I to do? What if someone looked in my room to remind me of dinner and found a gentleman lying on my bed and repeating, "I am in the Light . . . I am in the Presence"?

Mr. P. stayed in the Light for hours of our time — an eternity for him. Then he returned to our plane of consciousness, elated but shaken. We met the next day, and to his inquiry as to what I had done and what had happened to him, I confessed that I hadn't the faintest idea. Mr. P. then said,

"It was an extraordinary experience. There is a famous psychiatrist who lives here in Florence and knows all about these spiritual states: Let's try to see him."

The following day we met Dr. Roberto Assagioli, a lively, pleasant man in his sixties. Assagioli was interested and amused by this whole episode. At some point in the conversation, Assagioli asked me in a very gentle way, "But, Miss Archera, tell me, what do you do with people?" And I answered, "Well, I don't do anything really; I just help them to get rid of their garbage. And what do *you* do?" Promptly came the reply: "I do just the same thing you do."

How much I learned from this brief encounter! Dr. Assagioli's interested but not patronizing listening, his delight in our report, and finally his simple statement—"I do just the same thing you do"—gave me a whole course in the art of human communication in the most unpretentious way. I, a neophyte who had not gone past the seventh grade, was delighted to hear that the famous doctor did just what I did!

For many years I did not hear about Assagioli, except once in a while, and then I would think, "Oh yes, that is that man who does what I do!" In 1963 Assagioli sent me a charming letter of appreciation for my book, *You Are Not the Target*. I showed it to Aldous, who was very pleased and sent him *Island* with the following inscription: "To Roberto Assagioli, in the hope that he may find something to interest him in this utopian essay on psychosynthesis."

* * *

In 1969 Piero Ferrucci came from Italy to visit me. I was then giving seminars, and the moment he came to the house I knew that he was the one I wanted as a co-leader.

Piero Ferrucci had had the most exacting and classical academic training (he had just completed his doctorate in philosophy and education), all of which was totally different from the kind of work I did in my seminars. Yet I always felt that he had a tremendous insight into people, a great capacity for empathy, and a sort of self-effacing quality. I was going to give a seminar in San Francisco and asked him to be my co-leader. This was the beginning of a wonderful collaboration. We presented seminars and workshops together, and later we teamed to write *Between Heaven and Earth* (Farrar & Straus, 1975).

Aldous's memorable lectures were tape recorded. The task of research and transcription from tape to paper requires dedication and scholarship. Piero Ferrucci's discreet editing of *The Human Situation* (Harper & Row, 1977) has been highly praised.

In 1970 Piero wrote me that he had gone to Florence to work with Assagioli. Their close collaboration went on for several years until

Assagioli's death (1974). On my trips to Italy I saw Assagioli a couple of times and had brief but remarkable contacts with him. There was a good, light feeling. Speaking of Piero Ferrucci one day, he told me, "He will carry the torch of psychosynthesis in the world." While reading *What We May Be* I remembered that phrase and the loving way in which Assagioli spoke about Piero.

What We May Be is the first comprehensive presentation of psychosynthesis. The wisdom of Assagioli and the flower of his practical spirituality spring from every page. In *What We May Be* the reader can find an extensive variety of techniques, reaching the many levels of functioning of a human being. The training of the will and of the intuition is emphasized. There are ways to reach the famous (or infamous) unconscious, which are direct and even pleasurable. Some exercises have an Eastern flavor, which, however, is never dissociated from sane Latin common sense. The boundless power of beauty, so often neglected in psychotherapy, is an ever-present offering to the reader. Here and there one hears the unforgettable bubbling of the fountain of joy—according to many mystics, the highest spiritual quality. By bringing forth our highest qualities, these techniques help to solve everyday problems in a new and unexpected way.

This book does not offer the promise of an easy and instant illumination, which breeds the twin sisters of hope and disillusion. But I couldn't imagine anyone giving it an honest try for one month without experiencing remarkable, even surprising developments—within and without.

Bookshelves are nowadays flooded with works on self-realization. Among the few valuable ones, I find *What We May Be* unmatched in its class.

Laura Archera Huxley
June 1981

ACKNOWLEDGMENTS

Roberto Assagioli devoted sixty-odd years of a long life to developing a comprehensive understanding of the human being. Psychosynthesis. It has the virtues of being open to the great contributions of science, art, and the spiritual traditions; inclusive of the essential dimensions of human existence; and at the same time fundamentally practical. I was fortunate enough not only to study psychosynthesis with Assagioli, but also to know him personally—a truly wise old man, an inexhaustible source of joy and humor.

This book, which Assagioli encouraged me to write, aims to give a basic, comprehensive, and practical account of the main themes of psychosynthesis in the field of self-realization as I learned them from him and have used them in my practice. All the general principles and the techniques described here were created or described by Assagioli. The specific details, the casework, and the ways of wording and presenting the exercises are mine. I should like to express here my enduring gratitude to Roberto Assagioli for all he has given me on all levels.

I would also like to thank Stuart Miller for his invaluable contribution of intelligence, kindness, and, above all, good taste in editing this book; Kenneth Leslie-Smith for his great patience and precision in correcting my mistakes; Laura Huxley for her inspiring hints and practical help; Diana Becchetti-Whitmore for the quality of her humor in editing and for collaborating with me through the years—a fact that has left a deep trace in all my work; Massimo Rosselli, whose basic suggestions have greatly improved the book; the late Ruth Hagy Brod, my former agent, for her tireless efforts and some excellent advice; Lisa Mitchell for being a skillful mentor in the art of writing; David Grabijn for his careful reading of the manuscript and lucid observations; Philip Winsor for his kind co-operation; Millie Loeb for her care and her editorial work; and Jean Bond for being there when it all started. And then also Madeleine Shaw, Ida Palombi, Beverly Besmer, Andrea Bocconi, Naomi Emmerling, René van Hiersel, Matilde Santandrea. Furthermore, nothing would have happened without the unchanging support of my family.

Finally, I would like to thank all my clients, students, and colleagues, who — with suggestions, reports, experiences, or just their presence — have helped in countless important ways.

The techniques presented in this book can elicit within us transformations of great interest and importance. Also, they can be used in many contexts such as individual and group therapy, the school, social work, art, and business.

The outcome of this work goes beyond the boundaries of this or that school, and touches a much wider area; *the actualization of human potentialities and the realization of the Self.* And this is one of the fields where in-depth study is most needed. Whoever is interested in this work can send the author (Piero Ferrucci, piazza Garibaldi 12, Fiesole (Firenze), Italy) written descriptions of experiences and results emerging from the use of techniques offered by this book, or from their application in a specific professional area.

Any such report would be welcomed, and regarded as a contribution to research in this field.

HOW TO USE
THIS BOOK

A few hints may help you to maximize the beneficial effects the exercises are meant to bring about:

1. *Take time*. Devote some undisturbed period of time to an exercise. Even if this is only five minutes, make sure it is a universe of its own, uninvaded by outer disturbances.

2. *Prepare*. Take a comfortable position, with spine erect and muscles relaxed. Close your eyes and breathe deeply and slowly a few times. Take at least two or three minutes for this stage. (No preparation is needed for the more active exercises.) I also suggest recording the instructions for some exercises on blank tape cassettes, so you can work with them repeatedly and listen to them without interruption.

3. *Persist*. Pick one exercise you like and stick to it for some time, even if you do not notice immediate results. Repetition of an exercise multiplies its power.

4. *Connect*. After you have performed an exercise, it will keep working silently for you. But if you want its influence to be greater, remind yourself of the experience and its meaning right in the midst of everyday life—your true and ever-present laboratory.

5.   *Work in silence.* Sharing your insights prematurely with people who may not understand them often dissipates the psychological energy you have built up.

6.   You may also want to *keep a workbook* in which you write about the insights and subtle transformations that take place.

What We May Be

Introduction:

THE VISION OF WHOLENESS

A fter years of searching, the seeker was told to go to a cave, in which he would find a well. "Ask the well what is Truth," he was advised, "and the well will reveal it to you."

Having found the well, the seeker asked that most fundamental question. And from the depths came the answer, "Go to the village crossroad: there you shall find what you are seeking."

Full of hope and anticipation, the man ran to the crossroad, to find only three rather uninteresting shops. One shop was selling pieces of metal, another sold wood, and thin wires were for sale in the third. Nothing and no one there seemed to have much to do with the revelation of Truth.

Disappointed, the seeker returned to the well to demand an explanation, but he was told only, "You will understand in the future." When the man protested, all he got in return were echoes of his own shouts. Indignant for having been made a fool of—or so he thought at the time—the seeker continued his wanderings in search of Truth. As years went by, the mcmory of his experience at the well gradually faded until one night, while he was walking in the moonlight, the sound of sitar music caught his attention. It was a wonderful music, and it was played with great mastery and inspiration.

Profoundly moved, the truthseeker felt drawn toward the player. He looked at the fingers dancing over the strings. He became aware of the sitar itself. And then suddenly he exploded in a cry of joyous recognition: the sitar was made out of wires and pieces of metal and wood just like those he had once seen in the three stores and had thought to be without any particular significance.

At last he understood the message of the well: we have already been given everything we need; our task is to assemble and use it in the appropriate way. Nothing is meaningful as long as we perceive only separate fragments. But as soon as the fragments come together into a synthesis, a new entity emerges, whose nature we could not have foreseen by considering the fragments alone.

The process of synthesis is visible everywhere in the natural as well as the strictly human world: cells assemble to form an organism, letters join to form a word, musical tones combine to form a melody, and so on. Much empirical evidence shows that synthesis can also take place in the psychology of human beings, and, conversely, that its lack causes serious difficulties.

The Italian psychiatrist Roberto Assagioli noticed several years ago that a great deal of psychological pain, imbalance, and meaninglessness are felt when our diverse inner elements exist unconnected side by side or clash with one another. But he also observed that when they merge in successively greater wholes, we experience a release of energy, a sense of well-being, and a greater depth of meaning in our lives.

Seeing that this process tends to occur naturally in all human beings, but that it often gets blocked, Assagioli devised techniques to evoke and facilitate it. After he had initially been involved with psychoanalysis (he was considered by Freud as one of its representatives in Italy during the beginning of the century), Assagioli grew dissatisfied and developed his own system, a practical psychological approach open to all contributions, that has since been applied in such fields as education, therapy and medicine. To that system he gave the name of psychosynthesis.

Assagioli's approach is not just a form of self-improvement (which promises more and more of the same thing: more energy, more concentration, more relaxation, etc.) or another form of therapy (where we only try to get rid of something). Rather, it aims to evoke wholeness and the dawn of a new and wider frame of reference in the human psyche. A woman having experienced psychosynthesis writes: "The internal process of psychosynthesis makes me think of a kaleidoscope. When the pieces of colored glass are being shaken up they are just a jumble. Then you hold the kaleidoscope steady, and they form a beautiful pattern."

To help this process take place, simple psychological exercises—such as the ones presented in this book—are used. The techniques of psychosynthesis have been tested by Assagioli and his colleagues over the past seventy years in various cultures. And they have been found to be particularly effective when used regularly. As in all disciplines, from mountain climbing to piano playing, from learning a language to dancing, practice is essential for mastering something new.

The resulting change is gradual. Years ago, when I first started to use psychosynthesis exercises on myself, I expected instant fireworks. But nothing much seemed to happen right away (though it does for some people). Like many novices, I was not always able, at first, to perform the exercises as directed: I would be distracted, get stuck in a blank state, or become restless and think of something else to do. Only after a while did I realize that big changes were going on. I have subsequently seen this pattern occurring in the majority of people who use these exercises. We become aware of the transformation long after it has started.

There is a reason for this delay: our unconscious needs time. As Assagioli puts it:

> One of the main functions of the unconscious, and at the same time one of the most important stages in the educational process, is the elaboration of experiences which one has made, the vital assimilation of what has been perceived and learned.
>
> This elaboration can be regarded as a real "psychic gestation" having strict analogies with physical gestation. Both occur in the depths, in the mystery, one in the mother's womb, the other in the intimate recesses of the unconscious; both are spontaneous and autonomous functions, but so sensitive and delicate that they can be easily disturbed by external influences; both finally climax in the crisis and the miracle of "birth," of the manifestation of a new life. [1]

This notion of gestation reminds us that in psychosynthesis we stimulate forces already present in ourselves. These forces are usually latent, but at times we can see them directly at work. They operate, for example, when an emotional wound is slowly healed; when, in a crisis, we find unsuspected strength; when, after thinking about a problem, the solution suddenly presents itself to our mind; when a second wind of energy and inspiration comes after a time of fatigue; or when a sudden and spontaneous transformation takes place in us. The effectiveness of psychosynthesis exercises stems from the activation of these positive forces.

The moment we see the range of possibilities opening in front of us, we are filled with a sense of wonder and enthusiasm. But we should also beware lest this enthusiasm lead us astray; certain distortions and consequent dangers are particularly widespread today because of the intense interest in self-realization.

Perhaps the most fundamental distortion is the belief that the technique itself is the main transforming agent, rather than the way in which it is used.

An example can perhaps illustrate this danger. A psychiatrist had been working with an autistic child. For a long time he had been trying to communicate with him, but the child had always remained locked in his own world. At last, one day, in the wake of an intuitive impulse, the psychiatrist took a pencil, threw it on the ground, and told the child: "Now pick it up and give it to me." His tone of voice carried the weight of all the hopes of all the failed attempts of the past. The atmosphere was ripe; the child did as he was asked, and in that magic moment a link of consciousness was established between the two.

The psychiatrist later talked about this experience to a group of colleagues in a conference. Soon after, many of them started mechanically throwing pencils before autistic children and waiting for the children to pick them up. Of course, what had come to be known as "the pencil technique" failed.

The same distortion may occur with psychosynthesis techniques. The all-important factor is the *attitude* with which they are used. We can use them with attention and patience as tools to transform our lives. Or we can use them mechanically or as parlor games and just waste our time. We can make of them what we want; in themselves, they hold no guarantee.

A second major distortion is narcissism—being so completely engrossed in one's inner processes and growth as to exclude any concern for other human beings and society at large. Victims of this distortion forget that no technique we employ in personal growth has any value unless it affects our relationships and that, conversely, relationships themselves can be a major stimulus to individual evolution. As Martin Buber said, "Man becomes an I through a You,"[2] and there is no true growth that remains purely within the circle of the individual.

A recent wave of criticism, however, has gone to the extreme of condemning all forms of interest in personal growth as a form of narcissism. Some critics equate self-realization with self-absorption, seeing it as "a retreat to purely personal satisfaction."[3]

Such a way of thinking, however valid it may be in some instances, ignores the fact that the way people act—what they produce and express and the way they relate to others—depends on what they *are*.

If a person's thinking is sloppy and prejudiced, for example, he or she cannot participate intelligently in the decisions of the community. Those who lack sensitivity to beauty and a sense of the whole cannot be ecologically aware. Those who have not met their inner demons will not be able to take part in building a more open society. And if their relationships are polluted, they won't be able to contribute to social harmony in any effective way or to envisage a future consistent with their highest potential.

Any social change brought about by such people hopelessly perpetuates and multiplies their shortcomings on a collective scale. For this reason we focus on the individual, while avoiding the pitfall of narcissism.

A parallel danger is the inordinate thirst for experiences, unaccompanied by any effort to understand them or to anchor them in everyday life. This thirst for stimulation causes individuals to move from one "trip" to another, collect all the psychotechnologies on the market, and become true "consciousness junkies." These people hanker for excitement, change, and "altered states of consciousness"; and, if mere variety of experience—rather than its assimilation—were the measure of maturity, they would be the most evolved people around.

A sense of grandiosity is another trap in which we may easily get caught: a momentary euphoria leads us to expect instant, total, and permanent results. The magical wish to live happily ever after lurks in the back of our minds, ready to entice us into the false belief that we have achieved more than is possible. But the only way to accomplish valuable results in the work of self-realization is by being realistic about our human limitations. We have to be conscious of our relative smallness, of how many difficulties life presents, how weak the body and volatile the feelings can be at times, how easily we can be influenced, how complex human existence is, how many vectors impinge on all of us, how little we as a species know about anything, how likely chance is to interfere with our plans, and how mysterious life is at the core.

Not that we should look upon these facts as fatal handicaps—on the contrary, awareness of them can be incorporated into our unfoldment wisely and can lead us to realize more completely the full significance of being human.

For the reasons suggested above, psychosynthesis values times of darkness as much as periods of joy and enlightenment.

It emphasizes the importance of using obstacles as steps to growth rather than promising their complete disappearance.

It opts more for doubting and risking rather than for guaranteed safety or ecstasy.

It prefers the creativity of confusion to the deceptive "clarity" of ready-made answers.

It reminds us of effort as much as effortlessness.

It acknowledges the immense variability of human beings and therefore promises no standard results.

It praises the unexpected event that shatters in one moment our model of how it all should be.

In short, psychosynthesis recognizes our complexity as well as the intricacy of the human situation, and it sees no possibility of a universal recipe. As Assagioli was fond of humorously saying to those protesting against this reality, "It's not my fault if the universe is so complicated!"

This realization leads us to consider perhaps the greatest and most common of all dangers: one-sidedness. Were we to develop only one part of our being to the exclusion of all the others—be it the body, or feelings, or "spirit," or what have you—that part would be invested with a power it doesn't deserve. It could become demonic and make of us limited and, perhaps, even fanatical beings. A story told to me by a student of psychosynthesis is quite illustrative in this regard:

> When I was a child I played in bed at night with all kinds of fantasies. My favorite one was that I was a submarine, moving in the depths of the ocean. But that limited me from going on land, so I had to imagine I was a tank, free to roam on all lands of the earth, on the mud, on the sand, on the stones—everywhere.
>
> But as a tank I also felt incomplete. Because how could I reach the sky? So I had to become an airplane. But then airplanes can only fly. Finally one night I decided that I was going to be all three at the same time—some kind of fantastic machine that could fly in space, explore the abysses of the ocean, rapidly and easily move on land. I could reach everywhere, and that gave me a real joy.
>
> Working in psychosynthesis reminds me of that distant insight of my childhood. It equips me to move at all levels; it has taught me familiarity with all the various parts of myself.

When it is balanced and healthy, human growth proceeds in all directions: it looks like an expanding sphere rather than a straight line. It is for precisely this reason that psychosynthesis endeavors to take into consideration all the dimensions of human life which truly matter and which, if left unacknowledged, lead to a fragmented, even absurd existence:

The emergence of will and self-determination

The sharpening of the mind

The enjoyment of beauty
The enrichment of imagination
The awakening of the intuition
The realization of love
The discovery of the Self and of its purpose

Chapter 1

FOCUS

The other day I had a fight with a taxi driver. The man was rude and brutal, and I was so upset that afterward my hands were trembling. Later I couldn't get the experience out of my mind. This lasted for the whole day until I performed the exercise, which immediately enabled me to see the situation in its right proportions. My reactions are often melodramatic, but performing this exercise throughout the past week has had a liberating effect on me.

The "exercise" this woman refers to is remarkably simple. With eyes closed, she visualized a number and held it in her mind for three minutes without thinking of anything else. Although it generally takes time and practice to acquire the ability to perform this visualization without being distracted, it is surprising to see what progress people can make in this direction in the course of only a few days of training.

Miracles? No. Through the psychological exercises contained in this chapter and in the rest of the book, we can gain a sense of mastery over our psychological processes. We are already used to working well with material things: steering wheels, typewriters, toothbrushes, knives, buttons and so on. We can now become equally accustomed to dealing consciously and effectively with the stuff of our inner world.

The woman mentioned above was able to focus her scattered energies by doing this simple exercise and this achievement in itself had a healing effect on her whole personality. In addition, focus brings concentration—one of the most basic psychological skills. As the philosopher Keyserling puts it, "The ability to concentrate is a real propelling power of the totality of our psychic mechanism. Nothing elevates our capacity of action more than its development. Any success, no matter in which area, can be explained by the intelligent use of this capacity. No obstacle can permanently withstand the exceptional power of maximum concentration."[1]

Any human function—be it physical or psychological—atrophies when it is not used. Uncultivated and unexercised, our psychological functions tend to waste away, so that only those which habit compels us to use will survive. This truth was elegantly expressed by Sir Francis Galton, writing on the function of imagination:

> The pleasure its use can afford is immense. I have many correspondents who say that the delight of recalling beautiful scenery and great works of art is the highest they know; they carry whole picture galleries in their minds. Our bookish and wordy education tends to repress this valuable gift of nature. A faculty that is of importance in all technical and artistic occupations, that gives accuracy to our perceptions, and justness to our generalizations, is starved by lazy misuse, instead of being cultivated judiciously in such a way as will on the whole bring the best return.[2]

The following brief exercises can be done at any time during the day and do not require much time or call for special conditions.

VISUAL EVOCATION

Close your eyes and visualize the following:

A pen slowly writing your name on paper.

A single-digit number. Then substitute a two-digit one, then a three-digit one, and so on until you reach the limit of the number of digits that you can retain. Keep that number in front of your inner eye for two minutes.

Various colored shapes: a golden triangle, a violet circle, a blue five-pointed star, and so on.

Abstract images like letters of the alphabet or numbers on a blackboard may be more difficult to visualize than more complex ones with some appeal or familiarity. Thus you will probably find it easier to visualize people you love than a blue triangle, to imagine your favorite landscape than to see the number 716 on a blackboard. But for this very reason, the simpler and emotionally more neutral objects often prove particularly effective for *training the imagination*.

Do not be discouraged if, at first, you are unable to perform even such simple inner actions as these. If the images do not appear, if they are unstable and fuzzy, or they are vivid but vanish quickly, these are the precise reasons why such exercises can be useful. Therefore, try to hold a single image in your mind for some time—at least two or three minutes. It will probably change or disappear, and you will find yourself thinking of something else. Gently and patiently, bring your attention back to it.

These exercises are preparation for the more complex techniques described in later chapters. Though simple, they are more than basic drills, and they can also be profoundly useful by themselves in a variety of ways. A schoolteacher reports:

> I started a twelve-year-old child visualizing geometrical shapes and numbers. At that time she was having a lot of difficulty in school, and her marks were very low, especially in English and mathematics. She had, for example, great trouble in learning the present tense of the English verb "to be." I asked her to visualize a blackboard and imagine writing the English and the Italian forms with chalk and then reading two or three times what she had visualized. After a short time she remembered the verbs perfectly. After she had done some of the exercises for a few days, I saw a radical change in her behavior in school. She was alert, and as soon as she encountered some difficulty she would come and ask me to explain it to her so as to understand where she was wrong. Finally, she began to find the explanations by herself, I being just a prop.

TACTILE EVOCATION

Now imagine the following, this time focusing on the sensations of touch:

Shaking someone's hand. Feel its surface, its temperature, its pressure on your own hand.

Stroking a cat or dog. Feel its hair.

Holding a lemon in your hand. Feel its surface.

Touching:

the bark of a tree
some freshly fallen snow
the surface of a flower—but very gently, so as not to bruise it
sand
the water of a waterfall
a feather.

When you first do this exercise, combine the imagined tactile sensations with the visualization of what you are touching; then imagine the tactile sensation only. Through the tactile sensations, *receive* the thing you are touching.

We can learn to direct our attention through these exercises. This is not as easy as one might assume, since we are often bombarded by external and internal stimuli rather than being under our own control. In using these exercises we gradually come to see how focusing our attention can be made to replace its usually scattered state. For a few moments, the image we have deliberately chosen to focus upon will remain in the foreground of our awareness, and everything else will disappear. In time, the result will be an ever greater facility in placing and holding our attention at will on any object we choose.

OLFACTORY EVOCATION

Imagine that you are smelling:

Your favorite perfume

Gasoline

A flower

An herb

Clean mountain air in a pine forest

Burning wood

The ocean

Mint

Bread coming out of the oven

KINESTHETIC EVOCATION

And now for the kinesthetic sense, the sense through which we are aware of the body and its movements: Imagine that you are

Walking and then running along a beach: feel every movement of your muscles.

Driving a car: sense with precision each movement you make in turning the steering wheel, pressing the pedals, and so on.

Swimming, playing tennis or basketball, or practicing any other sport you enjoy.

Chopping wood with an ax.

Whenever we explore and voluntarily make use of a new part of ourselves, we experience intrinsic joy. There is a special delight in learning a new skill which is also subtle and delicate.

TASTE EVOCATION

In imagination, experience the taste, temperature, and texture of:

A banana

Yogurt

Almonds

Whipped cream

In imagination, sit down to your favorite dish and eat it. Pay attention to the taste and texture of each mouthful. Feel the knife and the fork in your fingers and the way they manage the food.

How do you feel when you perform these exercises? One important reminder: it is of the essence that you do not make yourself tense. A fencing master used to say, "Hold the foil as if you were holding a bird: not too tight, otherwise the bird dies; not too loose, or the bird flies away." The same rule is true for attention. Whenever you find yourself frowning or tense while doing these exercises, stop. You are killing the bird. Whenever you find your mind wandering, stop. The bird has flown away.

AUDITORY EVOCATION

Evocation of imaginary sounds is for some people more difficult than evocation of perceptions associated with the other
senses; yet, like the others, it increases the keenness of our
actual perceptions surprisingly. A colleague of mine writes:

After performing the exercise without apparent success for fifteen days, a forty-year-old man came to see me to tell me about
his great wonder. He had awakened one morning and thought
he had been dreaming of the sound of bells. He then realized
that the sound of bells was real and coming from a church near
his home. His astonishment was due to his hearing this sound
for the first time since he began living there.

Close your eyes and listen to these imaginary sounds:

> A voice calling your name
>
> The noise of traffic
>
> The sound of rain
>
> People at a party
>
> Waves breaking on the shore
>
> Children playing
>
> A squeaking door
>
> A gong, very gradually dying away into silence

Chapter 2

GLEAMS OF A
REMOTER WORLD

Some of the attitudes operating within us which once had meaning may now be obsolete. To illustrate this fact, the Swiss psychologist Baudouin used the following example:

> A bus passenger conforms to the official rule that he must hold his bus ticket at all times available for inspection. Leaving the bus, he goes on a shopping trip. Hours later, while juggling bulky packages, wallet and pocket change, he realizes that he has continuously held that ticket handy for inspection.
>
> What psychological mechanism was responsible for this exercise in futility? Some might classify it as inertia or automatism. However, if automatism is at work here, it is not a pure automatism: the original command became an unconscious directive in the man's functioning, but in addition it set off a series of ingenious and complex contortions requiring initiative and determination, in order to fulfill the rule as conscientiously as though life itself depended on the dutiful display of the expired bus ticket.[1]

We still have fears when there is no reason to be afraid. We cling to outdated resentments. We are depressed without cause. We hang onto our ticket long after we have left the bus. When the patterns that force us to such useless expenditures of energy are exposed, they are de-energized and often disappear, as in the example of the bus ticket, so new, creative tendencies can take their place.

This task is easier to undertake with the help of a guide because the old patterns have a tendency to perpetuate themselves and to employ all kinds of tricks to avoid being unmasked. However, we have at our disposal some direct and powerful means for discovering by ourselves the existence as well as the origin of our unconscious, obsolete habits.

By definition, the unconscious is that part of us which is not immediately accessible to our awareness. We can know it only through accidental occurrences, like slips of the tongue, or by using specific techniques devised to bypass conscious censorship: dream analysis, imagery, writing, body movement, free association, various kinds of tests, stimulus words, and so on. To these can be added free drawing, which is perhaps the easiest and most practical technique.

In free drawing we picture whatever comes to mind, without any particular concern for style, method, or subject. Then we look at the product and try to interpret it.* The results can be several:

Cleansing. We regard a lack of physical hygiene as uncivilized. But what about psychological hygiene? Our contemporary civilization elicits a great variety of feelings while at the same time inhibiting their expression. The result is that repressed emotional material determines our attitudes, blocks free movement within our psychophysical system, and generates a number of minor and major disturbances. Free drawing gives a visible shape outside ourselves to the unconscious psychic energy blocking us from within, and thus it loosens its hold on us.

Understanding. By observing this manifestation of forces objectified on paper, we can gain a better perspective on our inner worlds.

To account for variations in the orbit of Uranus that could not be explained by the action of known forces, the French astronomer Leverrier postulated the existence of an unknown planet. Thus was Neptune discovered. The unconscious forces within us might be compared to the unknown planet: they exert an influence on our behavior without our knowledge. With understanding of our free drawings will come insight into what determines our actions and attitudes.

---

*Drawings could also be made on a predetermined *theme*: we can draw a quality, a problem, a project, an obstacle, a trauma, the future, a relationship, a situation, and so on.

We could also put it this way: it is as if we had a machine similar to a television screen, and this machine could tune in to our unconscious and transform its subtle, invisible impulses into visible manifestations of colored energy fields on a screen so that by looking at it we could clearly and visibly perceive the interplay of forces within ourselves. As we shall see, free drawings display, with richness and often with precision, the energies and feelings that mysteriously motivate our lives—tendencies that no words can describe.

Liberation. Understanding leads to release from the control of unconscious energies. Just like the man who realized that he need not retain his ticket any longer, we may find ourselves able to let go of what was previously directing us in a blind and automatic way.

FREE DRAWING

1. Take several colored pencils or crayons and some pieces of paper. Before beginning to draw, allow yourself a few moments of relaxed, calm awareness.

2. Now let your hand draw, and watch with mild curiosity what is taking shape on the paper.

3. Allow your hand to draw absolutely anything it wants, abstract or concrete. Let the quality of what comes up be whatever it wants to be, even if it does not coincide with your present image of yourself. And as you draw, let your hand movements be the way they need to be—jerky or flowing, quick or slow, etc.

4. When you feel that you have finished, study your drawing. Is it really finished, or does it lack a final touch? If so, complete it in any way you like.

We should greet our drawing as if it were a person coming from a distant land whose customs are very different from those of our own country. Instead of judging it in an intellectual manner, we should listen to the drawing's story. This drawing may represent something new and different from what our surface mind feels like. We seek to resonate with it and intuitively capture the message it gives us about ourselves.

Then we look at it again, in a more analytical way. What is its style? (Is it childish, elaborate, nervous, mechanical, etc.?) What use did we make of color? (Note the presence or absence of color, contrast or harmony, bright or dark hues, and so on.) How is space represented? (Is it crowded, empty, oppressive, impersonal, cozy, irregularly occupied?) Is the drawing static or dynamic? (If movement is present, note whether it is flowing, jagged, impeded, violent, etc.) What are the mutual relations of the elements represented? (Are they in contraposition, isolated, dancing together, drawing apart?) What is the general atmosphere (gloomy, joyous, intense, etc.)?

After transforming inner forces into visible shapes, we try to transform visible shapes into ordinary understanding and words. As we stay with the drawing, its colors, forms, and various details may arouse in us a series of free associations, a nuance of feeling, a forgotten memory, an intuitive flash.

After a while, we turn the drawing over and write what comes to mind. It should be clear by now that interpretation is more than an intellectual operation; that we do not need any fixed code with which to decipher our drawing; and that it is insight that counts, not speculation. If insight does not occur, we lay our drawing aside and look at it after we have made some other drawings, or after a period of time. Our perception of it may then be richer. And even when our drawings remain meaningless hieroglyphs, we will have at least partially satisfied a vital need—the need for expression. Many people find a new, childlike delight in playing with pencils or crayons, in bypassing the control of the intellect, and in experiencing the pure fun of gratuitous creation.

As we make several free drawings, we may observe the emergence of a multiplicity of forms. We may find ourselves drawing flowers side by side with demons, UFOs, headless people, gigantic ants, unfamiliar faces, and so on. In this way we become conscious of the unbelievable variety of energies within us. Each of them can be regarded as a real psychic entity with a life of its own. And the fact that we are normally unable to see these lives directly or touch them does not mean that they don't exist. A young man writes:

> I used to have nightmares about rats and mice. To me rats have always instinctively symbolized something terrible, loathsome, disgusting, and unmentionable. Something I did not want to look at directly, so horrifying was the sight. So when I was asked to do some free drawings, rats came to my mind, and I drew them: rats with big teeth, rats with red eyes, rats coming out of filth, rats that brought destruction and rage, rats threatening the world, rats lurking in darkness waiting to attack, rats hungrily devouring corpses and gnawing bones, rats jumping out of closets and running all over the place.
>
> To me they represented the essence of evil. I didn't stop to ask myself if that meant just my own evil side or evil-in-the-world. I

just drew it. It felt scary in the beginning; then I even enjoyed it and felt a release.

Two nights later I had a dream. It was a dream of rats, but not a nightmare. It was the paradise of rats. They were all playing and dancing, and singing songs, and were in some way transfigured. Some of them wore nice clothes, and the fur of the ones without clothes was nice and soft—I almost wanted to touch it. The whole atmosphere was joyful, and I woke up with these words in mind: "the joy of recognition." It was as if the rats were happy because I had acknowledged their existence. As soon as I accepted them, they were transfigured.

Although I still have a lot of work to do, I feel much more solid and comfortable with the irrational within myself.

Sometimes the transformations are such that one hesitates to give free drawing the whole credit. Take the case of Ilaria. While she had previously used several psychosynthetic techniques, one free drawing intensified her awareness of what she was doing to herself and thus brought about her release. It was a drawing of two men wrestling. "They are trying to castrate each other," explained Ilaria. "The woman standing by, without arms and without legs, powerless, is me." The drawing was all in black except for the heart of the woman, which was red but shackled with two black bands. Two insights came to Ilaria as she pondered the meaning of this drawing. One was about her attitude toward what had been happening around her: "I was withdrawing, and impotently watching the cruelty of the world," she said. The other insight concerned that red shackled heart, inside which Ilaria sensed great vitality. When I asked her how she was able to utilize these insights to transform her everyday life, Ilaria replied:

Before, when I found myself in a group of people, I would leave or be silent unless they invited me to talk. Now that I am aware of this self-limiting pattern, I just go ahead and speak even if I am not asked.

In my yoga practice I am succeeding with postures I couldn't reach before, because my body was all tensed up with this fear of expressing myself.

When I see sad people, I no longer think I'm the cause of their sadness, I break through my blocks, and a word or a gesture is enough to start communication.

A gesture.... One thing I had noticed about Ilaria was that when she talked to me she kept her hands out of sight, behind her back, most of the time. This pattern she later unknowingly represented in the woman without arms in her drawing. Now, when she talks about her discoveries, Ilaria draws graceful designs in the air with her hands.

We should not, however, necessarily expect such major insights from any one drawing. The work is usually humble and slow. Gradually we get acquainted with our unconscious styles, moods, and drives. And we accomplish results of real value by making a series of free drawings. From such a series we can discover basic patterns in ourselves which we couldn't possibly notice by looking at a single drawing. Interpretation becomes easier because our perspective is wider. Moreover, really important themes will manifest themselves again and again in various forms, so that having more material at our disposal enables us to discriminate between the casual and the essential in what we have drawn. Finally, we may discover that in a series of drawings made over a short period of time, a true transformation may take place: the stormier but more ephemeral feelings are first materialized on paper, allowing deeper and more serene layers of our being to subsequently come to light. A woman writes:

> I was going through a period of fear because of having to be alone at Christmas time. I was in a very emotional state and didn't quite know how to cope with it.
>
> So I started to do free drawing. Each drawing took me into another dimension, and each was accompanied by a sense of letting go. I continued to draw every day, until finally a sense of completion came. At that point I experienced tremendous clarity, I was in touch with my intuition, and several synchronicities started to occur.
>
> I felt as though I had moved above the clouds, in the light of the sun.

After some practice in free drawing, we can continue our self-exploration in at least three other ways: body movement, imagery, and writing. As in the case of drawing, they can be used freely or they can focus deliberately on a specific theme or block.

With body movement, we become aware of the organic resonance of a block or psychological contents at the physical level, and then we express it in a posture or a movement, as if we were a statue symbolizing that block or a dancer representing it in our own choreography. In this way we gain a greater understanding of it, and at times we trigger some change. People who are more "into their bodies" than others sometimes feel it is particularly useful to work at this level; they discover that as long as they work at psychological or mental levels only, they cannot fully grasp what is going on inside them.

Using imagery consists in letting the psychological content we are working on take a concrete shape in front of our mind's eye. We are working on, say, fear. What color is it? What is its size and shape? How does it feel if we touch it? How does it smell? What does it sound like, and, if it has a voice, what does it say to us?

Valuable personal changes can occur, especially with highly charged negative images. On countless occasions, I have seen my clients meet octopi, mice, bats, giant spiders, imaginary monsters of all kinds and shapes, witches and sorcerers, and many other sinister beings. My clients were often frightened by them and felt they pictorially represented some deep-seated, unresolved aspect of themselves. Almost invariably I asked them to simply face those frightening creatures, become familiar with them, understand them, listen to their messages. The secret is always to have the courage to face the negative image and the patience to stay with it. Very often a transformation happens when we face it long enough and let the corresponding feelings freely emerge.

However, if you come up with some image that is frightening even after you have fully confronted it, I suggest making a drawing or drawings out of it. In time, the expressed image may more fully reveal itself and assume its rightful transformation into something more obviously useful.

Sometimes it is helpful to work with body and imagery at the same time, either by starting with a body sensation or block and then letting an image emerge that represents it or by being aware of specific, even subtle bodily reactions which may be going on as we work on an image.

Writing, the third method, can be much more powerful than we may think at first. If we start by freely writing about the issue that concerns us, we will find ourselves expressing things not previously thought of. We have to formulate *explicitly* that which we feel implicitly, thereby clarifying to ourselves what may have been a confused morass. In this process we may also come to new conclusions and ideas about courses of action to take.

We should not be surprised that unconscious material surfaces so readily in our writing. No great barrier separates the underworld of the unconscious from the lighted area of consciousness. On the contrary, a continual osmosis goes on between the two. Writing stimulates this interchange and allows us to observe, direct, and understand it.*

In all these methods, awareness is the first stage. After becoming familiar with our limiting patterns, after looking at them objectively, something will already have changed, for any pattern that is discovered—and

*Each one of these modes—free drawing, body movement, imagery, and writing—is a specific way of working on a problem or exploring a part of ourselves. In future exercises, use the modes you find yourself most comfortable with, even when you are not specifically instructed to do so.

fully faced, changes. After this first stage of assessment, it is then possible to replace destructive tendencies with more functional ones. We create a new line of force it is like cutting a new pathway in the jungle. Having become aware of the nature of our fear, for example, we substitute courage for it; we replace a tendency to depression with joy, or an attitude of suspicion and hostility with openness.

At other times we may see how an apparently negative element or pattern holds in itself the seed of a natural unfoldment. Anger can become self-affirmation, excessive sensitivity can evolve into love, stubbornness can be transformed into tenacity. In this case, as we shall see later in this book, it is our task to facilitate that unfoldment by the appropriate means.

To sum up: in an allegory by Plato, the guardian of a big beast observes it carefully. He gradually learns how to recognize its desires and irritations, how to approach it, where it should and should not be touched, at which moments it becomes restless or calm, what sounds it makes according to what mood, by which words it is soothed or upset. Consequently, the guardian creates a *method* out of all these observations: he calls "good" what the great beast likes and "bad" what it is disgusted by, and he subordinates his perception of reality to the beast's whims. He then calls his overall outlook "wisdom."

For Plato, of course, the big beast represents society intimidating the individual into submission and then flattering him with the illusion of lucidity. But the metaphor is also valid for what happens *within* an individual. The great beast can then be seen as representing our opaque, unconscious, unregenerated side. We may be totally at its mercy and not even know it. But we can face the great beast and transform it from an all-powerful master into a useful ally.

Chapter 3

MAPS

A fter the first exercises aimed at exploring the unconscious, in the following chapters we will proceed to the other basic themes of psychosynthesis. But before continuing this venture, it is wise to get acquainted in a general way with the various dimensions we are visiting and the words we will adopt. To do this, we will use two maps: visual, schematic representations of our inner reality. Like all maps, these are impoverished, static versions of the actual territory. Nevertheless, they are useful tools to facilitate exploration and prevent misunderstanding.

Assagioli's so-called "egg-diagram" (Figure 1) represents our total psyche. The three horizontal divisions of the oval stand for our past, present and future. All three are active in us, although in different ways. The *"lower unconscious"* (1) mainly represents our personal psychological past in the form of repressed complexes and long-forgotten memories.

As we have seen in the preceding chapter, if we wish to consciously encourage our growth we need to investigate our lower unconscious. Otherwise, it may be the source of trouble, storing repressed energy, controlling our actions, and robbing us of our freedom.

The *middle unconscious* (2) is where all skills and states of mind reside which can be brought at will into our *field of consciousness* (4), which—for you at this moment—is this book and the words you are reading.

Our evolutionary future comprises the states of being, of knowing, and of feeling which we call the *superconscious* (3). In the words of Assagioli, the *superconscious* is the region from which "we receive our higher

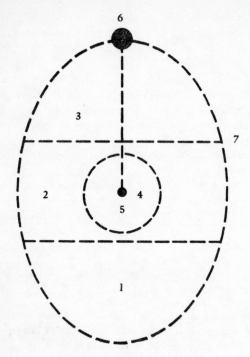

1. "Lower" unconscious
2. Middle unconscious
3. Superconscious
4. Field of consciousness
5. Personal self, or "I"
6. Transpersonal Self
7. Collective unconscious

Figure 1. Our Psyche

intuitions and inspirations—artistic, philosophical or scientific, ethical 'imperatives' and urges to humanitarian and heroic action. It is the source of the higher feelings, such as altruistic love; of genius and of the states of contemplation, illumination, and ecstasy."[1] The exploration of the superconscious is one of our great tasks.

The distinction between the "lower" and the "higher" unconscious, or superconscious, is developmental, not moralistic. The lower unconscious merely represents the most primitive part of ourselves, the beginner in us, so to speak. It is not *bad,* it is just *earlier.* Conversely, the superconscious constitutes all that we still can reach in the course of our evolution. It is not, however, a mere abstract possibility, but a living reality, with an existence and powers of its own.

Our psyche is not isolated. It is bathed in the sea of what Carl Jung called the collective unconscious (7). In Jung's words, the collective unconscious is "the precondition of each individual psyche, just as the sea is the carrier of the individual wave."[2] Notice that all lines are dotted to signify that no rigid compartments impede interplay among all levels.

Who experiences all these levels? The *self* does. In the early stages of human development, awareness of the self is nonexistent. For most of us, it now exists in a more or less veiled and confused way. Our task is to gain experience of it in its pure state as the personal self, or "*I*" (5).

The personal self is a reflection or an outpost of the Transpersonal Self (6)—enough to give us a sense of centeredness and identity. It lives at the level of individuality, where it can learn to regulate and direct the various elements of the personality. Awareness of the personal self is a precondition for psychological health.

Identification with the Transpersonal Self is a rare occurrence—for some individuals, the culmination of years of discipline; for others, a spontaneous extraordinary experience. It was described in ancient times with the Sanskrit words *sat-chit-ananda:* being-consciousness-bliss. The Transpersonal Self, while retaining a sense of individuality, lives at the level of universality, in a realm where personal plans and concerns are overshadowed by the wider vision of the whole. The realization of the Transpersonal Self is the mark of spiritual fulfillment.

Personal and Transpersonal Self are in fact the same reality experienced at different levels: our true essence beyond all masks and conditionings.

Assagioli's "Star diagram" (Figure 2) represents *our psychological functions*. It clarifies other aspects of our inner world, particularly the relationship of our several psychological functions to the self and the will.

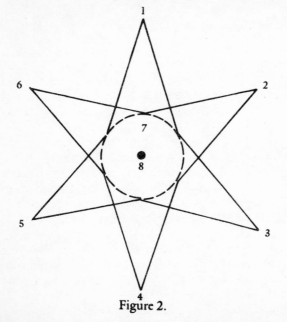

1. Sensation
2. Emotion-feeling
3. Impulse-desire
4. Imagination
5. Thought
6. Intuition
7. Will
8. Personal self, or "I"

Figure 2.

In the process of psychosynthesis, a person passes from being a disordered collection of clashing tendencies to being a meaningfully harmonized whole around a center: the self. Through the action of the will, the self can then regulate each function of the psychophysical organism.

Chapter 4

A MULTITUDE
OF LIVES

O ne of the most harmful illusions that can beguile us is probably the
belief that we are an indivisible, immutable, totally consistent being.
And finding out that the contrary is true is among the first tasks—and
possibly surprises—that confront us in the adventure of our psychosynthesis.

We can easily perceive our actual multiplicity by realizing how often
we modify our general outlook, changing our model of the universe with
the same facility with which we change dress. Thus, life may appear to us at
any time as a routine, a dance, a race, an adventure, a nightmare, a riddle, a
merry-go-round, etc.

Our varying models of the universe color our perception and influence our way of being. And for each of them we develop a corresponding
self-image and a set of body postures and gestures, feelings, behaviors,
words, habits, and beliefs. This entire constellation of elements constitutes
in itself a kind of miniature personality, or, as we will call it, a subpersonality.

Subpersonalities are psychological satellites, coexisting as a multitude of lives within the overall medium of our personality. Each subpersonality has a style and a motivation of its own, often strikingly dissimilar
from those of the others. Says the Portuguese poet Fernando Pessoa, "In
every corner of my soul there is an altar to a different god."[1]

Each of us is a crowd. There can be the rebel and the intellectual, the seducer and the housewife, the saboteur and the aesthete, the organizer and the bon vivant—each with its own mythology, and all more or less comfortably crowded into one single person. Often they are far from being at peace with one another. As Assagioli wrote, "We are not unified; we often *feel* that we are, because we do not have many bodies and many limbs, and because one hand doesn't usually hit the other. But, metaphorically, that is exactly what does happen within us. Several subpersonalities are continually scuffling: impulses, desires, principles, aspirations are engaged in an unceasing struggle."[2]

RECOGNIZING SUBPERSONALITIES

Our job begins by recognizing our major subpersonalities; getting acquainted with them will take us a long way toward being able to control and ultimately harmonize their energies. The following exercise will introduce you to this concept in a more direct manner:

1. Consider one of your prominent traits, attitudes, or motives.

2. With your eyes closed, become aware of this part of you. Then let an image emerge representing it. It may be a woman, a man, an animal, an elf, an object, yourself in disguise, a monster, or anything else in the universe. Do not consciously try to find an image. Let it emerge spontaneously, as if you were watching a screen, not knowing what will shortly appear on it.

3. As soon as the image has appeared, give it the chance to reveal itself to you without any interference or judging on your part.

Let it change if it tends to do so spontaneously, and let it show you some of its other aspects if it wants to.

Get in touch with the general feeling that emanates from it.

4. Now let this image talk and express itself. Give it space, so to speak, for doing so; in particular, find out about its needs. Talk with it (even if your image is an object, it can talk back to you; anything is possible in the imaginary world).

You have in front of you a subpersonality—an entity with a life and intelligence of its own.

5. Now open your eyes, and record in a notebook everything that happened so far.

Then give this subpersonality a name—any name that fits and will help you to identify it in the future: the Complainer, the Artist, the

Bitch, Santa Claus, the Skeptic, "Jaws," the Insecure One, the Octopus, the Drunken Sailor, the Clown, "I Told You So," and so on.
    Finally, write about its traits, habits, and peculiarities.

6. After you have identified and exhaustively described one subpersonality you can go on to the others. But take your time and work on each one alone until you feel finished. The process requires merely picking a few more of your prominent traits, attitudes, or motives and going through steps 1 to 5 for each one.

You can also discover other subpersonalities by taking stock of the various ways in which you look at life, by reviewing your behavior in various situations, and by considering your various styles of being you. Discovering our subpersonalities in these ways gives us a quick means to gain a relatively clear picture of our inner life. In turn, this clarity can enable us to be more at home with all those unknown inner guests having their own party—or battle—inside us.

When we recognize a subpersonality, we are able to step outside it and observe it. In psychosynthesis we call this process *"dis-identification."* Because we all have a tendency to identify with—to become one with—this or that subpersonality, we come implicitly to believe that we *are* it. Dis-identification consists of our snapping out of this illusion and returning to our self. It is often accompanied by a sense of insight and liberation.

At certain other times subpersonality recognition is also accompanied by a healthy feeling of dismay or alarm, as, for instance, when a woman who had suddenly recognized her Victim subpersonality exclaimed: "If I stop complaining, what else can I do?" Still other people, after having recognized a subpersonality, especially a very deeply ingrained one, suddenly feel naked and defenseless, as if their armor had dissolved—which is exactly what has happened. In all cases, however, no matter what the initial emotional response, there is more real awareness and, therefore, more freedom. But let's look at a few concrete examples.

Robert, a young doctor, is blocked by an inner rigidity which interferes with his relationships and is otherwise a nuisance. A subpersonality is continuously judging and criticizing whatever he and others do or say. It's like having a nonstop internal moralist preaching all the time.

When he deliberately evokes this quality and tries to let an image emerge, Robert sees a bespectacled, old-fashioned priest, grim, stern, and dressed entirely in black. As soon as he can see the image clearly, he also discerns the outlines of the rigidity which has been controlling him. While before he would feel this as a vague discomfort and merely endure it, now for the first time he is able to shake it off.

After repeatedly dis-identifying from the rigid priest subpersonality, Robert writes: "I am less judgmental with others now, especially my parents, and I am more able to understand why they behaved the way they did. I am also less impatient with myself and feel more secure. I can see that life is complicated and mysterious, and my sense of understanding and compassion for others and myself has increased."

Marco is a tall man in his early thirties. When he comes to my groups he is often attacked by some of the other members. Without being aware of it, he has a strong holier-than-thou attitude that puts other people off. They then become angry with him and often make him a scapegoat.

Marco soon finds out that all this happens because of a subpersonality which he calls "the Baron." The Baron is the result of various mannerisms that Marco adopts to astound others with how much he knows so they will hang on his words. This is how he describes it:

> The image that represents this subpersonality is that of myself in the middle of one of those old university lecture halls, constructed like a Greek theatre, with steps around a semicircle. I, The Baron, stand in the middle of the hall inside a glass cage, wearing a white gown and declaiming. The content of what I say is irrelevant. What counts is my theatrical style.
>
> The people around me are reached by my voice and are able to see my movements. But there is a total, sharp, and frightful separation between myself and them. I see the people around me as fish moving silently in an aquarium, and their lack of reality and feelings is terribly disturbing to me.

These images correspond to a very definite pattern in Marco's life: those times when he starts shooting names, dates, and quotations at people in order to attack them and make them feel inferior. It is a way of expressing himself that leaves no space for others. After he has contemplated these facts for a period of time, Marco sees and admits that this subpersonality is born of fear and, in turn, generates aggression in others. The discovery comes to Marco with sudden shock. He is temporarily filled with dismay.

Now we come to a crucial point. What happens after Marco has recognized this pattern in himself? Here is his description:

> I felt different right away. I now feel much more intensely and frequently joyous. And my contact with other people is also much more direct. In my everyday life I catch myself as soon as I am about to enter this subpersonality. I have become aware that as soon as I am The Baron my language changes totally. I

start talking in an out-of-date, heavy, pompous way. But now that I am conscious of this fact, as soon as it starts to happen I put things into reverse gear.

Marco's last remark is quite important. Awareness by itself is not enough: *it must be joined by mastery.* We need gradually to develop a steering ability to keep ourselves from slipping mechanically into this or that sub-personality. Thus we become able to identify with each part of our being as we wish. We can have more choice. It is the difference between being impotently transported by a roller coaster and, instead, driving a car and being able to choose which way to go and for what purpose to make the journey.

Kees's work on subpersonalities illustrates this difference. Kees is a Dutchman in his early thirties, a brilliant and humorous person who has been a citizen of many subcultures—the political and the psychedelic, the academic and the mystical. His work on subpersonalities is exemplary in several regards, including its enthusiastic thoroughness as well as its play-fulness:

> For me it was the most fruitful work I did in psychosynthesis. I talked with my subpersonalities, I collected comic books with characters representing various parts of myself, and I even thought of subpersonalities in terms of the Greek gods and goddesses. I talked to other people about subpersonalities and their experiences with them. I was very much into it.

Very soon, Kees became conscious of "The Golem"—the nasty part of himself. Its very existence came as a shock to him, for he had always considered himself to be as gentle as indeed he looked and acted. The image Kees gets for Golem is of an animal furtively dwelling underground, very reluctant to expose itself to his searching mind:

> I looked at this sneaky animal, and my whole image of myself as a decent, good person collapsed. It was a filthy creature, with green eyes and a mean disposition. Without a sense of personal centeredness, I wouldn't have been able to confront it. I would have been afraid that it was all I was, that it would overpower me, and so on.

But when such nasty monsters are brought out in the open they lose their threatening air, and we are even able to appreciate the vital contribution they can offer to the whole personality:

If I didn't possess that personality, I later realized, I would have gotten myself into all kinds of trouble. Though he first emerged as nasty and sneaky, at bottom he was only trying to say "no" when I was always and automatically inclined to say "yes" to everyone and everything. As I gradually understood this, I was able to concentrate on his underlying good quality and bring that out. Without Golem, I would have completely lacked discrimination. Like a child, I could have floundered my way into dangerous situations.

Such an account rightly suggests that there are no good or bad subpersonalities. All subpersonalities are expressions of vital elements of our being, however negative they may seem to us at first. After all, The Saboteur may have a strong sense of humor, and The Mystic may be at times only a boring moralist. The Bon Vivant may drink a bit too much, and The Rebel may come in handy once in a while and even save a life.

Subpersonalities become harmful only when they control us. One of the aims of this work, therefore, is to prevent us from becoming dominated —and consequently limited—by them, and to aid us in identifying with and dis-identifying from them at will. Here again, Kees's experience has value for us:

One afternoon, some time after I had started my work on subpersonalities, I had an image of myself sitting in the middle of a circle of African huts, and in each one of them were living my subpersonalities. Up to then they had been so strong that they could take turns in grabbing at me until one succeeded in holding me prisoner for a while. It might have lasted for ten minutes or ten years; I had no control.

What does it mean to be held prisoner by a subpersonality? It means that it imposes its characteristic patterns on us to the exclusion of all others. But if a certain attitude is the only one I can take, it becomes an idiosyncrasy. If a certain kind of behavior is the only one I can perform, it becomes a compulsion. If a particular viewpoint is the only one I can hold, I end up being narrow-minded. Kees continues his account of how the image of himself unfolded:

But then as I was sitting there, I sensed that this domination was coming to an end. Suddenly, for the first time, I truly felt, "I can go into this hut or that one, and I can come out. And I don't have to stay there if I choose not to." And, afterwards, this mastery started to take effect not only in an imaginary, static situation, like that of the African huts, but also in the dynamics of life, when I had to respond to various situations.

The ultimate aim in subpersonality work is to increase the sense of self or center by deepening our acquaintance with our own subpersonalities so that instead of disintegrating into a myriad of subselves at war with each other, we can again be one: "Sometimes I feel the center like a little flame which is not going to be blown out," says Kees. "Or like a place which remains absolutely quiet while outside it may be very noisy."

From the center, we can get into this subpersonality or that, we can regulate them, correct them, care for them. The knack to be learned is flexibility, so as not to be dominated by our subpersonalities nor to suffocate their expression and ignore their needs—in other words, to have a sense of compassionate, playful mastery.

Working on each of our subpersonalities one by one is the first, essential step. Later we may become aware of the dynamic interplay between them and notice the ways in which our wholeness is infringed.

Although the possession of several subpersonalities makes us rich, their many different needs may also cause dispersion. Such an inner experience of dispersion is especially likely to occur during times of great outer changes and activity. But even in this case there is a lot we can do. When Kees, for instance, for the second time in his life had to fly to England, and, on the plane, felt very scattered, he decided to call the roll of all his subpersonalities, one by one, just to make sure they were with him. He recalls:

> Before I left, my attention had been divided over a number of matters and I felt dispersed. So while I was sitting on the plane I evoked their images and the presence of the particular part of me which each one of my subpersonalities represented. I tried to sense if they were really with me, and found they were. And this simple checking in with all of them made me feel not only that all these aspects were with me, but that I was *together*.

Singing the praises of subpersonality work, as Kees and I have been doing, makes it important that I also say that one can go on forever finding new subpersonalities; they are not finite in number. Subpersonalities shift and change over time. Moreover, each one of us tends to have some of every human quality (from anger to zeal and beyond), and a subpersonality can be found for each. As in psychoanalysis, there is always something more to get hold of. Here, a fundamental attitude should be cultivated: *a sense of just proportion.* A moment comes at which one begins to create new mazes instead of finding his or her way among the existing ones. As in all situations, we have to sense the moment when it's right for us to stop, long before we feel that we have had too much. Moreover, our task is not just finding more subpersonalities, but consists mainly in gaining increasing mastery over them and gradually facilitating their harmonization within the context of a flexible whole. A man writes:

> I dreamed there were lots of people in a big room, all looking at me. All of them were doing different things on their own, completely ignoring the others. Chaos was rampant. I couldn't communicate with these people. Then I clapped my hands and all those "me's" came and arranged themselves in a row in front of me. My feeling was that they were all accessible to me. There was a sense of cohesion. This dream illustrated exactly what is now happening to me in my waking life.

Before we work with them, subpersonalities are fairly distinct universes, ignoring or misunderstanding each other. But as soon as awareness penetrates them, their communication tends to increase. Awareness not only liberates, it also integrates. An analogy is useful here. Consider two people, one of whom is intolerant or even sarcastic about cultures different from his or her own. Implicitly this person believes his or her own world view to be the only right one. We call such a person "provincial," in the derogatory sense of the term. The second person, instead, has access to the soul of many countries. By virtue of much wider experience, this individual is prepared to be at home in all cultures and knows the culture of his or her own country to be but a relative and not an absolute model. We call this person "cosmopolitan." Similarly, we may say that subpersonalities, before we recognize them, are "provincial" and gradually, as we work with them, become "cosmopolitan."

People often experience this process as an *unfreezing*. They talk about subpersonalities suffusing one another while still retaining their original traits. The ice has melted among the people inside them, and the party is more relaxed. As further progress is made, however, it is as if the relaxed jumble of voices gradually gives place to the kind of harmony created by a choir, in which each voice blends with all the others to express the theme of the musical work at hand.

In order for us to reach this stage, a general transformation has to take place in the way we understand our subpersonalities. Instead of looking only at their surface aspects—at which level no true unity is possible among them—we have to learn to look at them as *degraded expressions of the archetypes of higher qualities*.

Any content of our psyche can be *degraded* (literally, "stepped down from its higher state"). Compassion can become self-pity, joy can become mania, peace can become inertia, humor can become sarcasm, intelligence can become cunning, and so on. But the converse is also true: contents of consciousness can be *elevated;* self-pity becomes compassion, and so on. In fact, nothing is ever static in the life of the psyche. And the higher we rise, the closer we will be to unity. Conflict is among distortions—but there is no clash at the source. As Teilhard de Chardin puts it, everything that ascends, converges.

Subpersonalities, too, are degradations or distortions of timeless qualities existing in the higher levels of the psyche. For example, the hyperactive subpersonality can be seen as a distortion of the archetype of energy; the compulsive seducer is a distant relative of love in its higher aspect; the obstinate subpersonality may be seen as a distortion of will; and so on.

Anybody wanting to know more about the degradation of archetypes should read *Exiled Gods,* by Heine. In this delightful work the German poet asks himself what happened to the Greek and Roman gods after the advent of Christianity. According to the medieval legends, stories, and superstitions that Heine traces, the mythical gods lost their power and became demons. During the day they hide with the owls and the toads among the dark ruins of their former splendors, while in the night they wander around seducing or deceiving some unwary wayfarer. Other traditions, which Heine also records, represent some of the Greek and Roman gods as having suffered such a change from their original archetypal natures as to be now totally unrecognizable: Mars, the god of war, has become a mercenary soldier; Mercury, the god of commerce, has ended up a shopkeeper; Venus, the goddess of beauty and love, is depicted as an insatiable female vampire; and Jupiter, the former king of the gods, has been reduced to making a living by selling rabbit skins.

Subpersonalities are like the exiled gods—caricatures, degraded specimens of the original, luminous archetypes. But there is a difference: while there seems to be little hope for the exiled gods (in Heine's poetical vision, at any rate), subpersonalities are clearly susceptible to transformation. Instead of degraded archetypes, they can be regarded as psychological contents striving to emulate an archetype, as a gross version of what is to appear later in a much more refined form.

If we keep this dynamic conception in mind, subpersonalities won't look to us like a bunch of nonsensical patterns anymore. On the contrary, they will reveal to us the hidden potential they carry. However far a subpersonality may be from its origin, it may well come to serve us as a means for reconnecting ourselves with it.

We can best facilitate this process through purposeful imagery that deliberately uses the symbolism of ascent. The imagery of climbing a mountain represents, for example, the inner act of rising to the higher levels of our being, going back to the source of all life. In the words of the French psychologist Desoille, "The effort of ascent, carried out by the subject in his imagery, causes the appearance of increasingly luminous images, accompanied by euphoric feelings of various kinds. On the contrary, descent provokes dark images and feelings of sadness, uneasiness, and anguish."[3]

If we imagine climbing a mountain while carrying a particular subpersonality with us, we may be able to bring about surprising changes in it: we may be able to return from distortion to archetype, or at least to understand the meaning of the subpersonality and its present and future contribution to the overall mosaic of our personality.

Let me mention a few specific examples here. A client of mine had a subpersonality which was quite childish, capricious, and self-assertive. Through ascending, this subpersonality became first a youth and then a warrior—a powerful symbol of strength. And after that happened, my client was able to relate to authority figures in a much more calm and centered manner rather than in his usual defensive way.

In another case, a young man visualized his "self-concealing, reluctant, fearful, resentful, aggressive, curling-up-when-in-danger, trying-to-outwit-others subpersonality" as Quasimodo, the monstrous hunchback of Notre Dame in the story by Victor Hugo. After having made contact with Quasimodo in the valley, he reached the very top of the mountain with him. The light of the sun shining on them there brought about a surprising transformation: under its beneficial rays, Quasimodo became a golden plow—a symbol, as we later learned, of the inner beauty which comes from experiencing life in all its aspects, even the basest ones, and from the resultant seasoning and tempering of the personality.

WORKING ON A SUBPERSONALITY

The following exercise may be similarly fruitful for you. Remember that repetition of the exercise and attempting it in a relaxed state facilitate its usefulness.

Choose a subpersonality with whom you are already familiar.

Imagine yourself in a valley with this subpersonality. Together, the two of you experience your surroundings. You look around and see the grass, the flowers, the trees, and a mountain. Take some time to become aware of the sounds of nature around you—the chirping of the birds, the sounds of the leaves in the wind, and the like.

Now start walking up the mountain with your subpersonality. As you keep ascending, you can imagine seeing all kinds of scenery, climbing through woods and rocks, walking on wide meadows or near precipices. Keep in touch with the increasing sense of elevation, feel the air becoming purer and more energizing, and listen to the utter silence of the heights.

Throughout the ascent, keep in contact with your subpersonality. You may see it going through subtle transformations—like a variation in mood or facial expression or dress—or even a radical transformation: the subpersonality changing completely into something else.

When you reach the top, let the light of the sun shine on the two of you and reveal the very essence of your subpersonality. You may see a transformation taking place once more. At this point, let the subpersonality express itself for what it is now, and let it communicate with you.

It is possible, of course, that a transformation may not occur when we first try the exercise. The subpersonality may even degenerate, slipping further away from its archetypal source. This may happen if we have not recognized and accepted the subpersonality for what it is, with all its needs and limitations.

As long as we impose our negative judgment on a subpersonality, we impede its journey back to its source. One woman, for example, had a very powerful subpersonality, which she called the "I'm sorry" subpersonality. It was the part of her which always felt guilty about something, which was always afraid of bothering others, and which preferred to have her suffer herself rather than cause the slightest disturbance to another person. This apologetic subpersonality appeared in her imagery as a tiny, shy old man. She couldn't stand this part of herself and was very angry at it, regarding it as the source of all her problems. There was real truth in this supposition, but the effect of her anger was to make the little old man feel even guiltier for causing all the trouble.

In other words, *by not accepting a subpersonality, we cause its involution*. As soon as this woman was able to accept this subpersonality as being a part of herself, its constructive side emerged. The image of the tiny old man became a young, strong one with sensitive eyes symbolizing empathy and understanding. At least temporarily, the woman had transcended her guilt feelings and recovered her sensitivity. Subpersonalities are like people. We have to treat them with understanding in order for them to open up and give us the best of themselves.

To sum up, subpersonality work has several benefits:

1.   We learn to recognize our various and contradictory faces and thus undergo a miniature psychoanalysis. In this way we forthrightly own the maternity or paternity of all our parts instead of exiling them into unconsciousness.

2.   We learn to be able to free ourselves from the control of the forces which usually dominate us, throwing us in this or that direction like a ping-pong ball.

3.   We increase our integration by allowing our subpersonalities to become synergistic rather than antagonistic with each other.

4.   We can raise each subpersonality to its highest potential and thus discover that every psychological aspect has in itself the seed of its own transformation.

5.   Finally, by peeling off each mask, one by one, we move ever closer to discovering our underlying core—our true self.

Chapter 5

TOTALLY
IMMEASURABLE

A few years ago I happened to be watching the movie *2001: A Space Odyssey*. At one point one of the astronauts leaves the spaceship, remaining connected to it only by an air tube.

But then the tube is cut and the astronaut drifts away into the distance, abandoned in space. You see him writhing desperately as he dies and becomes a piece of cosmic debris, floating in infinite space.

When I watched that scene, I felt an incredible wave of panic. My heart started pounding, and I felt that the fear I was experiencing was more than just my own fear—it was universal fear, if you know what I mean.

Since then I have had periods of sudden and intense anxiety for no apparent reason. I certainly used to feel anxious before, but the *2001* episode made the situation much worse.

David, the author of these lines, is a student, age twenty-six. He is highly intelligent, loves music and nature, and has a wide variety of other interests. He is tall and thin, and the look in his eyes is crystallized fear, as if he himself were that astronaut, condemned to die alone in the immensity of space. He writes:

When that fear strikes I feel fragmented into a multitude of pieces, with each piece going off on its own. It's like losing the ground I am standing on, like being deprived of a reference point to get hold of.

During the year following the writing of these notes, David's acute crises gradually ceased. He was able to resume his interrupted studies and succeeded in having acceptable relationships with the people around him. When he felt able to carry on on his own, we decided to end our work together. And when I asked him what, in his view, had caused his transformation, he had no doubts and answered right away:

The factors that contributed to my growth were many—finding someone who understood me, exploring the unconscious, awakening my latent love . . . But one star is brightest among all: the self. I found the source of livingness inside me, something I didn't even know existed.

And the most exciting fact is that it was not you who gave me this strength. I did not get it from friends, from favorable circumstances, or from a pill. I myself found it. At times I still feel fear or estrangement, but now I am much stronger than these feelings so that they just slide over me without involving me, the way a drop of water slips off a leaf.

What does David mean, exactly, when he talks about the self as the "brightest star"? The word "self" is used in so many ways that it may be worthwhile to stop a moment and look into some of its meanings.

First of all, the self is commonly referred to as the factor differentiating each one of us from other human beings and the rest of the universe, providing us with a sense of "I-ness" and therefore allowing each to become an individual.

Every morning when we wake and rise up from the darkness of sleep to awareness of our surroundings, of time, and of our individual presence, we recapitulate in a few moments an adventure which took many millions of years: the awakening from the depths of unconsciousness. This saga started when the first forms of life came into being on the planet, and it eventually culminated in the emergence of self-consciouness and individuality.

It is precisely this awareness of self that makes it possible for us to experience solitude and love, to be responsible to other human beings, to be aware of the past and of the future, of life and death, to have values, to be able to plan ahead, to be conscious of our evolution and perhaps be able to influence its course.

Aware of its central importance, psychologists have attempted various descriptions of self (sometimes called the "ego"). It has been seen as the executive function of the personality, as the coordinator of behavior, as the meeting point of conscious and unconscious, or as a constellation of attitudes and feelings individuals have about themselves. Still others describe the self as the result of our interaction with others, as the whole psychophysical organism, or as an illusory aggregate of transient elements. ments.

Psychosynthesis brings the matter to a point of extreme simplicity, seeing the self as the *most elementary and distinctive part of our being — in other words, its core.* This core is of an entirely different nature from all the elements (physical sensations, feelings, thoughts, and so on) that make up our personality. As a consequence, it can act as a unifying center, directing these elements and bringing them into the unity of an organic wholeness.

Seen in this perspective, the self not only differentiates us from other human beings, but it also differentiates us from our own ever-changing contents of consciousness. What saved David from his deep fear was the realization that his essence or self did not coincide with it. He, as a self, could step back (or dis-identify) from that fear and observe it as something other than himself. The fear could be seen out there, so to speak, becoming merely another psychological object with its own clear contours.

The self can also be defined as the only part of us which remains forever the same. It is this sameness which, once found and fully experienced, acts as an ever-present pivot point for the rest of the personality, an inner stronghold to which we can always refer in order to regain a sense of poise and self-consistency. Then we can see that the self remains the same in ecstasy and despair, in peace and turmoil, in pain and pleasure, in victory and defeat. As Tagore poetically puts its, "The same sun is newly born in new lands in a ring of endless dawns."[1]

Sure enough, if we take a look at our psychophysical organism, our first impression is that there is no such pivot point, that everything is in a state of continual flux. To begin with, our body is sometimes tired and sometimes full of energy, healthy or ill, young or old, sleepy or awake, hungry or satisfied. It certainly isn't an immutable reality. Our feelings are not permanent either. Through some mysterious illusion they sometimes assume a character of changeless presence. But then they disappear and other feelings take their place, bringing with them the same old illusion of permanence. Finally, our thoughts are not permanent. They pop in and out of our minds, one after another, in a matter of moments.

Yet if we look within ourselves carefully enough, we will find that there is a permanent element. Body sensations change, feelings fade, thoughts flow by, but someone remains to experience this flow. This "someone" is the self, the experiencer. It can be said, then, that *the self is consciousness in its essential state, undiluted, chemically pure*. It is a state of psychological nudity in which we have taken off all our psychological clothes—thoughts, feelings, images, physical sensations—and only pure being remains.

The way things usually work, this pure consciousness spontaneously takes the form of whatever it comes in contact with. If I am glad, my consciousness is my gladness. If I have a toothache, my consciousness is my toothache. If I think of ice cream, my consciousness is the thought of an ice cream, and so on. This process we call *identification*, and it is present in all of us. With training, it is possible to detach our consciousness from the states that mold it *(dis-identification)*, and to experience it devoid of any content or support *(self-identification)*.

Identification can be equated with a loss, a dream, or an illusion. We identify with our feelings and our desires, with our opinions, with our roles, with our body. The problem is that if, for example, I identify myself with an idea which I particularly cherish and believe to be true, and then that idea is proved to be wrong, I feel that *I* am wrong. If my body is the focus of my attention and the source of my power and success, and I perceive myself primarily as a body, then when my body becomes weak, sick, or old, *I* feel weak, sick, or old. If I equate my identity with my role ("I am a businessman," "I am a teacher," "I am a wife," etc.), then when that role ceases to be, I also feel that my sense of being is diminished or annulled. If I experience myself as a desire and that desire is frustrated, *I* am frustrated.

Since all the contents of consciousness change and at some moment inevitably cease to be, identification with any of them inevitably leads to a death of some kind. On the other hand, identification with the self leads to the experience of our permanent being, that unconditioned core which remains the same throughout all of life's events. As one woman put it, "When I say 'I am,' I know that *I am* before thinking, before feeling, before acting. I am aware of being pure possibility." The look in the eyes of a newborn baby can remind us of this same openness to all possibilities—an openness unobstructed by any past experience, without veils, without thoughts, without exclusions. Similarly, the unbound nature of the self makes it the place in a human being where freedom is maximized.

As long as we are identified with sensations, feelings, desires, thoughts, it is as if our sense of being were sewed onto them, and therefore they can submerge us, control us, limit our perception of the world, and block the availability of all other feelings, sensations, desires, and opinions. On the other hand, when we are identified with our self, it is easier for us to observe, regulate, direct, or transcend any of our contents of consciousness, because we are dis-identified from them.

At this point, one may well ask, "Isn't the process of dis-identification an ascetic denial of a part of ourselves?" An answer to this important question comes from someone who had felt the same doubt:

> In the beginning, dis-identification seemed to me a very dead affair, rather like going into the center of some dead place, while all the aliveness was on the outside, on the periphery.
>
> And what could possibly happen here? I was more for what I thought of as the way of Blake and Whitman—to identify with everything. Nevertheless, I decided to give this process a try. And then I found out that I could identify *better* with everything than before. I realized that up to then I had never been able to identify completely before because of fear.
>
> Now I can identify myself much more easily and fully with any aspect of myself that I choose. Surrender has become easier.

This report clearly reveals how dis-identification does not prevent us from subsequently identifying with any aspect of ourselves, if we so choose. On the contrary, this ability is expanded. What we want to avoid is a continual, unknowing identification with any random process of our personality. This latter kind of identification always brings a thickening or freezing of some sort.

Thus, when we persistently identify ourselves with it,

> A body state tends to become a tension.
>
> A feeling tends to become a hangup.
>
> A desire tends to become a compulsive craving.
>
> An opinion tends to become a prejudice.
>
> A role tends to become a mask.

Conversely, by turning back to the self, we allow our hangups to become feelings again, our prejudices to become opinions, and so forth. A woman, for instance, writes:

> I was almost obsessively immersed in some work I was doing. Once started, I was impatient to get it done. Instead I decided to dis-identify, as if nothing else in the world counted. As I did so, I experienced calm and a sense of well-being. Then I went back to work, without the previous anxiety and haste.

Figure 3

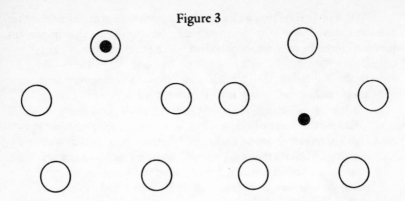

1. Empty circles indicate contents of consciousness: feelings, sensations, ideas, and so on. The point indicates the self. The self passes unintentionally from identification to identification throughout the day: "I am angry," "I am tired," "I am happy," etc.

2. It is possible to experience the self as pure consciousness, apart from any content: "I am." From this psychological place, the self has a panoramic view of all the personality contents instead of being identified with just one of them at a time.

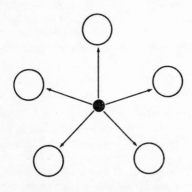

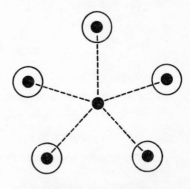

3. In the psychosynthetic conception, the self is neither the passive spectator extraneous to the show nor the actor completely involved in it. It is the producer, who stages the whole show with expertise, good timing, and tactful handling of the actors.

4. When clearly experienced, the self can decide to identify fully and easily with any personality content, from romantic love to furious anger to physical appetite. But it is also able to dis-identify from the content. The experience of self allows choice at all times. Thus the whole personality is available to the self.

We dis-identify by observing. Instead of being absorbed by sensations, feelings, desires, thoughts, we observe them objectively without judging them, without wanting to change them, without interfering with them in any way. We see them as distinct from us, as if we were looking at a landscape. We calmly observe those psychic arabesques from a detached viewpoint (see Figure 3).

This attitude of serene observation can be practiced at any moment of our life, and its first effect is that of liberation. I am fearful, I observe my fear, I see its contours clearly, I see that the fear is not me, that it is a thing outside myself; I am free of that fear. This attitude of contemplation was exemplified by Pythagoras in the metaphor of the festival. Some people, he said, come to the festival to compete, some come to show off, some come to ply their trade, and some come to meet other people. But some individuals come just to watch. They do not have to prove anything or try any harder. And they are the freest.

Likewise, the Self is the part in us that can watch any content of the psyche without getting caught up in its atmosphere. This fact allows the whole personality to find a balance of which it would not otherwise be capable. The Oriental story of the ten fools illustrates the situation: Ten fools crossed a river, and, having reached the other shore, wanted to make sure that all of them had crossed safely. One of them started counting the others, but in doing so left himself out, and therefore counted only up to nine. "We are only nine," he declared, "One of us must have been drowned in the river." "Are you sure you counted right?" asked another fool, and also proceeded to count; but he, too, omitted himself. And no matter how many times the ten fools tried to count themselves, the result was always nine. They began to weep because they were convinced that one among them had been drowned—but they could not think which. A passerby asked them what was happening, and they explained. In seeing all ten before him the man realized their mistake, and he started to count them by touching each one in turn. As each one was touched, he was to call a successive number. "One," said the first; "two," said the second, and so on, until they came to the last fool, who said, "ten." The fools, astonished, thanked the wayfarer and rejoiced that one of their number had not been drowned.

This story points out what easy prey to illusion we are without a unitary point of perspective—wandering from one identification to another and continually experiencing a sense of loss. Only in an element independent of the interplay of the various forces has the possibility of achieving a clear, true perspective. In the case of the human personality, this condition is achieved through self-identification.

Self-identification can be compared to being on top of a *belvedere*—an Italian word meaning that point on high ground which gives us a panoramic view of the landscape below—because from the vantage point of the self we can obtain an overall view of the ever-changing contents of our personality. The first four steps of the following exercise are designed to lead us to the belvedere position of our inner space. The fifth step, which follows naturally from the others, is planned to yield the experience of the self as pure consciousness.

SELF-IDENTIFICATION

1. Become aware of your *body*.

   For some time, just notice in a neutral way—and without trying to change them—all the physical sensations you can be conscious of.

   Be aware, for example, of the contact of your body with the chair you are sitting on, of your feet with the ground, of your clothes with your skin.

   Be aware of your breathing.

   When you feel you have explored your physical sensations long enough, leave them and go on to the next step.

2. Become aware of your *feelings*.

   What feeling are you experiencing right now?

   And which are the principal feelings you experience recurrently in your life? Consider both the apparently positive and negative ones: love and irritation, jealousy and tenderness, depression and elation . . .

   Do not judge. Just view your usual feelings with the objective attitude of a scientific investigator taking an inventory.

   When you are satisfied, shift your attention from this area and proceed to the next step.

3. Turn your attention to your *desires*.

   Adopting the same impartial attitude as before, review the main desires which take turns in motivating your life. Often you may well be identified with one or the other of these but now you simply consider them, side by side.

   Finally, leave your desires and continue with the next step.

4. Observe the world of your *thoughts*.

   As soon as a thought emerges, watch it until another one takes its place, then another one, and so on. If you think you are not having any thoughts, realize that this too is a thought. Watch your stream of consciousness as it flows by: memories, opinions, nonsense, arguments, images.

Do this for a couple of minutes, then dismiss this realm as well from your observation.

5. *The observer*—the one who has been watching your sensations, feelings, desires, and thoughts—is not the same as the object it observes. *Who* is it that has been observing all these realms? It is your *self*. The self is not an image or a thought; it is that essence which has been observing all these realms and yet is distinct from all of them. And you are that being. Say inwardly: "I am the *self*, a center of pure consciousness."

Seek to realize this for about two minutes.*

The self is the most fundamental psychological experience we can have: crystal clear, limpid consciousness. And yet this experience doesn't usually come spontaneously, and eliciting it by means of this exercise may take some time. We should remember, too, that the self is not some state located out there, which we must look for and strive hard to reach. On the contrary, we already *are* the self all the time. Moreover, the experience of the self does not mean blotting out all other contents of consciousness. Feelings and thoughts may still be coming and going—but now they are in the background of our awareness, which is becoming aware of itself.

Finally, the self is not a reality to be experienced only with closed eyes. It is a realization that can be retained in the midst of daily life. While the self is by definition pure inner silence, it does not necessarily take us away from our everyday moods and activities; on the contrary, it can increasingly manifest an effective presence and self-reliance, as the following story illustrates.

An airplane never used and full of spider webs; a heap of ruins; a wrecked ship; a lifeless puppet. These images appear to Lia at different times when I ask her to close her eyes and give free reign to the spontaneous flow of her imagery. And they all obviously show how she feels about

---

*In Assagioli's original version of this exercise, a radical formula is used for all levels:

"I have a body, but I am not my body."

"I have feelings, but I am not my feelings."

"I have desires, but I am not my desires."

"I have a mind, but I am not my mind."

You are not only led to create a psychic distance between yourself and what you observe, but you are also asked to affirm this distinction by voicing the corresponding statements. While some people find this wording particularly effective for dis-identifying, others prefer to perform this exercise without any particular formula.

herself: "I feel this sense of neglect, of uselessness, the way you feel when there is nothing you can do. One builds an airplane and then leaves it there to collect cobwebs. One exists, but the whole world is too busy to take notice.

"I feel a sense of torment. One asks why, with despair. Nobody knows that the airplane exists. *Something happened, but nobody knows about it.*"

What is happening without anybody knowing about it is the fact that Lia exists. Lia is a teacher in her thirties. Her father died when she was a child, and she can hardly remember him. Her mother has persistently rejected her. When she was a little girl, she had to spend long periods away from home at boarding school. This situation may account for her sense of being forgotten and for her "sweet and intense desire to dissolve." She is hurt by people's indifference. She is uncertain of her image, and every time she comes to see me she dresses and has her hair done in a different style. Despite all this, she is a warm and intelligent person. She is hungry for all the experiences of life and is always striving for authenticity. I find it a real pleasure to work with her.

One thing Lia tells me about herself helps me to grasp the core of her predicament. She compares herself to Gurdulù, a character in Calvino's novel *The Nonexistent Knight*. Gurdulù is only one of his innumerable names; he is "without names and yet has every possible name." He exists but does not know that he exists. Therefore, he becomes whatever he sees: if he sees a bunch of frogs, he becomes a frog and starts croaking; if he sees a pear, he believes he is a pear; if he sees a big cauldron of soup, he dives into the soup, believing that he is soup and that *everything* is soup.

Lia feels the same way. When she is with the others, she is absorbed by their wants, their opinions, their worlds, and she goes along with them without even being aware that she is doing so: "When I start feeling unreal, an increasing sense of anxiety builds up, and it seems almost to solidify inside me. This mask goes forward to talk to other people, saying whatever the anxiety wants it to say. This happens especially with people by whom I feel dominated, or who I think are better than me."

Lia's entire psychosynthetic adventure up to now could be summed up as a search for the self—what she rightly calls her "center." During the same period in which she comes to see me, she takes part in a psychosynthesis group. She also comes to the weekly exercise sessions held at the Institute, which are open to everyone. Gradually the experience of self dawns on her. She realizes that she exists independently of other people's recognition and that this fact is intrinsically *right*. She learns to switch back to the self in the course of stressful daily events and to be more present to herself while relating to others.

Lia sums up her experience with the following words: "I needed other people's judgment in order to convince myself that I *existed*. Without asking them too openly, I wanted to know my friends' opinions of me, so as to create an image of myself. I don't feel like that anymore now. The strong vital energy of the self dispelled this excessive need of the approval of others and allowed me to regain my own balance."

In Lia's story (as well as in David's), we see one crucial consequence of the discovery of the "I": *self-reliance*. A great number of people preserve from their childhood years an unresolved need to lean on others, as if their center of gravity were elsewhere than within themselves. In much of their outward behavior and attitudes, these people may seem to be mature. They have not, however, truly faced a crucial fact of existence—the basic alone-ness which is the lot of each human being. In an implicit, obscure way, they expect the environment to supply what they illusorily believe not to have themselves: strength, direction, even life itself.

Because their wishes are seldom satisfied, these people are almost constantly off balance. They tend to interpret any signal of unavailability from someone else as a rejection or a defeat. They see the necessity to stand on their own feet the way their childish part wants them to—as a senseless and supremely uncomfortable duty. At times they are overwhelmed by the unbearable terror of solitude.

The discovery of the self teaches these people the hard lesson that other people are not functions of their own existence, that we are all funda-mentally on our own, and that this natural fact—far from being a tragedy—can stimulate them to use their creative resources. It may later show how, paradoxically, facing their solitude is a needed step on the way to recogniz-ing their essential solidarity with other beings.

The entire long-range process which seems to be at work here brings us well beyond the boundaries of personal identity. To make a long story short (but we shall come back to this subject in later chapters), we can say here that once pure consciousness (the personal self) is detached from the ordinary psychological elements which structure it and increase its density, it has the tendency to rise spontaneously to its origin (the Transpersonal Self). From the discovery of self-reliance and individuality there can be a progressive transition to an all-embracing realization of universality. As pure consciousness gains in clarity and fullness, a fundamental shift takes place whereby we make a direct approach to the creative vitality at the very source of our being.

This last point requires an explanation. *We usually experience aliveness in connection with a situation:* being with a person we love, being successful, feeling healthy, earning money, riding a motorcycle at 100 mph, whatever. If that connection is not present, it is not possible for us to experience a sense of aliveness. If my lover doesn't love me, if I don't earn money, if my motorcycle is out of order, I don't experience my basic aliveness. My basic aliveness is tied to these "ifs."

But the experience of basic aliveness is possible without any "ifs." To reach it, we have to discover what in ourselves is truly independent of any "ifs," totally and unconditionally alive: *our Transpersonal Self.*

Even though its full realization is a rare, extraordinary phenomenon, we know that the Transpersonal Self has been contacted by a number of famous as well as ordinary people through the ages, in both the East and the West, and deserves most attentive consideration and study. The Transpersonal Self has been called, among many other names, the "Diamond Consciousness," the "Jewel in the Lotus," the "unconquerable mind." Of it, Plotinus says, "It is not measured by size nor circumscribed by the limitation of any figure, not to be increased in magnitude because unbounded . . . totally immeasurable."[2]

Chapter 6

THE WILL

The Italian opera composer Rossini, we are told, was as lazy as he was brilliant. Of the many anecdotes that circulate about his indolence, one portrays him lying in bed in the morning while composing an overture.

It was wonderfully cozy there, and it was just too cold to get up. At one point, however, a sheaf of the pages he had been writing fell to the floor and scattered all over so that Rossini had to get up and gather them together if he wanted to continue composing. But what an effort that would have been for him! Unwilling to go to that trouble, Rossini simply started over again—and wrote a completely new overture, much more brilliant and lively than the one that had slipped from his hands.

This anecdote can be seen as a victory of inspiration over brute effort and unimaginative self-discipline. It is a victory that, especially in recent times, seems to be complete, so much so that feelings, spontaneity, and "going with the flow" are the ultimate conquerors—in keeping with contemporary trends of thought. On the other hand, discipline and the will, which have increasingly come to be considered forms of useless self-torture, are the apparently hapless losers in this story.

This change of attitude toward the will started when Western culture became more psychologically aware. The mechanism of repression was discovered, and people realized the immense power of those forces they naively had been trying to dominate—while they themselves were actually dominated *by* them. They saw that however much the will boasted of being able to control life, it was often itself controlled by factors of which it wasn't even conscious. Its leadership began to look dubious.

Accordingly, well-meaning, enlightened folk took the will down from its throne of omnipotence and began considering it an artificial, pompous intruder, telling everyone what to do. Finally, prevailing thought exiled the will to the Land of Disrepute and Insignificance.

But that was a mistake, because the will in its true essence can explain a host of human attainments, while its absence can account for legions of psychological disturbances. If understood in its proper perspective, the will is, more than any other factor, the key to human freedom and personal power.

In fact, the will can be seen as an expression of what Angyal called "autonomy"—the capacity of an organism to function freely according to its own intrinsic nature rather than under the compulsion of external forces. In fact, all of evolution can be seen in terms of the emergence of this freedom.

To begin with, the passage from the vegetable to the animal kingdom is marked by the achievement of freedom of movement. This passage is evident in certain kinds of medusae, which during part of their lives cling to rocks and live as vegetables, and then spend the rest of the time as animals, freely moving about.

The less evolved organisms within the animal kingdom show little more than the capacity to move. In the case of insects, for instance, behavior is completely determined by rigid programs, and no choices are permitted by their rudimentary nervous systems. As we rise on the ladder of evolution, we find that the brain is enriched by associative cells, enabling the animals to perceive the environment through more than one sense at a time. But their behavior is still exclusively ruled by fixed programs. Certain species of fishes, for instance, are programmed to move in groups, and this tendency is so strong as to make them give up any food or prey for the sake of blindly following their leader with the rest of the group.

It is only as the level of birds and mammals is reached on the evolutionary scale that behavior stops being completely prearranged, and some space is left for contingency and variability. The brains of these animals have a selective ability and can *distinguish* between stimuli that are significant for survival and stimuli that are purely contingent. If the stimuli are recognized as urgent, the animal proceeds purely according to program. But if they are not urgent, the cortex elaborates a response based either on trial and error or on a previously learned strategy.

A monkey, for instance, if it is not in a situation threatening its survival, will do all kinds of unpredictable things—play with the toothpaste, jump on the piano keyboard, and otherwise drive us crazy. Animals at this level can choose among innumerable outer stimuli. However, they also depend on them: they are environment-bound.

With human beings we enter a different kingdom. Just as animals are freer than vegetables because they can move in the physical world, humans are freer than animals because they can move in the world of ideas, plans, and visions of infinite variability—and they can do so independently of the environment. Our nervous system enables us to be the least predictable of all species, because we are the least dependent on programs to provide us with step-by-step courses of action.[1]

True, at any moment we may find ourselves going along with outer pressures: social constraint, propaganda, and so on. We may fall into the grooves of habit and act on automatic pilot. More rarely, we may even function purely according to instinctive mechanisms. But—and here lies the great novelty—we can also invent new behavior and become an intelligent cause. *We can truly and freely choose, bearing the full responsibility of self-determination. It is to this evolutionary acquisition, still very much in development, that we give here the name of will.*

At times we are all dramatically confronted with situations which invite us to make use of the will. If we do so, our psychic voltage rises and we can move on to greater freedom. But if we don't, we are crushed by the circumstances of life. A woman I once worked with had an experience with this choice; I would like to describe her story, because I believe it shows the birth of will in a particularly clear way.

Left by her husband with a small child, Cinzia felt alone and totally vulnerable. She had stomach trouble, and her general health had been seriously undermined by years of too many tranquilizers. She felt overwhelmed by crowds, and every time she entered a department store she was overcome with anxiety. The future looked so frightening to her that at the age of thirty-two she did not want to live anymore.

When I met Cinzia she looked pale, and her eyes revealed an idealistic sensitivity which had been badly hurt by contact with a reality too rough for the delicacy and wealth of her feelings. An image bubbling up from the depths of her being most clearly described what she felt: "I am in a dark tunnel. Its walls are black and spongy and the ceiling is low. At first the tunnel seems completely blocked, but then I see an exit in front of me and the green outside. But no one is waiting for me there, and this prevents me from coming out of the tunnel. I turn round and round inside the walls, with my ten thousand thoughts of despair." Another phrase was even more revealing: "The will does not exist in me. I am being carried along by this grey everyday life, with the regret for what might have been. Why has everything been swept away? I believe it is a black destiny which has always persecuted me."

Cinzia's self-diagnosis was correct: her will was nonexistent. Or, more precisely, she had not yet discovered it. Since she lacked the capacity to determine her own life, she felt a victim to "black destiny." Having never learned how to use her autonomy, she felt fragile and vulnerable. Brought up to deny and disown her personal power, she felt lifeless.

Cinzia's situation brings us to consider a general principle: whenever the will of an individual is ignored, suppressed, or violated in a consistent and enduring way—or if it is stillborn or even nonexistent—pain and illness arise. And, because the will is the faculty closest to our self, when it is infringed upon, the hurt goes all the way to the core.

REVIEWING THE WILL

Take a look at your own will.

Is it frequently:

pushed around by the will of other people?

subjugated by your feelings, such as depression, anger or fear?

paralyzed by inertia?

lulled to sleep by habit?

disintegrated by distractions?

corroded by doubts?

Do you generally do what you wish, from the depths of your being, because you have willed it, or does some other factor prevail?

Take some time considering the major aspects of your life and your most important relationships. Then write down your answers in detail.

THE WILL IN EVERYDAY LIFE

Despite many obstacles, the discovery of the will is quite an elementary experience. If we want to facilitate this process, we can start in the simplest of all ways: *we can discover or intensify our will by using it*. Each moment offers such an opportunity; if we look at it that way, life becomes a laboratory for experimenting with and developing our will. Here are just a few of the ways—thousands of others can be invented—of activating it in various situations of everyday life:

Do something you have never done before.

Perform an act of courage.

Make a plan and then follow it.

Keep doing what you are doing for five more minutes even if you are tired or restless or feel the attraction of something else.

Do something extremely slowly.

Say "no" when it is right to say "no," but easier to say "yes."

Do what seems to you the most important thing to be done.

When facing a minor choice, choose without hesitation.

Act contrary to all expectations.

Behave independently of what other people might think or say.

Refrain from saying something you are tempted to say.

Postpone an action you would prefer to begin right now.

Begin, at once, an action you would prefer to postpone.

Perform the same psychosynthesis exercise every day for one month, even if it seems useless.

Eliminate something superfluous from your life.

Break a habit.

Do something that makes you feel insecure.

Carry out an action with complete attention and intensity, as if it were your last.

Any action can be transformed into an exercise of will, provided it is not done from habit or experienced as duty. An "avalanche" process is thereby set in motion; once we have discovered our will, it enables us to perform further acts of will. In this way we increase our reservoir of will and therefore become able to develop it even further. We begin to create a virtuous circle: will generates will.

But do not imagine that things always run so smoothly. We may start performing these exercises but forget them the next day; on the third day they may appear to be of no use; and at a still later date we may like them again and want to start all over. Or, fired by sudden enthusiasm, we may perform a great number of acts of will in order to accumulate as much will-energy as we possibly can, only to find later that we have created a sort of indigestion of the will. A client of mine, at a certain point in this process, once remarked, "Now, whenever I try to perform acts of will, I just can't do them. Something in me rebels against them." This was a signal that he had done too much and needed to take a break.

Clearly, acts of will must be done without yielding to the temptation of doing too many at a time. We must bear in mind that continuous linear progress in all fields is a relatively rare achievement. Therefore, we must approach acts of will in a sporting spirit, as if we were training to get in better shape.

In Cinzia's case this process took several months. She had first come to see me during the darkest days of winter. With the arrival of spring, however, she manifested the first buds of determination, although her new tendencies were still intermingled with old ones. She wrote:

> I want to learn to live alone, serenely, without absurd hopes, without torturing myself about the mistakes I have made, and without thinking about a future which anguishes me, about my terribly boring job, or about aging without a partner.
>
> Spring is near; how many perfumes, how many feelings, how many wishes! I wish to dive into the sun and feel its warmth, inviting me to live. Does hope still exist? I don't have much hope in my potential. In fact, I have none.

In these few contradictory lines we can already see the emergence of a clear determination ("I want to learn to live alone . . ."), accompanied by the ups and downs characteristic of emotional life. Cinzia kept working on herself in the midst of her recurring difficulties until one day a further change occurred. At that time she wrote in her journal: "I want to love. I want to be available to others. I want to get out of this oppressive solitude. And most of all, I want to be a person."

I watched Cinzia's evolution over this period, during which she came regularly to see me. I knew that a deep discovery of the will was lying ahead of her, but I didn't know when or how she would actually get to it. Finally she succeeded:

> I worked a lot on will exercises, because there was a period in which I wasn't able to rouse myself. So I tried in all ways to release my will. And the will came—I don't even know how. One day I just found myself able to do everything I wanted. I became aware that I was throwing my life away. I wasn't living, I was destroying myself.
>
> And here the will to live came in. It was not the will to live because I had a family, but the will to live for my own sake, to show myself that I was a person who, faced with life, had every chance of living without killing herself.

The last time I saw Cinzia, she told me that she still felt lonely occasionally, but that this did not stop her from making plans for a new life, such as leaving her job and finding some activity in which she could help other people. She wanted to train to be a nurse. She showed me pictures of her child, who, as a consequence of the atmosphere of dejection in their home, used to be lifeless and would not play with other children. Now the child looked strong and happy.

At this point, however, a doubt may creep in. "This is all fine and nice," one may say, "but the amount of stiffness associated with exercising the will makes me wonder if I wouldn't become too rigid. I want to live without trying so hard, without the constant imposition of controls. So any talk of willpower arouses my suspicion."

The point here is that the experience of real will is not to be confused with Victorian willpower. The fact that many people have been calling "will" what was actually stern self-restraint should not tempt us to throw out the baby of the true will with the bathwater of Victorian self-denial.

We can clear up this misunderstanding as soon as we realize that *the real function of the will is to direct, not to impose.* An example can help to illustrate this basic fact. Let us suppose that you are in a rowboat in the middle of a lake, and you want to return to the shore. To do so you will have to make use of two functions: first, you must *decide* in which direction to steer the boat and maintain that direction; second, you must *use* your own muscular energy to row the boat.

Now suppose, again, that instead of handling a rowboat you are working a sailboat in a mild breeze. What you need this time is skill in handling rudder and sail so as to take advantage of the interplay of natural energies. No muscular effort on your part is required to move the boat. Your only function is to choose and maintain the direction in which you want to sail—a much easier and more relaxing task than that of supplying the propelling force, as before. In the sailboat you are not an agent: you are a meta-agent. This means that you let the wind, the sail, the waves, and the currents interact with one another. All you have to do is skillfully regulate this interaction without directly participating in it, as you would have done in a rowboat.

True will is likewise a meta-agent or, as Alyce and Elmer Green called it,[2] a "meta-force" which can direct the play of the various elements of the personality from an independent standpoint, without mingling or identifying with any of them. But we don't usually realize that this is possible.

The way we habitually handle ourselves resembles the act of rowing a sailboat while the wind is blowing. We thrash about needlessly, determined to act as agents, even when no effort is required of us. We waste so much energy because we do not only decide *what* to do, we also "try," applying ordinary "willpower." But we could accomplish just as much without "trying" and with much less expenditure of energy.

Once, when the conductor Herbert von Karajan was coaching his students, he made the distinction between laborious doing and effortless direction in a marvelously clear fashion. He recalled the days when, as a child, he took riding lessons. On the night before his first jump he was sleepless with worry: "'How can I lift this enormous thing up into the air and over the fence?' I thought to myself. Then I realized no one lifts the horse. You set it in the right position and it lifts by itself. The orchestra will do the same thing."[3]

Do not misunderstand me here. Using the will may at times involve effort and striving. It may run against our ingrained attitudes and habits. It may be a will that breaks through barriers, that overcomes fear, that compels even the most improbable things to happen. And it may still be a healthy will, immune from the harsh grimace of "willpower" and different from it in nature. What makes the difference is identifying with decision *only*, and not with action and effort. For this to happen the will has to spring from the very core of ourselves, without being contaminated or deviated by other forces. This, however, rarely occurs. Consider, for instance, the following people:

A fifty-year-old man is prey to periods of depression. When they come, he loses all confidence in himself, feels physically weak, and does not enjoy life anymore. He is told by friends to "react" to his depression by "strength of will." But he finds that the more he does so, the worse his condition becomes.

A businessman has set up a very ambitious goal for himself in his corporation. He works overtime, denies himself any sort of amusement, and deprives himself of his nurturing relationship with his family. He sacrifices himself on the altar of achievement.

A woman has been left to herself since she was a young girl. She has learned that in order to survive, she has to be tough, and she puts out a "shield of obstinacy, strength, and denial." Only later does she become aware that she has "tried too hard and too much" and has lived in a constant state of emergency reaction—and that at the core of her hardness is fear.

While indeed they *will* with great intensity, these people are also controlled by a feeling or a desire—be it rebellion against pain, ambition, or fear. They do not will as *selves*. Instead, their efforts become "trying," absurd effort, blind push. In each case, the will is not a meta-agent, but only an agent on the same plane with innumerable other psychological agents.

The best way for us all to offset the danger of "trying too hard" is to remember that we can truly will only from the center of our being, the self. All other forms of willing are psychological monsters: the will is captivated and distorted by a feeling, a subpersonality, and so on.

When it springs from the center, the will can express itself in many different ways and can be regarded as a constellation of inner events rather than a single, clear-cut psychological manifestation. At times we realize the will in an instantaneous event, quick as a bolt of lightning, as in the case of a spontaneous act of courage or a sudden decision from which we cannot draw back. At other times, we may experience the will as a steady flow of strength, as when we concentrate our attention on some subject independently of outer distractions, or when we apply ourselves steadfastly to some project which we want to carry out regardless of the difficulties involved.

At certain moments the will consists in doing what needs to be done for its own sake, without any promise of future reward, without any hedonistic prop or threat or sense of guilt. At times the will may show us that life is also a struggle to be fought without compromises, while on other occasions it is the factor that energetically projects a bridge between people — a bridge across which the warm flow of human communication can pass. At other times the will comes into expression when we aim at a goal with undivided tension, untouched by those ambivalences and fluctuations which, functioning in the twilight regions of the mind, so often succeed in undermining even the strongest determination.

The will can be clearly seen functioning in a person like Amundsen, who fulfilled his determination to become a polar explorer despite apparently insuperable obstacles, despite ridicule, danger, and physical hardships. But then will is equally present in somebody like Emile Zola, who produced a total of fifty-eight books by writing four pages a day — and never missing a day.

To clarify these issues further, it may be useful to look at another example. Mario is an architect and university professor. The story of his search for will begins when, at the age of 41, he saw that things had started going downhill for him. He had just recovered from an acute attack of ulcerative colitis, coinciding with the birth of his first baby. "I was the sick father of a newborn baby, and this filled me with anguish," he says. On top of that, his summer had been catastrophic. Mario had gone to Sardinia on his boat for his summer vacation, together with three friends. But everything conspired to make the vacation difficult. All of Mario's journey, in fact, was an example of lack of will. He picked his friends randomly, and his choices turned out to be wrong. There was a continual shirking of responsibility among the four, and a great part of the dialogue on board was made up of unpleasant exchanges: "Why didn't you fill up the container of drinking water?" "I thought *you* were going to take care of that!" Everybody was unprepared. One of the voyagers had come without bringing the compulsory life raft and had had to buy one at the last moment—but then it was too big to fit easily in the boat, and it got in everybody's way throughout the trip. It was a "boat of confusion," where nobody could find what he was looking for, where space was poorly utilized, and where there was either too much or not enough of anything.

Even the beginning of the journey had been chaotic. "We left in a completely unconscious way," says Mario. Instead of waiting until morning, to start out rested and refreshed, they impulsively decided to leave at night after a large meal. At three A.M. they found themselves in the middle of the sea, utterly sleepy, and without enough fuel—which they hadn't thought of checking before leaving. "It was a way of doing the least with the most effort," says Mario in retrospect. "I acted as if I were totally free of all ties, without responsibility. In this way, the whole trip was for me a return to childhood. But it was a childhood full of mistakes and inexperience."

If a journey in a boat can be a small-scale model of one's style of living, this was the case with Mario. When he came to see me the following autumn, one of the main traits I noticed in him was a lack of will. He was uncertain about his goals in life. He would start something and not finish it. Overly discouraged by small adversities, he postponed commitments, hesitated in taking initiatives, and allowed himself to be walked over by colleagues or even friends. The models he related to most easily were Charlie Brown and Woody Allen.

When the will is missing, the psychological space it should occupy is taken over by anguish, depression, resentment, and confusion; and this was what had happened to Mario. A great part of our work together was devoted to discovering the will in its various aspects and helping Mario deliberate on which goals he truly wanted to reach in his life.

The central aspect of working with the will consists precisely in being conscious of what we will do and how we will to do it. Unlike Mario, or the depressed fifty-year old, the businessman or the woman we met before, we act from the clarity of self rather than from impulse, desire, or drive. We ask ourselves what our present main purpose is. We decide to reach it. We deliberate on how to do so in the most effective way possible. And we search out and discover what can facilitate us in this task. Then we can resolutely plunge into conscious action, facing obstacles in our way with firmness and intelligence. At the same time, we can be flexible enough to change our plans if the need arises, without being too serious about it, so that we can still have a good time and enjoy what we are doing. Conscious willing is the key.

The next summer, Mario again decided to go on a sea journey. "This time I wanted to make it as perfect and as beautiful as a sonata," he says.

"And it later turned out to be some kind of general model of what life should be for me."

First came the preparation in all its details: checking the sail's seams, lubricating the machinery, taking care to do everything that would guarantee efficiency and safety. Then came the decision on where to go and where to stop on the way. Mario resolved to follow the coast of southern Italy and then head towards the Greek islands. This year, the choice of people for the trip was not random. Mario picked friends with a sporting spirit and good will—men who fit well with one another and who did not suffer from seasickness. Then came the elimination of all the superfluous stuff on board; not much was needed for a trip like this, and the lighter the boat, the faster it goes. Elimination, like any form of choice, is an act of will.

Mario put great energy and commitment into this adventure, a degree of commitment that he had rarely experienced before in his life:

> The beauty of the trip came out of the joy of being able to see the forecasts come true. I would write methodically in the journal the time we were leaving and the time we were stopping, when we were using the sail and when we were using the engine, and so on. So I gradually became able to forecast that at such and such a time such and such an island would appear to our view. And the island regularly appeared.
>
> The whole trip went like an arrow that reaches the target in the right way and at the right time. It was a microcosm of what life can be, so many were the elements involved: living with other people, survival, security, planning, enjoyment, reaching the set goal.

Assagioli talks about seven groups of qualities displayed by the will in action: energy, mastery, one-pointedness, determination, persistence, courage, and organization. In his journey Mario expressed each of those qualities. Indeed, the whole trip became a symbol of his new approach to life. Later, Mario decided that his main purpose was that of expressing himself and his talent in the academic world. Therefore he gave priority to a series of targets that would help him along this way, such as writing articles, publishing a textbook, following a course of specialization in aerial photo interpretation, exploring new fields, and in general affirming himself more in his profession. Without denying the joy of the unexpected, Mario has made his life like his journey to the Greek Islands: harmonious and purposeful.

PURPOSE

Like Mario, we can use a capacity which is most eminently human: *the power to choose*. By selecting our own right purposes and abiding by them, we can streamline our life and bring to it much more potency and ease. The following exercise can be of help in this respect:

1. Take some time and think of what the *main purposes* in your life are right now. Jot down a list of all the most important purposes that come to your mind—abstract or concrete, difficult or easy, far or near.

They may range from self-realization to painting the garage, from developing a better relationship with a person to learning a new language. Anything goes, as long as (a) it is important to you and (b) it is a real purpose and not just a mere possibility, a hope, or a "should."

2. Now choose what feels to you at this moment to be the most important purpose on your list.

3. Close your eyes and let an image spontaneously emerge that symbolizes this purpose for you. It may be the image of absolutely anything—an object of nature, an animal, a person, etc.

4. With your eyes still closed, imagine that in front of you lies a long, straight, clear path reaching directly to the top of a hill. On top of the hill you can perceive, from afar, the image you have chosen to symbolize your purpose.

5. On both sides of the path you can see and hear and feel the presence of beings of various kinds who will try to divert you from your path and prevent you from reaching the top.

They can do absolutely anything they want except for one thing: they cannot obstruct your path, which remains straight and clear before you.

These entities represent various situations, persons, secondary aims, and inner states of your life. They have a great number of strategies to divert you—they will try to discourage you and seduce you, to frighten you and hypnotize you. They will give you logical reasons why it is not worthwhile or why it is even absurd for you to go on; they will try to intimidate you or make you feel guilty; and so on.

6. Experience yourself as clear will, and proceed on the path. Take some time to understand the strategy of each entity. Feel its pull. You

can even have an imaginary dialogue with the entity—but then move on, and, as you do this, experience yourself *willing*.

7. When you reach the top, face the image representing your purpose, stay with it for a while, and enjoy it. Realize what it means to you, what it has to communicate to you now.

8. Open your eyes and write about your purpose as well as about all the forces that tried to prevent you from going forward.

9. Repeat the exercise, on succeeding days, for your second and third most important purposes. In general, the remaining ones will tend to take care of themselves, because the habits of conscious willing you develop in applying yourself to your main purposes make you generally more effective, and also because as you accomplish your main purposes, enormous energy may be released that makes other tasks easy. Feel free, however, to repeat the exercise for as many targets as you wish, keeping in mind that it is always your main purposes, especially your first choice, to which you have decided to devote most of your attention and energy.*

---

*This exercise was devised by Dr. Massimo Rosselli.

Chapter 7

TIGERS OF WRATH

S enselessly, constantly, aggressive energy is misused everywhere on our planet. Every day this fundamental energy, more elusive than the most fleeting phantom and yet—as its victims would all agree—more powerful than a storming sea, causes innumerable kinds of pain. Every day, through the most sophisticated and respectable means or, on the contrary, through the most primitive ones, physical and psychological murders are committed. Every day, people's rights to physical and emotional safety and survival are threatened. Every day people are insulted, discriminated against, attacked, tortured, and killed.

Moreover, millions of persons involuntarily direct their aggressive energy against themselves, causing (psychosomatic medicine tells us) such disturbances as heart disease, hypertension, obesity, stomach diseases, and intestinal, sexual, respiratory, skin, and rheumatic troubles. And this same energy of aggression is found to be one of the determining factors in various psychological ills such as certain forms of depression, guilt, obsessive and paranoid syndromes, and perhaps some cases of psychosis.

Even more common are the countless ways in which aggressive energy poisons our everyday psychological lives and our personal interactions. As this partial list suggests, this problem can assume an immense variety of forms:

Cold, silent hatred	Passive sabotage
Criticism	Cruelty
Self-destructiveness	Bitterness
Sarcasm	Quarrelsomeness
Irritation	Malevolence
Resentment	Unreasoning dissent
Pique	Sulkiness
Vicarious enjoyment of violence	Blind rage
Grumbling	Frustration
Brooding	Spite
Aggressive fantasies	Vengefulness
Sneering	Hostility

Is aggression, then, merely sickness to be cured and eliminated? Far from it. Many factors can distort and exaggerate aggression and even transform it into violence: personal isolation and lack of communication, the absence of love (especially during the early years), overcrowding or scarcity of resources, repression, negative environmental models, improper nutrition, and so on. Effective, systematic action on these problems will alleviate many of the negative results of aggression. We can best understand aggression in itself, however, not by looking at its worst forms, but by seeing it in its simple essence—in the words of Assagioli, "a blind impulse to self-affirmation, to the expression of all the elements of one's being, without any discrimination and choice, without any concern for the consequences, without any consideration for others."[1] Then we realize that we have at our disposal a form of *natural energy*.

All natural energies are neutral. The energies of the wind, of the sun, of the atom, of a river can cause catastrophes or prevent them. They can kill or they can sustain. It is a sad fact that we are much more proficient in directing and using physical energy than in mastering and channeling our own aggression. Yet the two tasks are parallel, and we can succeed in one as we have succeeded in the other.

REVIEW ON AGGRESSION

The following questions will allow you to look at the ways you experience aggression:

1. What form does aggressive energy take for you?

Take a few minutes and think of the ways in which you manage your aggressive energy; see what your favorite channels and habitual modes are.

2. Do you express or repress your aggressive energy?

3. What is your attitude about aggressive energy—do you fear it, despise it, enjoy it, harvest it?

Or do you, perhaps, fail to experience it at all?

4. Are there specific patterns to your aggressive energy? And situations or people that specifically tend to arouse it?

We can look at it as a natural process—a wave of aggressive energy arises in the individual, becomes powerful, and pushes forcefully forward to express itself. At this point at least two possibilities are presented: First, the person may be frightened, shy, or unwilling to break his or her own standards of courtesy, so the aggressive wave is repressed causing all kinds of psychophysical harm, from psychosomatic to purely psychological ills. *Or*—and this happens especially with extroverted, action-oriented people—the wave finds an outlet in the shape of words and deeds, sometimes constructively and sometimes not.

No general rule can be made about expressing aggression. On the one hand, you have individuals who, being generally shy and easily walked over by others, are at a loss in the jungle of everyday life. They rightly take the act of boldly asserting themselves as a victory, and they rejoice in being able to speak up frankly and courageously and, sometimes, to explode.

Some individuals also find that expressing their anger with persons who understand and love them may help their mutual relationship; after the initial shock, the situation is changed and a new clarity can emerge. As Blake beautifully expressed it,

> I was angry with my friend:
> I told my wrath, my wrath did end.
> I was angry with my foe:
> I told it not, my wrath did grow.

But it would be a great mistake to generalize such experiences and believe that freely expressing aggression is right and helpful at all times. Words said in a moment of exasperation can cloud a relationship forever. Many forms of anger can hurt and even destroy what is soft and beautiful in another person, stifling growth, generating misunderstandings, kindling the desire for revenge, and so on.

Fortunately, we can also choose to harmlessly *discharge* our aggression. Simple but excellent methods of doing so have been described by many authors: punching a pillow or tetherball, repeatedly and violently hitting a mattress with a tennis racket, tearing up newspapers, writing a cruel letter to a person we are angry at (and then not sending it). Such methods work equally well with current hurts as with accumulated resentments, and they should become part of our habits as a culture. They enable us to eliminate emotional debris which would otherwise impede the free flow of our functioning. Unfortunately, people who most need to use these methods often rationalize their fear of adopting them, calling them ridiculous, useless, or undignified.

Another important possibility is available to us: We can *transform* aggressive energy—we can alter its target and mode of expression while leaving its intensity intact. Let's go back to our wave; the wave emerges and pushes forward, but this time it is given a shape and a target different from those it originally had. None of its momentum is repressed, but its new expression is now positive and congruent with the course of our lives.

To quote from a couple of reports:

> Whenever I feel anger rising in me, I immediately convert this energy into putting my apartment in order. And I always have a *very* tidy apartment.

> When I got low marks in an exam I became very angry, and I invested that anger right away into studying for the next exam. I fed my desire to study with my own rage, which improved my concentration tremendously.

Some basic points emerge as we consider the attitude underlying these examples. First, we can most easily transform that from which we are dis-identified. For this to happen, we must see our anger, our aggressive impulses, with an objectivity and a lack of judgment which, as we shall see, is the mark of true love. These impulses are elements of our being and therefore intrinsically valid. There has to be a fundamental respect: any condemnation of our aggressive energies is an act of psychological clumsiness which makes transformation impossible. Second, there is something beautiful and profoundly vital about aggressive energy. Unfortunately, many people look at it with dread. They often automatically associate aggression with violence and wrongly assume that by concentrating on developing higher qualities they will make it dissolve. Usually they only succeed in repressing it.

While aggressive energy at its most primitive levels can become destructive, in its more evolved form it becomes creative power. Many spiritual leaders have warned against despising or deprecating aggression, pointing to the consequent dangers of helplessness and resignation. Ramakrishna, for example, used to narrate the story of an incredibly fierce and venomous snake. One day this snake met a sage and, overpowered by the latter's gentleness, lost its ferocity. The sage advised it to stop hurting people, and the snake resolved to live a life of innocence, without harming anyone.

But as soon as the people in a nearby village realized that the snake wasn't dangerous anymore, they started to throw stones at it, to drag it by the tail and tease it in innumerable ways. The snake was having a very hard time.

Luckily, the sage passed by the place again, and after seeing how badly battered the snake was and listening to its complaints, he simply said: "My friend, I told you to stop hurting people—I didn't tell you never to hiss at them and scare them away." Ramakrishna concludes, "There is no harm in "hissing" at wicked men and at your enemies, showing that you can protect yourself and know how to resist evil. Only you must be careful not to pour your venom into the blood of your enemy. Resist not evil by causing evil in return."[2]

Let us now look in greater detail at an example of how one person succeeded in starting to turn her own aggressive energy from enemy into friend. Julia is a powerhouse with immense energy. She doesn't walk up the stairs—she runs. She doesn't enter my office—she rushes in. She doesn't talk—she shoots out her words. But all this energy is not utilized in healthy ways. Besides expressing some of it in harmless forms, Julia has the tendency to keep much of it inside, turning it against herself. She says, in retrospect: "I used to avoid any aggressive act, because I had the feeling that as soon as I did the slightest thing there would be an explosion capable of tearing the whole world apart."

She adds: "My aggressiveness has always been turned against me. Sounds like an epitaph, doesn't it?" No other words could better describe her situation. She has received a lot of aggressiveness in her life and held it in. Her father used to beat her regularly, and her mother imposed a rigid, obsessive control on her. "I have incorporated this aggression," Julia says, "and elevated it into a way of life. I have made it mine, and kept it inside. How else could I have managed not to kill my parents?"

For Julia, the outcomes of aggression turned inward are a self-destructive attitude (leading her to an attempted suicide during her adolescence), depression, disturbances in her sleep cycle, "inability to surrender to the joy of life," and obsessive thinking. It is as if the energy not expressed kindles her thoughts, forces them into repetitive patterns and ideas which never find an outlet but just turn in infernal, never-ending circles of torture. Another prominent trait is Julia's "bitter satisfaction," as she calls it, an attitude of reveling in her pain and of turning into agony whatever she would naturally tend to enjoy. She also calls this attitude her "sadomasochism." To try to suffocate this pain, she gorges herself with food.

Julia was twenty-one and a university student when she started working with me. Her husband was sixteen years older, and the marriage was troubled. She has, however, managed to survive her many difficulties and shows a brilliant mind and a passionate interest in everything. Moreover, she has a highly developed sense of beauty, an urge to share and relate, and the extraordinary but disorderly vitality of which we have already spoken.

Over a considerable period of time the key for Julia has clearly been to learn how to invest her aggressive energy in an activity she likes and values, instead of turning it against herself. To a considerable extent she has systematically learned the knack of using aggression as *fuel* for her activities. "I chose studying," she says, "because that is a natural channel of expression for me." As soon as she gained some facility, Julia was able to transform studying—previously a painful, empty duty for her—into an activity filled with life and interest.

Now Julia elaborates on and utilizes what she reads, and her attention is so passionate that she sometimes becomes aware that "two hours have passed only after they have gone by." After studying, she feels tranquil and satisfied. As the process has continued, she has broadened the range of her energy investments: she has become involved with mime, started acting, found a part-time job in a school, and written her thesis. Meanwhile, I must add, she regularly beats her bed with a tennis racket in order to discharge her surplus aggressive energy.

Julia did not achieve these results by imposition. Instead she learned the new knack gradually and introduced it into her life almost as a subterfuge. She merely utilized the exercise described later in this chapter and let it seep into herself, and eventually the new attitude spontaneously emerged in her everyday life. She puts it simply: "The more exercises I do, the better." Whenever she tries to impose a new habit rigidly and mechanically, however, her psychophysical organism rebels. This reaction is quite understandable in her case, endowed as she is with a sensitive alarm system against all imposition—a residue of her suffering at the hands of her authoritarian parents. But such sensitivity in introducing a new attitude is important for other people besides Julia; indeed, we may take it as a universal rule if we want to avoid contrary reactions.

Julia now feels her aggressive energy to be "the greatest problem" and at the same time "the propelling force" of her life. At times the old patterns show up again; they have been learned through the years and cannot be wiped away overnight. But the new skill is hers, gradually becoming part of her life. "When I succeed in not killing myself with my own energy," she says, "I realize all the wonderful things I am able to do."

Here is the exercise that Julia used with such good effect. It should be performed *only* when one is actually experiencing some form of aggressive feelings or is close enough to retrieve them easily. If that is not so now, simply read the exercise and come back to it later.

TRANSFORMING AGGRESSIVE ENERGY

1. Pick a project or an activity to which you want to give more "steam."

2. Now, laying that project aside for the time being, get in touch with your aggressive feelings. Feel their vigor, their vibrancy, the effect they have on your body, and, perhaps, the hurt which they cause you. Give them, so to speak, space—that is, observe them without judging them or immediately labeling them in some way.

3. Now realize that these feelings are energy at your disposal, energy that is precious and can *do* things. It can hurt, but it can also become the propelling power for the project or activity you have chosen.

4. Now vividly imagine yourself in the midst of your project or activity. Call to mind as many details as you can with your imagination. Imagine the moves involved, but see them now kindled and intensified by the vitality you have chosen to invest in them.

The transformation of aggressive energy is no artificial gimmick. Our task is to master the laws of this process rather than letting it happen only by chance. It is useful, therefore, to take a look at how creative people of all times have used aggression. Aggression in many forms has often been the key to their trade. "Facit indignatio versus," wrote the Latin poet Quintilianus: "My anger creates my verses." In a different culture and occupation, Einstein was described by his friend Infeld as using "unbelievable obstinacy"[3] to pursue his mathematical problems—which ten years later emerged as relativity theory—without any need of encouragement or help from outside sources.

At other times indignation at existing circumstances has been transmuted into actions aimed at changing those very circumstances. As Emerson put it, "Good indignation brings out all one's power."[4] And, when asked what had been the motivating factor behind her immensely productive work in hospitals, Florence Nightingale answered with one word: "Rage."

Let us end with the examples of two great artists who succeeded to an unusually high degree in expressing their struggles and their inner power in their work: Michelangelo and Beethoven.

In listening to the music of Beethoven, one is often impressed by the way its dynamic potency sharply differentiates it from the classical elegance of the other works of his time. And in viewing many of Michelangelo's statues and paintings, one is struck by what his contemporaries called "terribilità"—the sense of sublime grandeur and intensity. Naturally the few scattered documents we have are insufficient to reconstruct in detail the complex inner process of creation. A few words here and there, however, suggest that the propelling agent behind much of the work of these two geniuses was aggressive energy in the widest sense of the word—a spectrum of psychological hues from rage to vigor to the creative urge. A French visitor, for instance, reported at that time:

> Michelangelo could hammer more chips out of very hard mar-
> ble in a quarter hour than three young stonecarvers could do in
> three or four, which has to be seen to be believed, and he went at
> it with such impetuosity and fury that I thought the whole
> work must go to pieces, knocking off with one blow chips three
> or four fingers thick, so close to the mark that, if he had gone
> even slightly beyond, he ran the danger of ruining everything.[5]

No wonder that his biographer, Vasari, tells us Michelangelo himself used to say that "using the hammer kept his body healthy."[6]

Beethoven, too, despite his irregular life and the difficulties and despair caused by his deafness, found a way to nurture his work with his aggressive energy. We are told, for instance, by a contemporary English visitor of what happened when Beethoven played the piano: "He seems to feel the bold, the commanding, the impetuous, more than what is soothing and gentle. The muscles of his face swell, and its veins start out; the wild eye rolls doubly wild; the mouth quivers, and Beethoven looks like a wizard, overpowered by the demons whom he himself has called up."[7]

But perhaps the best evidence is given by Beethoven's own words, as reported verbatim by a friend, to whom he explained how the process of creation occurred for him: "You will ask me where I get my ideas. That I cannot say with certainty. They come unbidden, indirectly, directly. I could grasp them with my hands; in the midst of nature, in the woods, on walks, in the silence of the night, in the early morning, inspired by moods that translate themselves into words for the poet and into tones for me, that *sound, surge, roar,* until at last they stand before me as notes."[8]

To conclude: on this planet one person kills another every twenty seconds.[9] One dollar out of six is given to military expenses. It costs $14,800 per year to maintain a soldier versus $230 to educate a child.[10] A gun is sold in the United States every 13 seconds.[11] The tragically clumsy way in which humanity handles its own aggression generates massive destructiveness. We all realize that the solutions to this immense problem are difficult and extremely complex. But these shocking statistics suggest the importance of personal transformation as one of the many ways needed to deal with this critical situation. Sometimes we can succeed in turning our aggressive energy from destructive into constructive action.

Chapter 8

THE PRIMORDIAL FACT

During my training with Assagioli, we would often walk up and down his small garden, discussing a variety of topics—from diet to Buddha's conception of the not-self, from Dante to the significance of perfume, from the dangers of "psychic smog" to cybernetics, from mandalas to the structure of the universe. Because of the difficulties in hearing Assagioli had during the last years of his life, I always wrote my questions to him, but often, in order to make myself heard, I needed to shout other questions or objections that came up during the conversation. My earnest youthfulness in querying the older and wise master, the humorous awkwardness of the shouting and the occasional difficulties in understanding the quiet of the garden just one wall away from Florence's noisy traffic, and finally the inspired good sense of Assagioli's thoughtful but quick replies all combined to give a joyful magic to those lively times. I recall them with the gratitude that one reserves for life's most beautiful gifts. But one moment stands out in my memory as being curiously striking. I had written a question in which, among other things, I casually referred to "following our feelings," taking for granted that that was the attitude toward living we should all assume. When Assagioli reached that point in his comments, he looked at me and, very gently but firmly, stated: "But you must *not* follow your feelings." He spoke as if this were perfectly obvious. "Your feelings must follow *you*."

I was taken aback by this remark. After all, I thought, weren't we all supposed to be listening more to our feelings, which were so often brutally repressed or maltreated in our over-achieving society, thus accounting for so much of the psychological malaise we see around us? Surely we had to give in fully to the natural demands of our emotional life. That was my credo. And here was this old man telling me that my feelings had to follow *me!* How authoritarian, how unfamiliar that sounded! At the same time, the statement—perhaps because of the disarming way in which it had been uttered—awoke my curiosity. I soon realized the importance of the problem. Should we acknowledge our feelings as the primary factor in deciding what to do in our various life situations? And if not, which part of us *should* determine our course of action?

If we take a closer look at the situation, we clearly see that feelings are necessary ingredients in everyone's life: they are an inexhaustible source of enjoyment, they facilitate communication, they add power and color to whatever we do, they vitalize ideas and reflect intuitions.

And yet just following our feelings may subject us to invasion by other individuals' emotions; distort our perception of the world; cause us to fall into prejudice, confusion, and hysteria; let us be tortured by excessive sensitivity; and stimulate regression to our ancestral past. The point, clearly, is that we cannot trust our feelings indiscriminately, as if they were oracles: to do so might lead us astray. On the other hand, we cannot disparage them because that would repress a precious dimension of our being.

The key to keeping our feelings in proper perspective—and this is what Assagioli meant by his remark—lies in evaluating the situation each time with fresh eyes and with a centered outlook. From the self we can see a particular feeling in its real dimension. We can know how truthful it is, and we can decide what to do with it. From the center of our being we can choose which feelings on the stage of our psyche deserve the magic spotlight of our attention and which ones are better left in the dark. It is our show, and each one of us has the ability to direct it as he or she wishes.

But how are we to deal with those feelings that distress us? When depression, resentment, envy, fear, anxiety, and other such feelings arise, at least three possibilities are open to us: we can give them total attention, listen to them, understand them, and express them. Or we can decide not to pay any attention to them. Or we can do both in succession—often a necessary and useful choice.

Attention feeds. Many individuals have found that if they want a feeling to loose its grip on them, they can withdraw their attention from it.

They switch the spotlight off it and plunge themselves into some activity, as if that feeling did not exist. It may then grumble in the dark in which they have confined it, but they can still ignore the feeling and act independently of it without submitting to its capricious dictatorship. Within a short time, the intensity almost always lessens. Withdrawal of attention can truly enable us to realize astounding economies of psychic energy.

The following story of a man named Enrico provides a good example of a person's extricating himself from the control of negative feelings and learning the skill of directing the vitalizing power of attention. Enrico first came to see me when he was in the throes of a powerful depression, which at times brought him "very far away from reality." Now, two years later, he recalls:

> Depression gave me a radically altered way of looking at life and the external world (of this I became aware only later, when I started to free myself from it). A lamp in my room, say, would take on an incredibly dismal appearance. Some fairly ordinary object like a tape recorder would assume dimensions of fearfulness and even terror. The whole external world looked like it was falling in on me. A rainy day, for instance, would be an intensely oppressive experience.

Enrico was nineteen when I first saw him. Despite his average build, he felt himself to be too small. The scantiness of his beard greatly distressed him and helped to intensify his feelings of inferiority. He had already been to a psychologist and a physician. The psychologist, after seeing him a dozen times, had concluded that his problem was physical. The physician had found nothing wrong with him. Enrico had no confidence in therapy and believed that only some sudden and miraculous event could save him. When he began his work with me, he lacked the ability to clearly perceive what was going on inside him. He was simply and painfully aware of the end results—depression, fear, and apathy. And it was very hard for him to conceive of the possibility of working on these conditions psychologically.

The work with Enrico has been long, and I won't go into the details of our exploration of the causes of his problems: his relationship with his stern and emotionally distant father, his childish dependency on his mother, his jealousy of his younger sister, and so on. Suffice it to say that, as Enrico began to understand that his troubles had a psychological origin, he became more open, and his will to grow was energized. Now I had before me a collaborator rather than a suffering antagonist. Despite this change, however, Enrico's troubles persisted—a reminder that awareness of the causes of a psychological problem does not necessarily liberate us from it.

It was at this point that I introduced Enrico to what gradually proved to be the key element in his psychosynthesis: the art of directing attention. I asked him to withdraw attention from his depression and fear by acting as if they were nonexistent. In the beginning it was hard: "It was very difficult to muster that necessary minimal determination to act as if these oppressing forces didn't exist, because my habitual reactions made me respond to them. They were like a vortex that dragged me down."

A vortex is a very appropriate symbol for psychological identification. As we saw in previous chapters, identification is a recurrent process in which we mistakenly lose our identity in some particular content of consciousness: for example, if I *have* a depression, I tend to *be* that depression —to implicitly believe that depression is what I am and what life is all about. Depression (or any other identification, including the more pleasant kinds) becomes a vortex, a force that absorbs me and sweeps me into itself. This emotional entanglement tends to color one's whole way of perceiving. As Enrico says, "it was only later that I was able to understand that I was too immersed in my feelings to be able to perceive things objectively."

After a time, things started to change for Enrico. Whenever a wave of anxiety or depression swept over him, he ignored it and focused on some activity: from gymnastics to calling a friend, from working to putting his desk in order to going out to meet girls. Little by little he saw that the oppressive forces were only as real and powerful as he allowed them to be. Now he has made progress in acquiring some control over them:

> As soon as I feel anxiety or depression building up in me, if I think, "Yes, all right, it's there, but I won't pay any attention to it, right now I am doing something else," I can keep going with whatever I'm doing, whether anxiety is there or not. I find that I can see these negative thoughts as a river flowing before me, carrying these emotions along on its surface. And I can look at the river from a stable point, remaining unaffected. This gives me a marvelous sense of strength, of peace and well-being.

From this stable point, Enrico adopts an attitude of indifference to his anxiety and fears. He lets them dwindle into insignificance.* He adds:

---

*Let me reiterate: I am not implying that all depressions and all anxiety can be dealt with by acting as if they didn't exist. First and foremost, one must come to an understanding of their causes. We can afford to ignore only what we have understood. If, for example, we act as if a depression did not exist without having first acknowledged its presence and understood its . causes, we may repress it rather than devitalize it. In some form, the depression will return. For this reason, prior to "as if" work of the kind I have been describing, it is vital to do some methodical self-exploration. Simple means for facilitating this task are described in Chapters 1 and 2.

All this worked and yielded big results on a long-range basis. It helped me to the point of really developing a new personality, one which was no longer depressed and fearful. Moreover, I came to live in a completely different dimension; I was able to see things in their true light. I can see now that a rainy day is not an oppressive, terrible event, but is just what it is—a rainy day.

The art of placing or withdrawing emphasis can be employed not only with our feelings, but also with *all* elements of our being. The fundamental importance of this technique was described by Keyserling with his customary philosophical vigor:

> We can accent in ourselves absolutely everything which exists. What is accentuated is elevated into being the dominant element and in the long run transforms all the other elements in conformity with its proper character ...
> ... no state exists which cannot, by conversion, disruption, or remoulding of the personality, be abruptly changed into a completely different state. It depends solely on the position of the accent of importance and on the growth or diminution which this accentuation has called forth.[1]

The act of shifting the accent of importance naturally and spontaneously takes place in all our lives, not only with inner elements but with outer stimulations as well. You are having a pleasant dinner with your family, let us say. The telephone rings, and you answer; you feel you have been in the house too long, so you decide to go for a walk; you lose interest in the magazine you are reading and pick up another one. Such shifts of attention, or—as we call them in psychosynthesis—*substitutions,* happen all the time, usually mechanically and semiconsciously.

Substitutions, as we have seen in the case of Enrico, can also be *conscious* and *intentional*. We can learn how to redirect attention, rapidly and neatly, and through this process redirect our interest and even our total involvement in life. We can learn to give emphasis to anything we want in our inner universe—a subpersonality, a feeling, an idea, an aspiration—as well as in the outer universe—an activity, a project, a relationship, and so on. Here is an exercise that will give you some practice in this process:

DIRECTING ATTENTION

1.   Visualize a yellow triangle. Let it take shape on the background of a white screen. (You may not be able to keep its shape steady in your

mind's eye, and its lines and colors may change or disappear; do not be concerned now about the quality of your visualization.)

2. Imagine a red triangle by the side of the first one. Keep both triangles in your field of vision.

3. Start shifting your attention from one triangle to the other. First focus on the yellow one. You see only that one now. Then shift to the red triangle, and focus only on that one.

4. Shift your attention from one triangle to the other a few times, and thus become aware of your capacity to make intentional substitutions.

5. Now that you are familiar with this capacity, imagine, instead of two triangles, two different situations, one pleasant, the other unpleasant. First imagine the unpleasant situation in detail. Experience it with all your senses; be there. Then shift your attention to the pleasant situation, and again experience it fully and in complete detail. Now shift your attention rapidly a few times between the two situations.

You can do this shifting experiment with the inner and the outer world, with past and future, lower and higher unconscious, etc. You can shift from any place in the universe to any other place. Always realize that you are the one in the center, the one who can direct the searchlight of attention wherever you will.

The ability to direct attention can, among other things, relieve us of several related and widespread habits: the urge to do many things at the same time, the anguish of never accomplishing all we want, the haste to finish one thing in order to start something else. Instead, we learn to do one thing—and only one—at a time, giving it our full concentration. One woman I know, aware of the calm power and ease this ability confers, has called it "regency." I have rarely met a person so busy and at the same time so centered. I once asked her what her secret was.

> I call "regency" the ability to handle my life without clenching my teeth, without sweating. It is a very different kind of attention from that of a person anxious to finish what he is doing. It is an attention which is independent from everything, which nourishes its object but at the same time easily withdraws from it when life demands it.
> Sometimes during the night, for example, I have to get up to feed my child. In a moment of non-regency I would be very

sleepy, and I wouldn't feel like feeding her. In a period of regency, instead, I can leave my sleepiness easily and honor life however it presents itself. It is a beautiful, exalting experience: at this moment life *is* this child, and at this moment I honor this child. I honor life whatever dress it wears.

Attention is an energy carrier, and knowing how to direct it is truly, as Keyserling says, the "primordial fact," as important in the handling of our lives as in learning how to walk or how to talk.

The psychic energy conveyed by attention is neutral in itself. How we use it, what we make of it, is up to us. The electrical energy in the circuits hidden by the walls of our houses can turn on a television set or a record player, a bomb's timing mechanism, a juice blender, or a lamp. The energy is pure and unqualified. It is the appliance we plug in which qualifies and transforms it into images or music, an explosion, a drink, or light.

Chapter 9

A MIND CRISP
AND INCISIVE

I n his novel *La Réponse du Seigneur,* Alphonse de Chateaubrillant compares the human mind to one of those butterflies that assumes the color of the foliage it settles on: "We become what we contemplate," he says. If our mind is only occupied with gossip, everyday worries, telephone bills, resentments, and the like, it will assume their hue. If it thinks about joy, infinity, or universality, its hue will again correspond. Many years earlier Marcus Aurelius made much the same observation when he said, "Your mind will be like its habitual thoughts: for the soul becomes dyed with the color of its thoughts."[1]

A fundamental principle is at work here: *our thoughts define our universe.* For thoughts do more than color our minds. Far from being ethereal and remote from life as we may sometimes believe, thoughts act on us in profound ways; indeed, we can literally say that thoughts are living beings. The French psychologist Fouillée remarked that pure ideas do not exist: each one has an energetic aspect. Consequently, every idea tends to actualize itself and would do so completely, were it not for the existence and pressure of many other ideas, differing and often opposed to it, which also tend to actualize themselves. Fouillée called such entities "idea forces."

Practice shows that we can create, vitalize and strengthen an idea-force by thinking about it. As we observe its possibilities, dimensions, and applications, it becomes more clearly defined. Feelings are attracted to it, and the new idea-force seeps into us, becoming part of our attitudes toward life and our habits of action. Thus by thinking about strength, love, or joy, we create strength, love, or joy in ourselves. The technique of deliberately picking a psychological quality and then thinking about it is called *reflective meditation*.

Reflective meditation is nothing more than systematic investigation of some idea. Let us say that we have decided to reflect on joy. We can think about the joyous people we have met in our life and the times when we experienced joy; the relationship of joy to a similar state, such as cheerfulness or humor; its origins and the hindrances to it; and so on. At some point our mind will be tempted to go off the track and think about something else. We then bring it clearly back to the subject of our reflection. Firmly but lightly, we bring all our power of focus, all the intensity of our understanding, to this endeavor.

REFLECTIVE MEDITATION

The following exercise is designed to introduce you to this practice:

1. Choose one of the qualities in the following list (or another one you have in mind):

Joy	Vitality	Wisdom
Gratitude	Simplicity	Cheerfulness
Love	Openness	Loyalty
Will	Strength	Peace
Courage	Creativity	Understanding
Calm	Power	Wonder
Generosity	Inclusiveness	Freedom
Humor	Clarity	Risk
Compassion	Energy	Truthfulness
Cooperation	Playfulness	Steadfastness

2. Reflect on the quality chosen for a period of ten to fifteen minutes.

3. As a subject for your reflective meditation, you may also want to choose a meaningful phrase such as one of the following:

"The greed for fruit misses the flower."—Rabindranath Tagore

"Gratefulness is heaven itself."—William Blake

"We are not troubled by things, but by the opinions which we have of things."—Epictetus

"It is in self-limitation that a master first shows himself." —Wolfgang Goethe

"A good runner leaves no tracks."—Lao-tse

"Love is the pursuit of the whole."—Plato

"The greatest discovery of any generation is that human beings can alter their lives by altering their attitudes of mind."—Albert Schweitzer

"If one advances confidently in the direction of his dreams, and endeavors to live the life which he has imagined, he will meet with a success unexpected in common hours."—Henry David Thoreau

"To be a whole and to live in the whole becomes the supreme principle, from which all the highest ethical and spiritual rules follow."—Jan Smuts

"One never loves enough."—Aldous Huxley

At some point during the meditation we will reach the stage of believing that we have exhausted the subject, covered its every aspect. Or we will become bored and want to do something else. Or we will feel that the subject lacks the importance we thought it had and start asking ourselves whether we should have chosen something else to meditate on. *This is precisely the moment not to stop, but to keep meditating.* This feeling of going up a blind alley often occurs just before achieving insight. If we go through and beyond this stage, our mind will shift onto a level at which the quality of thought is more lucid and meaningful.

After we have finished our ten or fifteen minutes, we may think that the process has also finished. But it is only beginning. Our thoughts sink into the unconscious, which keeps working at them, elaborating, connecting, developing.

In *Pattern and Growth in Personality,* Gordon Allport cites a psychological experiment in which subjects were asked to write down as many words beginning with the letter "c" as they could remember. After the experiment, however, words starting with the letter "c" kept popping into their minds, sometimes for days. This phenomenon is called "perseveration." Something similar, but deeper (because the subject concentrated upon is not neutral but desirable and because the experiment is repeated daily) happens in reflective meditation. Due to unconscious elaboration, the reflection later blooms into some unexpected insight, a subtle alteration of behavior, a gradual but pervasive change in attitude. As a client of mine humorously put it, "The more that damned meditation on love became a regular habit, the more my whole day was lived in the light of it."

Let us see in more detail how such a transformative effect can actually occur. Hugo, a forty-six-year-old businessman, is short, energetic and has an apparently positive approach to life. He owns his own plane, which he flies for fun, has many friends, and is successful in his job. He is very skillful at concealing his depression, his frequent headaches and his painful difficulties with women. He was left first by his wife and then by a lover.

When I ask him to do some free drawing, letting his crayon make whatever picture it wants, the most interesting image to emerge is a brightly colored flame. In discussing the meaning of the drawing, Hugo says this flame has been extinguished by life's circumstances, which have hurt him deeply and permanently. He complains of feeling inhibited in contacts with superiors at work and of experiencing a general uneasiness and uncertainty in his emotional life.

We soon find that Hugo's inner fire has not really been extinguished: it has only been temporarily suppressed. The cardinal root of all his trouble is his subtle but generalized reluctance to plunge into the new. In performing the visualization exercise of transforming the caterpillar into a butterfly, he gets stuck at the stage of the cocoon and is unable to get out of it. He writes:

> How much I have lost in my life! Feelings, beauty, ecstasy, enthusiasm. And I am still incapable of freeing myself from that gloomy grayness of the cocoon, to break toward the light, to float above the flowers, to enjoy their perfumes and their nectar, to contemplate their dazzling colors, to soar toward an apotheosis of beauty, of ideals, of joy. When I try to venture into this magnificient world something throws me back, and the grayness of a false security attracts me like a magnet.

Hugo's "cocoon complex," as he calls it, prevents him from manifesting his vitality, from having new relationships or asserting himself at work. It also obliges him to verify the correctness, the "safety" of whatever he does over and over again. Therefore, it keeps him locked in "total immobility."

I suggest to Hugo that he reflect on risk. He accepts this idea willingly, and the very first time he performs this exercise with me, he feels a release. As a result of his further reflection, Hugo starts doing small things that jolt him out of his usual grooves, such as calling up a person he hasn't seen in a long time, challenging his subordinates to ping-pong games, dealing with some of the scary issues he has been postponing for weeks, giving a party, parking illegally at the risk of being fined, starting a new hobby. Simple as these actions are, they represent for Hugo the first steps in breaking out of the cocoon and shedding it.

As the weeks go by, I remind him of the value of continuing to meditate on risk as a component to be incorporated into his everyday life. And this embodiment takes place surprisingly quickly. Where previously Hugo had tended to be exaggeratedly cautious, he soon finds himself much less reluctant to gamble in business negotiations. He undertakes an important trip abroad which is successful for his firm. The escalation proceeds, and, finally, he commits himself to a relationship with a woman—a relationship which hitherto a vague fear had prevented him from initiating and which turns out to be as worthwhile as he could ever have hoped. After a few months we can truly say that all these events were not just contingent. The attitude of risking stayed with Hugo as a stable acquisition. He has broken out of the cocoon.

We should not think, however, that reflective meditation works only on our personal attitudes and actions, as in Hugo's case. It may also serve as an avenue to *transpersonal* levels—areas and states lying beyond our ordinary awareness. The mind then functions as a carrier of superconscious energy. A physician, for instance, writes:

> As I am going to bed, a few minutes after the meditation on calm, I have the sensation of arriving at the threshold of the Self: I experience a sense of wideness, of power, of great amplitude. With some humor, I tell myself that perhaps it's too soon yet. . . . Then I fall asleep.
>
> The next day, during the visits and dialogues with my patients, I often have the sensation of being struck by light, as if I am walking or gliding through areas of light, along paths in a wood that open onto sunny glades.
>
> I feel tranquil and filled with radiance.

Using the mind for higher purposes is a beautiful experience. But it is precisely at this exalted point that we should stop to recall that if the mind can foster constructive personal attitudes and evoke superconscious energies, it can also be used for purposes far less commendable, even as an instrument of the worst irrational tendencies. Examples can be seen in those technological advances which are used without regard to some of the fundamental human issues, or even have a deliberately destructive aim to begin with, such as the sophisticated weapons in use today. In these cases, the mind—though functioning in a highly effective, instrumental way—is divorced from human needs and ends, such as love, solidarity, aesthetic appreciation, intuitive understanding, and positive relating with the cosmos. When this divorce occurs, the mind becomes demonic.

In the individual, the hypertrophy of the mind presents dangers as disparate as they are deadly: you have aridity and abstraction from living experience, ruthlessness and contempt for the less brilliant. You have the eclipse of intuition and a reliance on empty logic alone. And then you have a cruelty unresponsive to anything that lives, as in the case of vivisection.

Therefore, in the rest of this chapter, we will go on to explore further advantages of mental development, but as we do so let us remember its risks—risks always present when a part of our being is developed independently of the whole. And let us also remember the remedy for dangers of this kind: the cultivation of *all* our faculties in harmony, rather than any narrow emphasis on one.

Now we are ready to consider what can be the greatest benefit of mental development: the birth of independent thinking. In a world of prejudice and rampant irrationality, of opinion manipulation and standardized attitudes, of ideological indoctrination and occult persuasion, nothing is more needed than an independent, critical, and clear mind.

Think of how commonly deceptive techniques are used by various organizations—private and public—to capture our minds: appeals to authority (of the "experts," of "science," or what everybody else is doing); use of stereotypes; biased selection of data; repetition of slogans; oversimplification of issues; creation of scapegoats; the artful evocation of guilt and inadequacy.[2] Each one of these forms of deception can be effectively countered and often defeated with the help of an autonomous and well-developed mind.

In a great variety of situations we can use our mind to clarify issues. In addition to meditating on a quality or phrase, we can also purposively reflect on a situation or problem—a general problem or, even more important sometimes, a personal one. In this way we throw more and more light on the issue we have chosen, disentangling the knots and seeing the possible alternatives and their consequences. Whenever we skip this stage we act on the impulse of the moment, we laboriously trudge in an atmosphere of confusion, we establish the edifice of our action on the wobbly columns of careless thinking. Nobody needs to be brilliant to stop and think for a moment. All we need is to remind ourselves to do it—already an important achievement—and then have the patience to go through with it. Cultivating these habits is the road to truly independent thinking.

The birth of independent thinking is usually experienced as an increase in mental freedom and power. I have seen people who are unexpectedly discovering this faculty in themselves become exhilarated with its possibilities. They suddenly understand that they do not have to think as they have been told. They see that they can question long-accepted assumptions. They become conscious of wide new areas of interest. Finally, and most important, they feel capable of formulating their own original design.

There are still farther reaches of mind development, but to describe them we must look at mental training from another perspective: control, focus, and concentration. Reflective meditation is a process of deepening our mental abilities to the point where new powers and states become available to us. First, we begin with an increase in focus. Reflection teaches us the habit of concentrated thinking whereby, as soon as some foreign association arises, we bring our attention back to the subject. "Reflecting" means "bending back." This bending back is gentle, but firm and alert, and is analogous to the strengthening of muscles in physical training. It builds mental flexibility.

Reflective meditation creates a *qualified environment* in our mind. In such an environment some elements are given admittance and others are not. A home is a qualified environment, because only certain persons can enter it. So are a stadium, a convention, a church or a circus. A cell is also a qualified environment, because it lets in through its membrane all that is useful and excludes whatever is useless or harmful to its maintenance. A city square is not a qualified environment, because anybody can pass through it at any time.

Most frequently our mind is comparable to the square of a big town: it contains all sorts of thoughts and images and concerns and memories and expectations in a confused whirl. By giving sole admittance to thoughts concerning one subject, we create a qualified environment.

As our mind's area of attention becomes circumscribed, its grasp of the subject deepens. At first, it is the analytical mind that is brought into play. One tends to see various partial aspects of the subject. Related memories crop up. Constellations of ideas present themselves to our attention because we are allowing those insights to come to light which would otherwise have remained submerged under the throng of everyday thoughts and preoccupations. Then, as focus is held ever steadier—possibly after long practice—one finds that the vagaries of the mind's superficial layers are left behind; the mind deals more with the essential and less with the casual or accidental; we come to see the deeper and more general implications of the subject; and, finally, active thinking transforms itself into silent dwelling on the very heart of what it contemplates.

When speaking of this kind of concentrated attention, raja yoga may come to mind, in particular Patanjali's *Yoga Sutras*. But it would be a mistake to believe that the razor-sharp mind, educated to penetrate the essence of a subject, is the monopoly of the yogi. One can find it functioning among creative people of all kinds—scientists, artists, inventors, politicians, religious leaders, and so on. Let me briefly quote two beautiful accounts of deep and concentrated thinking. The first, by the poet Stephen Spender, describes his technique of composition, emphasizing the all-encompassing grasp of the focused mind:

> It is a focusing of the attention in a special way, so that the poet is aware of all the implications and possible developments of his idea, just as one might say that a plant was not concentrating on developing mechanically in one direction, but in many directions, towards the warmth and the light with its leaves, and towards the water with its roots, all at the same time.[3]

The second account is by a saint, Teresa of Avila. Her words come in the form of an instruction and describe the transition from the early to the later stages of meditation:

> As soon as you apply yourself to reflection, you will at once feel your senses gather themselves together; they seem like bees which return to the hive and there shut themselves up to work at the making of honey . . . At the first call of the will, they come back more and more quickly. At last, after countless exercises of this kind, God disposes them to a state of utter rest and perfect contemplation.[4]

Portraits of advanced mental development further underscore the point that there is no process of self-actualization without a well-trained mind. It is not only *what* we think, but also *how* we think—the style, the rhythm, the cogency of our mind—that powerfully determines the patterns of our life. Thus, a well-functioning mind:

- can concentrate at will and examine in depth any given topic, even in distracting situations.

- can organize ideas, memories, and images in inner files, which can be consulted instantly.

- can become conscious of the grooves it is functioning in and choose to get out of them.

- sees all sides of a question, not only those on is comfortable with.

- can build tight, qualified environments.

- can switch easily from one mental universe to another and be at home in all of them.

• can evaluate and modify its own ways of functioning.

• can examine details without getting lost in them and grasp general principles without forgetting the details.

• never takes anything for granted.

• is aware of its own limits and is able to transcend them.

• experiences its own working as effortless delight.

Such positive mental qualities take time to develop, but reflective meditation is a simple and astonishingly effective key to them. Some of the rewards of reflective meditation, as we have seen, are immediate, while others take patience to attain. The goal is worth the journey, however, for through steady application we can become the sort of person that Ernest Dimnet, the educator, dignifies with the name of "thinker":

> A thinker is preeminently a man [or woman] who sees where others do not. The novelty of what he says, its character as a sort of revelation, the charm that attaches to it, all come from the fact that he sees. He seems to be head and shoulders above the crowd, or to be walking on the ridgeway while others trudge at the bottom. Independence is the word which describes the moral aspect of this capacity for vision. Nothing is more striking than the absence of intellectual independence in most human beings: they conform in opinion, as they do in manners, and are perfectly content with repeating formulas. While they do so the thinker calmly looks around, giving full play to his mental freedom. He may agree with the *consensus* known as public opinion, but it will not be because it is universal opinion. Even the sacrosanct thing called plain common sense is not enough to intimidate him into conformity.[5]

Chapter 10

THE SCHOOL OF LIFE

O ne morning, after working for about a year with Assagioli, a very upsetting event took place for me: my draft notice came in the mail. In Italy, military service is compulsory for every male citizen. You can postpone it for a few years, as I had already done, but in the end you just have to go. I had almost completely forgotten that fact, so much was I taken by enthusiasm for my work in psychosynthesis. Now I had to leave in a few days, interrupting my search for a higher consciousness, my training in psychosynthesis, my learning from Assagioli, my stay in Florence — among the most exciting things which I had enjoyed in my life up to that time. All this was now going to be replaced by fifteen months of military training in some faraway place: fifteen months of dressing in a uniform, of marches and guards, of handling guns and bombs, of coexistence with loud, boorish individuals (or so I felt at that time), and of having other people inspect and control me at all times. I was furious and also very depressed.

When I broke the news to Assagioli, I thought he was going to join me in my complaint about the absurdity of this situation. But his response surprised me. He said, "Great. Now you will learn how to collaborate with the inevitable. This will be a most important part of your psychosynthesis training." He was suggesting that instead of grumbling about a situation

113

which was, after all, beyond my control, I extract out of it all the benefits I could.

I was so puzzled by Assagioli's response that, instead of getting angry at him for not participating in my annoyance, I tried to follow his indications as well as the indications which life itself was giving me at the time.

Military service turned out to be a profoundly useful experience in my psychosynthesis training — even if the generals and the colonels had not meant it that way. I learned how to be open and communicate with people whose background was different from my own; I acquired the skill of meditating in a noisy dormitory; I became able to utilize the time between one chore and the next for reading and taking notes; I learned to waste time without feeling guilty. Finally, I understood that realizations of a higher consciousness are not tied to this or that situation but can occur in any place and at any time. And of course, once in a while I would still be annoyed by the whole situation and look forward to its ending.

Assagioli's teaching was clear now. When an unpleasant event happens to us, we can decide to accept it as it is, without complaining, because the universe does not adjust itself to our plans. As Marcus Aurelius beautifully states in his *Meditations,* we "don't quarrel with circumstances."[1] Our first spontaneous reaction may of course be one of self-pity, evasion, or rebellion. But as we assume a positive, dynamic attitude of *acceptance* (not resignation or approval), we find that we can better understand what is coming our way, learn from its message, take advantage of the hidden circumstances it may offer, and, if we so decide, fight it effectively. In any case, we will be able to take responsibility for whatever choice we in fact have — choice about our actions, thoughts, and feelings — instead of simply blaming everything on the outside world. In the words of the Indian saying, "If you don't want your feet to be hurt by thorns, you can try to carpet the whole earth; but it is easier and less expensive to buy a pair of shoes."

Assagioli's ideas about collaborating with the inevitable were certainly not born out of abstract speculation. In 1938, when he was jailed by the fascists for his antiwar and internationalist views, he realized that only an attitude of conscious acceptance would enable him to maintain a clear view of his real options. He later recorded his insights in a few notes, which he intended to publish as a book titled *Freedom in Jail:*

> I realized that I was *free* to take one of many attitudes toward the situation, to give one value or another to it, to utilize it in one way or another.
>
> I could rebel inwardly and curse; or I could submit passively, vegetating; or I could indulge in the unwholesome pleasure of

self-pity and assume the martyr's role; or I could take the situation in a sporting way and with a sense of humor, considering it as a novel and interesting experience (what the Germans call *Erlebnis*). I could make of it a rest cure or a period of intense thinking, either about personal matters — reviewing my past life and pondering on it — or about scientific and philosophical problems; or I could take advantage of the situation to undertake personal psychological training; or, finally, I could make it into a spiritual retreat. I had the clear, pure perception that this was entirely my own affair; that I was *free to choose* any or several of these attitudes and activities; that this choice would have unavoidable effects which I could foresee and for which I was fully *responsible*. There was no doubt in my mind about this essential freedom and power and their inherent privileges and responsibilities.

In such ways acceptance becomes the quickest and most practical way to free oneself from a difficult situation, while rebellion inexorably tightens the knot. The transition from rebellion to acceptance may then have an extremely important consequence: the shift from a *reactive* to a *cognitive* attitude, in which we start seeing life as a training school, where a series of situations tends to teach us exactly what we need to learn. We understand that our growth does not happen only through predefined meditations and exercises, or in private therapy sessions, but takes place mainly in the ever-changing process of life.

Painful situations then become charades to be deciphered rather than nuisances to curse at. And instead of merely surviving by being hurt, weary or frustrated, we can emerge from them enriched and with greater understanding.

We can also practice acceptance with the inevitable present and future disturbances of our inner life. Fear, depression, and irritation can be greatly relieved in a variety of ways, but they cannot be completely eliminated from human experience. By fighting these conditions, we give them energy and create a vicious circle. By accepting them as they are, we take the wind out of their sails and greatly diminish their power. For instance, instead of being irritated at our own irritation, or depressed because of our depression, which would only aggravate the problem, we can accept our feelings. We can practice a form of psychological judo.

ACCEPTANCE

1. Think of something in your life for which you feel or have felt grateful. It can be the presence of a person you love, a talent you have,

a sense of physical well-being, the beauty of a flower, and so forth. Imagine it vividly, appreciate it, think of what it gives you and what you can learn from it.

2. Now think of something (or somebody) which you would like to avoid in your life. Again, imagine it, and watch closely any reactions which arise in you. Watch them as they emerge, without trying to stop them. Observe your *habitual strategy of non-acceptance*. Be aware of how it works at the level of your body, your feelings, and your mind.

3. Now suppose that life is guiding you by communicating with you in a code language made up of situations and events. What is the message contained in the situation or event you have chosen? Write down any ideas that come to you as you reflect on this question.

4. Now return to whatever it was you felt grateful for. Imagine it once more, think of it with appreciation, and be as fully aware as you can of your acceptance.

5. Now switch back again to the unpleasant situation, bringing with you the accepting attitude which you have aroused. Acknowledge the *temporary* inevitability of this unpleasant situation. Realize that the same universe which produced what was pleasant also produced the unpleasant, and assume—if you feel ready and are willing to—an attitude of conscious, deliberate acceptance.

Even if you couldn't find any message in the situation you have chosen, you may still be able and willing to accept it. Acceptance of the absurd leads to the deepest of all surrenders. Really authentic and full acceptance gives up all comparisons, all expectations, all manipulations. At its core we find gratefulness for the fundamental all-rightness of the universe. A Zen story beautifully conveys this point:

When Banzan was walking through a market, he overheard a conversation between a butcher and his customer.

"Give me the best piece of meat you have," said the customer.

"Everything in my shop is the best," replied the butcher. "You cannot find here any piece of meat that is not the best."

At these words Banzan became enlightened.[2]

Chapter 11

RESERVOIRS OF REVELATION

I am on the beach at dawn. A few stars of an incomparable delicacy twinkle in the clear sky; the air is fresh and the sea almost motionless. Suddenly a golden ray, warm and radiant, reaches my face, and I surrender to its light and warmth. The sun rises slowly from the sea like a golden diamond and opens a luminous path on the water towards me. Completely naked, I move toward this path.

The limpid water caresses my body and is almost cold. The sun's radiance envelops me completely, and I walk until the water comes above my waist; then I start swimming in this path of light toward the sun. At a certain point I become aware I am no longer swimming in the water, but in the light, and I enter the sun.

I surrender to its immense warmth and brilliant light; the solar energy acts on me, caressing my whole body, my hair, my face, and enters me through my vagina. It rises slowly, pervading all my organs, transforming them into light. When it reaches my heart, I feel my whole chest expand. For a moment I cannot breathe; the energy penetrates my throat and my brain. I feel my head almost opening up, and suddenly my body starts

117

emitting this luminosity within it. At last, my whole being blends with the sun and becomes the light of the sun. It is hard to describe this sense of expansion and the ecstasy that derives from it. After a while my body rebuilds itself little by little, but now it is all made of light.

These words, describing the results of a visualization exercise, were written by Veronica, a teacher in her late thirties. She has always been intensely emotional, often experiencing difficulties in her relationships with people. When she started to work with me, Veronica had just been rejected by the man she loved and was having trouble with her colleagues. I perceived her as bewildered, vulnerable, and resentful. Her emotional wounds were wide open. But her resources were surprising, and she was quite receptive to psychosynthesis from the start. The visualization of swimming into the sun came as the culmination of our work:

That visualization helped me save the femininity in me. I didn't want it to die, even if for the time being it was not being reinforced. It was a part of me that had remained latent for too long, and now I did not want to lose it. Doing this exercise made everything seem transformed. The light reached the darkest parts of my unconscious, transmuting my passions. I succeeded in transferring them to another level of my being.

Of course, the relief I felt after doing the exercise did not last long at first. Soon I was back where I had been before, and the crisis repeated itself several times. But I kept performing the exercise until all of a sudden a big change happened. Some sort of illumination and renewal occurred; the forces of life were coming back again.

For Veronica the image of the sun had acted as a symbol—a symbol of light, of regeneration, of warmth—and one of the many which can be used in such exercises. When we visualize them, symbols can have a profoundly transformative impact on our psyche. They can be used to undo past conditioning and to establish new and more desirable energy patterns within us.

Symbols can also have a cognitive function. As Jung put it, they "point to something that is very little known or completely unknown."[1] They connect us with regions of our being which are completely unavailable to our analytical mind. Thus they train us to understand by seeing directly, jumping the intermediary stage of discursive thinking, which is sometimes more of an obstacle than an aid to understanding. This deeper kind of understanding awakens a faculty whose importance is almost universally neglected: *the intuition*.

We become intuitively receptive to the essence of a symbolic image by holding it steadily in our mind, letting it irradiate our awareness with its subtle quality. Such contemplation of an image may lead to an *identification* with it. Whether it happens spontaneously or intentionally, identification enables us to understand symbols from within, and intuition is nothing less than the understanding from within of the formless reality which the symbol represents. A man, for instance, writes:

> When I visualize the sun, it is as if I were drawn out of my body into that Source and at the same time were more alive, more aware, and more into my body and into the world to spread and diffuse these energies, accomplishing a higher will whose scope and consequences my feeble mind can hardly comprehend. I would like to remain in this state of consciousness forever, for this is what *life really is;* this is eternity, the eternal NOW.

Naturally, such cognitive connections do not occur to everyone all the time, and, when they do occur, they do not necessarily produce identical insights. For example, for some people the diamond is a symbol of the Self and of the world of visions, of glittering harmony and unity. But for others, the diamond may just stand for social status and prestige. For still others, the diamond may not be symbolic at all. It may be just a diamond, and nothing else. In any case, nearly all of us will find that one or another symbol can be a true reservoir of revelations.

THE LIGHTHOUSE

Let us now turn our attention to a visualization exercise that focuses on another symbol—one coming from the man-made world this time: the lighthouse.

You are on a small ship at sea, at night. A storm is raging, and the rain beats down on the deck. The ship is rolling and pitching. All around is darkness.

Feel the rolling and pitching of the ship, hear the wind howling, feel the chill of the wind and the rain on your face. See the stormy sea at night. Experience the fatigue in your muscles and the difficulty with which you wrestle with the wheel.

Now, in the distance, you can see a dazzling light shining. Its source is a lighthouse. Its steady, radiant beam guides you through the night. You welcome this guidance with relief. Now you know where to steer. Concentrate on the lighthouse, and visualize its light radiating in all directions to help people who have lost their way, to give guidance to all who need it. The storm is raging, the wind howling, the rain falling, the night pitch-black. But the lighthouse stands solid and shining. Nothing can shake it.

After a time, let the visualization gradually subside, yet keep within you this sense of shining strength.

A student who has performed this exercise reports:

Long before the university office was due to open, a mass of about one hundred people had formed, waiting in front of the door. I was toward the back.

I have a strong aversion to crowds, lines, offices, and bureaucracy in general, and as I started thinking about what would happen when the door opened, I felt my anxiety mounting. And then the worst happened: everyone crowded into the office, carrying me with them. I found myself squashed in a small room in the middle of a hundred people! For me a situation like this is particularly traumatic. At first I just wanted to get out, and to hell with everybody and everything! Then I decided to stay despite the increasing anxiety nearly suffocating me.

At this point I thought to avail myself of psychosynthesis, and I chose the lighthouse exercise. Part of the time I kept my eyes closed as if I were resting; otherwise, I continued the visualization with my eyes open amid the crowd. At first, I easily identified myself with a small sailboat wildly tossed about by the waves. Then I visualized a lighthouse emitting a powerful beam, almost as brilliant as sunlight. At its foot the waves pounded relentlessly, but it stood solid and unshaken. Now its light, increasing in intensity, began to spread over the surface of the sea as far as the horizon.

Retaining this picture in my mind for some time brought me great relief from the difficult situation I was in. My breathing grew slower and calmer, my chest and throat relaxed, and I gradually experienced some kind of inner peace and strength.

Such an example illustrates how symbols, rightly used, will deepen their transformative function, allowing us to change our inner attitudes and outer behavior. The quality inherent in the symbols not only *reveals* to us new ways of experiencing ourselves and life, it also *creates* a new line of force in our psyche — one which can gradually become a trait in our personality and thus affect our actions. The student was able to assimilate the sense of solidity he felt in doing the lighthouse exercise and create a stronger pattern of behavior.

A series of visualization exercises based on symbolic images follows. Each one represents a subtle reality with its own particular quality. Hence, each opens the door to a new state of consciousness and can elicit psychological change. Consciously and deliberately pick one symbol from among those given in this chapter or in other sections of the book, such as the blossoming of the rose, the wise person, the ascent of a mountain, the temple of silence, or from among other symbols which you may already have in mind. Then, the technique is to unflinchingly concentrate on the subject you have chosen, visualizing it as vividly and consistently as you can.

The point here is that you do not have to just wait until a symbol spontaneously appears in your process of inner development. Rather, you can *choose* to work with this or that symbol because of the cognitive and transformative value it offers. The issue here is a general one: we can creatively intervene in our unfolding, playing with it and exploiting its possibilities instead of just passively letting it take any shape it wants.

In this respect psychosynthesis encourages deliberate choices, rather than leaving the initiative wholly to the spontaneity of the moment. It also emphasizes steadfast persistence in a gradual comprehension of any subject (in this case a symbol) instead of an aimless gliding on to other experiences. It is advisable, therefore, to stay with a symbol over a period of time — a few minutes daily for a week or more, for example — so that symbol will gradually reveal to us unsuspected inner realities.

THE BUTTERFLY

Imagine a caterpillar. You can watch it crawling about on the tree where it lives. Attaching itself to a branch of the tree, the caterpillar starts to form its cocoon. Gradually it surrounds itself with golden, silken threads until it is totally hidden. Observe the cocoon for a few moments.

Now be inside the cocoon. Surrounded by the softness of silk, you rest in the warmth of the golden darkness. You are only dimly aware, so you do not know exactly what is happening to you, but you sense that in this apparent stillness a hidden, transforming intelligence is at work.

At last the cocoon breaks open, and a ray of light penetrates through a chink. As the light touches you, you feel a sudden surge of vitality and realize that you can shed the cocoon.

As you feel the cocoon falling away, you discover that with it you have shed the defenses and supports of your safety and your past. You are now freer than you ever dreamed you could be; you are a beautiful, multicolored butterfly. You soon realize that your boundaries have extended infinitely: you can fly. You find yourself dwelling in a totally new realm of colors, of sounds, of open space. You experience yourself flying, being supported by the air, being gently borne up by the breeze, gliding down, flying up again.

Below, you see an immense meadow full of flowers of every kind and color. You settle on one, then on another, then on another still, so gently that the petals are not even disturbed. You experience each flower as a different being with its own color and perfume, its own particular life and quality. Take your time in experiencing the many aspects of your expansion, your freedom, and your lightness.

THE SUN

Visualize yourself on the beach at dawn. The sea is almost motionless as the last bright stars fade away.

Feel the freshness and the purity of the air. Watch the water, the stars, the dark sky.

Take some time to experience the silence before sunrise, the stillness filled with all possibilities.

Slowly, the darkness melts and colors change. The sky over the horizon becomes red, then golden. Then the sun's first rays reach you, and you watch it slowly emerging from the water.

With half the sun's disc visible and the rest still below the horizon, you see that its reflection in the water is creating a path of golden, shimmering light leading from you all the way to its very heart.

The temperature of the water is pleasant, and you decide to go in. Slowly, with joy, you start to swim in the golden radiance. You feel the light-filled water touching your body. You experience yourself floating effortlessly and moving pleasurably in the sea.

The more you swim toward the sun, the less aware you are of the water, and the more the light around you increases. You feel enveloped in a beneficent, golden light which permeates you completely.

Your body is bathing now in the vitality of the sun. Your feelings are pervaded by its warmth. Your mind is illumined by its light.

THE FLAME

Imagine a burning flame. See it dancing, drawing ever-changing designs in the air. Look into it as it moves; seek to experience its fiery quality.

As you keep visualizing this flame, think about fire and its manifestations in the psyche: personal warmth and radiance, flaming love or joy, fiery enthusiasm, ardor.

Finally, as you keep the flame in front of your inner eye, slowly imagine that you are animated by that fire, that you are becoming that flame.

THE FOUNT

Imagine a fount springing from granite rock. You see its pure water sparkle in the sun and hear its splashes in the surrounding silence. You experience this special place, where everything is clearer, purer, more essential.

Start drinking the water, and feel its beneficent energy pervading you and making you feel lighter.

Now walk into the spring itself, letting the water flow over you. Imagine that it has the power of flowing *through* each one of your body cells and in between them. Imagine it also flowing through the innumerable nuances of your sentiments and emotions, and through your intellect as well. Feel this water cleansing you of all the psychic debris we inevitably accumulate day after day—frustrations, regrets, worries, thoughts of all kinds.

Gradually you experience how the purity of this fount becomes your purity, and its energy becomes your energy.

Finally, imagine that you are the fount itself, where all is possible and life is forever new.

THE DIAMOND

Vividly imagine a diamond.

See all its shining facets, perfectly integrated into one whole.

See the perfection of its shape.

Hold the diamond in front of your inner eye, and let yourself be pervaded by its crystalline beauty.

The word "diamond" comes from the Greek *adamas*, "unconquerable." As you identify with this diamond, sense it connecting you to that part of you which is likewise unconquerable, your Self.

Your Self is unconquerable by fear, by obscurity, by the pulls and the pushes of everyday conditioning. It is untouched by the shadows of the past, the monsters of worry, the phantoms of the future, the demons of greed, the dictatorship of social conformity. It is your very essence, shining through innumerable facets and yet one. Realize that you *are* that Self, and, as the image of the diamond fades away, let this sense of Self strengthen and grow ever clearer in you.

THE SKY

Imagine that it's a summer afternoon and you are lying on the grass. You feel the softness of the grass under you. Lying on your back, you look up at the sky: limpid, uncontaminated, deeply blue. Spend some time contemplating it.

You see a butterfly cross your field of vision. As it flies above you, you notice how light it seems and how delicately colored its wings are. Then you watch it disappear.

Now you see, silhouetted against the sky, an eagle high in flight. Following the eagle with your eyes, you penetrate the blue depths of the sky.

Still looking at the sky, you project your sight even higher. You can now see, very high and far away, a small white cloud pass. Watch it as it slowly dissolves.

Finally, there is only the boundless sky.

Become the sky—immaterial, immemorial, all-inclusive. As the sky, realize that there are no limits. Realize that you are everywhere, reaching all, pervading everything.

THE SHIP

Imagine a big ship at the beginning of its voyage; the wind is filling its sails as it moves toward the open sea.

Vividly visualize the ship with its billowing sails, its bow breasting the waves. Realize the propelling power of the wind, and listen to the sound of the waves as the ship heads toward the unknown.

Now imagine being on the ship. You are at the helm, conscious of the open sea ahead. The water sparkles in the sunlight, and you can barely distinguish the point where, far away, sea and sky merge at the horizon.

You sense the smell of the sea and the wind beating your face. You feel the wooden surface of the wheel in your hands.

You turn the helm now to your right, now to your left, and you are aware of a sense of mastery over the ship. Concentrate on your power of aiming the ship in whatever direction you want. It is an effortless mastery in which each decision is immediately transformed into action. You feel in charge.

Be conscious of this sense of mastery and discover all its nuances, and then let the image subside.

THE BELL

Imagine that you are lying on the grass of a meadow surrounded by hills. Feel the softness of the grass under your body, and smell the fragrance of the flowers around you. Look at the sky above.

Nearby there is a small country church. It has a bell which you can hear pealing. Its sound is both pure and joyful. It travels through the ether and reaches you. It is *your* sound, a sound capable of evoking and stimulating your unknown, concealed joy.

Now you hear the bell again. This time its peal is louder. Feel its resonance within you. Realize that it is awakening your dormant potentialities. Then listen to this sound as it gradually fades, and be aware of the moment when sound ends and silence begins.

Once more, you hear the bell pealing. The sound is somehow closer to you, and you can feel it vibrating within you, in each one of your cells, in each one of your nerves. And at some moment, if only for a second, you *become* that sound, pure, boundless, vibrating.

THE ARROW

Imagine that you have a bow and arrow in your hands. Feel your feet and legs solidly in contact with the earth. Hold the handle of the bow with one hand and the notched arrow and string with the other. Experience the muscles of your arms extending as you bend the bow. Now see the target clearly and vividly in front of you. And watch the tip of the arrow pointing toward it.

The bow is now bent to its limit; the arrow is precisely aimed. Sense how much energy is stored in this static posture. All you need to do is release the arrow for that energy to carry it to its target. Realize how this letting-go will release dynamic energy.

Now the arrow is released. See it in its flight, and feel its extraordinary one-pointedness. Nothing exists for the arrow but the target— no doubts, no distractions, no deviations. Flying perfectly straight, the arrow hits the center of the target and stops there, quivering.

Calmly and confidently, shoot a few more arrows into the target, and, as you do so, experience in yourself their unwavering, one-pointed, concentrated power.

RECONSTRUCTION: THE VILLA

Imagine a neglected garden overgrown with weeds. It surrounds an old, uninhabited villa with dilapidated walls and many broken windows. Open the creaking, wooden front door, go in, and look at the empty, dusty rooms. The sight of this abandoned villa and its uncultivated garden may give you a sense of desolation and sadness. But think of what this house could become if you decided to restore it. Size up its beautiful surroundings: trees, a lake, mountains in the distance.

It is time to get to work and start fixing up the villa. Wherever a wall is crumbling, you repair it with bricks and cement. Replace the rusty hinges of the doors with new ones. Where the floorboards are rotten, you replace them too. You put new glass in the broken windows and new tiles on the roof where needed.

You weed the garden and turn over the earth in preparation for planting. When the soil is ready, you sow seeds of various flowers in different parts of the garden according to the picture you have in mind of how the garden will look in full bloom.

You clean the house, sweep and wax the floors, and paint the inside and outside walls. You water the garden and notice that some plants are beginning to come up.

The house is ready to be furnished. Imagine tables and chairs and beds and carpets and mirrors and chandeliers and paintings and wardrobes and ornaments and vases. It is your villa, and you can furnish it just as you like. Take your time and furnish each room.

You walk in the garden and notice that the flowers are already beginning to blossom. They are of many colors, of many shapes. Look at them all and smell their perfume. Arrange the garden in the way that pleases you. Would you like, say, to put a fountain in the middle or a statue with ivy climbing on it? Do what you wish.

The time has come to put life and energy in the villa. You turn on the lights and see that they work. Some wood is burning in the fireplace; you check the water supply and see that it flows properly. You put some food in the refrigerator in the kitchen and some flowers in the vases.

You look out the window and see the garden in full bloom, with the lake and the mountains in the background.

Part of the effectiveness of visualizing such symbolic images as these can now be explained. They serve to structure and direct certain unconscious energies. Part of our unconscious is fragmented, dispersed, and unpurposive. It could be compared to a group of children who have a lot of energy but do not know what game to play. As we all know, they won't just sit there and wait. If the energy inherent in the unconscious is not channeled, it generates a vague sense of dissatisfaction and restlessness. We experience a lot of nervous stimulation but end up by doing nothing. This free-floating energy can often cause exaggerated emotional ups and downs, produce dispersion and a sense of meaninglessness, or explode in sudden outbursts of anger. It can also manifest itself as some general feeling that something needs to be done — but we know not what — and in many other unproductive and disturbing ways.

The unconscious, and particularly this disorganized, chaotic part of it, needs to be coached. It needs to have a rhythm and a direction communicated to it. Evocative symbols can greatly help in this task, because they tend to focalize free-floating psychological energy without repressing it. Visualizing the blossoming of a rose, for instance, orients the unconscious vectors — which would otherwise dart everywhere — in the direction of blossoming, of positive evolution.

The mythical image of the charioteer and the horses, which we find in both the Western and Eastern traditions, symbolizes one's capacity to deftly handle internal irrational and unknown forces. As we gradually acquire that capacity, we succeed in utilizing our latent resources rather than being at the mercy of an alien, unpredictable, and unmanageable power. By coaching our unconscious, we also discover in it a potentiality for countless transformations. I believe that this potentiality is metaphorically represented in Greek and Roman mythology, where gods and human beings are transformed into all kinds of flowers, plants, animals, constellations, rivers, and inert stone. However, one character especially symbolizes this infinite moldability: Morpheus, the god of dreams, who visits people while they sleep and has the capacity to take the semblance of any human being he wants.

It is precisely in this moldability of the human psyche that lies the promise of unfathomable possibilities.

Chapter 12

ONE FLOWER OPENS

At some times in our life a mysterious inner barrier loosens, and we experience directly that which we have been yearning for or vaguely felt or perhaps just heard about—or never surmised at all. In that incomparable moment the most exquisite, the most prodigious flow of realizations enters our awareness: we have contacted the highest realm of our being, our *superconscious*.

"It all happened in a second, but it was the most important moment of my life," says a woman reporting such an experience. "This was Reality. I had been through a long sleep and suddenly woke up. There was this overwhelming love, and it wasn't I who was very loving, or something that was loving me, *love itself was just there*. Even the air seemed to be alive, the nothingness seemed to be scintillating with this love. It all suddenly made sense." And the practical consequences were certainly no less intense than the subjective feeling. This woman, who had been refusing to feed herself for several months and was on the point of dying of starvation, decided to start eating again after this experience and gradually regained her health.

Even though these phenomena are intrinsically valuable and practically relevant, for years they have been excluded from the study of psychology and relegated to the supernatural, explained away as pathological, or dubbed self-suggestion. Rarely have they been studied as natural facts, as we can study a leaf, for instance, a bird, or a planet. Fortunately, in more recent years studies have been published giving more satisfactory descriptions and explanations, and research has shown how superconscious or transpersonal states are not the monopoly of a few, but a rather common occurrence in the life of many. However, we are still far from being able to answer fully some fundamental questions concerning transpersonal states. For example, how do they manifest themselves? What influences can they have on the psyche? What is their meaning and function in human existence? What are the laws that govern them? Which techniques can be used to evoke them? Answering these questions is certainly an enormous task, and the considerations in this chapter and the next ones—very far, of course, from being exhaustive—are an attempt to formulate a few working hypotheses.

We can perhaps start by pointing out how inadequate it is to believe, as is sometimes implied, that there is a single stable state of "enlightenment" or "liberation," to be reached once and for all and to be enjoyed permanently. I particularly recall that when I tackled Assagioli on this point he replied, smiling: "Life is movement, and the superconscious realms are in continuous renewal. In this adventure we move from revelation to revelation, from joy to joy. I hope you do not reach any 'stable state.' A 'stable state' is death."

To understand how this is the case, it is sufficient to consider a few of the nearly infinite variety of forms which superconscious experiences are reported to take:

An insight

The sudden solution of a difficult problem

Seeing one's life in perspective and having a clear sense of purpose

A transfigured vision of external reality

The apprehension of some truth concerning the nature of the universe

A sense of unity with all beings and of sharing everyone's destiny

Illumination

An extraordinary inner silence

Waves of luminous joy

Liberation

Cosmic humor

A deep feeling of gratefulness

An exhilarating sense of dance

Resonating with the essence of beings and things we come in contact with

Loving all persons in one person

Feeling oneself to be the channel for a wider, stronger force to flow through

Ecstasy

An intimation of profound mystery and wonder

The delight of beauty

Creative inspiration

A sense of boundless compassion

Transcendence of time and space as we know them

The *rhythm* of superconscious experiences can also vary greatly. Because of their suddenness and beauty, they are sometimes compared to fireworks or to meteors crossing the night sky, rapidly appearing in all their splendor and then vanishing. At other times, they are more gradual and take the form of an unfolding revelation comparable to a wonderful landscape slowly becoming visible as the fog which concealed it disperses.

In spite of all their variability, there seems to be a recurring factor in the transpersonal experiences of people from many cultures, times, and walks of life: a rare glimpse of, or even a full contact with, *a timeless essence,* a living entity which is perceived as unchangeable, silent, pure being. In psychosynthesis we call this entity the Transpersonal Self. The working hypothesis here is that the Transpersonal Self is at the core of the superconscious, just as the personal self, or "I," is at the core of the ordinary personality.

However we may want to classify them, superconscious or transpersonal experiences are facts. It would be hard to deny their reality while so many people bear witness to their existence. But what is their meaning? Why do they exist? Are they exceptional or random or, perhaps, even bizarre and abnormal manifestations of the human mind?

Of the many answers given to these questions, possibly the most reasonable explanation of transpersonal experiences maintains that they represent the next steps in the course of our human evolution. This was already the thesis of Richard Maurice Bucke's book, *Cosmic Consciousness.*

Comparing evolution to a growing tree, Bucke says:

We know that the tree has not ceased to grow, that even now, as always, it is putting forth new buds, and that the old shoots, twigs, and branches are most of them increasing in size and strength. Shall their growth stop today? It does not seem likely. It seems more likely that other limbs and branches undreamed today shall spring from the tree, and that the main trunk which from mere life grew into sensitive life, simple consciousness, and self-consciousness shall yet pass into still higher forms of life and consciousness.[1]

Similarly, Teilhard de Chardin claimed that biological evolution—the version prevailing since Darwin's day—is only an aspect of the "mighty tide" of the evolution of consciousness, bringing humankind toward the "interminably and undestructibly new."[2] More recently, Abraham Maslow saw "peak experiences" and "meta-needs" (needs for beauty, love, truth, justice, order, and so on) as being the highest part of nature and the most recent acquisition in our evolution. He claimed that they should be seen as aspects of human biology, and that they should not be the exclusive property of theologians, philosophers, or artists, but also be the object of scientific study. "The spiritual life," he said, "is part of our biological life. It is the 'highest' part of it, but yet part of it."[3]

It is difficult to argue with total certainty that humanity is evolving—and concentration camps, nuclear weapons, the horrors of war, the unequal distribution of wealth, don't help prove the point. But we can surely agree that single human beings can grow. Their awareness can expand into realms that they experience as intrinsically valuable, that have a dimension of universality, that evoke mystery and wonder, and that possess a revelatory, healing, and transforming power. Superconscious experiences are subjectively felt as a step forward in personal evolution, as a wonderful unfolding of what was previously existent only in a potential state.

THE ROSE

To convey the sense of an unfolding process in the psyche, and at the same time to facilitate it, Assagioli—in his book *Psychosynthesis*—created the exercise of the blossoming of the rose. The following is a variation of that exercise:

Imagine a rosebush: roots, stem, leaves, and, on top, a rosebud. The rosebud is closed, and enveloped by its green sepals. Take your time in visualizing all the details clearly.

Now imagine that the sepals start to open, turn back, and reveal the petals inside—tender, delicate, still closed.

Now the petals themselves slowly begin to open. As they do so, you become aware of a blossoming also occurring in the depths of your being. You feel that something in you is opening and coming to light.

As you keep visualizing the rose, you feel that its rhythm is your rhythm, its opening is your opening. You keep watching the rose as it opens up to the light and the air, as it reveals itself in all its beauty.

You smell its perfume and absorb it into your being.

Now gaze into the very center of the rose, where its life is most intense. Let an image emerge from there. This image will represent what is most beautiful, most meaningful, most creative that wants to come to light in your life right now. It can be an image of absolutely anything. Just let it emerge spontaneously, without forcing or thinking.

Now stay with this image for some time, and absorb its quality.

The image may have a message for you—a verbal or a nonverbal message. Be receptive to it.

To those who have experienced it, the realm of the superconscious and the Transpersonal Self is intensely *real*.

It is not an intellectual concept.
It is not a byproduct of the superego.
It is not the result of suggestion.
It is not a parapsychological phenomenon.
It is not a state of lowered awareness.

In its ordinary state, the personality rightly feels itself to be incomplete. Indeed, it is constantly occupied with trying to reach a state of completeness. Its usual condition is a state of perpetual *busy-ness*. But the Self is in a state of plenitude and does not need to look outside in order to be fulfilled. The Self is pure *being,* beyond thoughts, beyond words, beyond actions.

Stealing precious minutes from her busy schedule now and then, Anna keeps doing the rose exercise and sees as the final image a long staircase ascending toward an intensely luminous source: "At each step I find flowers on both sides, and they blossom as I look at them. As I follow the stairway with my eyes, I see that its top merges with the light. I see that it is the meeting point of infinite other stairways that come to it from all directions, even opposite ones, and are made luminous by the source toward which they mount."

We have here a pictorial representation of the journey from *multiplicity* to *unity*. Multiplicity characterizes the realm of our ordinary personality. The eyes of the personality perceive multiplicity everywhere: in the inner life of the individual, with all its different subpersonalities, often at war with one another; in the world of contrasting opinions; and at the level of human relationships, where the personality perceives itself as an entity separated from other entities.

But as we move toward the Self, unity replaces multiplicity. The psychological life becomes harmonized as the diversity of its parts fuses into a synthesis. "Now I feel *I*," says a young man, "I feel *one*, while before I felt split into different conflicting parts." Unity can also be experienced at the intellectual level, as when we discover a law of nature which explains a multiplicity of apparently unrelated events. Unity is found in a work of art—be it a symphony, a play, or a painting—when all its elements fit into one harmonious whole. And finally, unity is also experienced in relation to others, as a sense of solidarity with the human race at large and an awareness of one single source common to all beings—a source in whose light all conflicting viewpoints and interests disappear or lose their importance.

Let us now look at another image that emerges in Anna's exercises: "A spring gushing from a divided stone. The upward spurt of limpid water shines at its top, because at every moment some water is illuminated by the sun. This image gives me a sense of the perennial, of timelessness."

The personality lives in *time*. At its level we come across the conviction that nothing is permanently reliable, nothing is permanently satisfying—a condition that Mircea Eliade has called "the terror of time."[4] But the Self lives in *timelessness*. The distinction between the two modes is beautifully stated by the English poet Henry Vaughan:

> I saw Eternity the other night
> Like a great *Ring* of pure and endless light,
> All calm, as it was bright,
> And round beneath it, Time in hours, days, years
> Driv'n by the spheres
> Like a vast shadow mov'd, in which the world
> And all her train were hurl'd;

Intimations of timelessness are much more common than we might think. It is easy, for example, to lose the ordinary perception of time when an activity or an encounter totally absorbs us —until we are called back to the old rhythm by some extraneous event. Or it can happen when we come in contact with an environment whose tempo is much slower than the human one: mountains, oceans, deserts, and, above all, the starry sky.

We can also have similar experiences through meditation, without the help of outer stimuli. I was once reminded of this fact in a curiously homely way. Assagioli relied on an egg timer to signal the end of a period of meditation with a loud "bing." When I asked him why he needed it, Assagioli answered that his reason for "sublimating" the egg timer from its humble work in the kitchen to such a dignified function was that in meditation the sense of time often fades out, so that it is difficult to know how long one is in it by the standards of our usual, human time. He mentioned this as something quite obvious, and I could see how real that experience was for him. Just as real was my own experience in meditation at that period: I was not getting into timelessness at all, but on the contrary struggling moment by moment with distractions, resistance, or drowsiness — the inevitable obstacles that any beginner comes up against at first.

To return to Anna, in another exercise, as she looks into the center of the rose, she sees the sky: "It is an infinite sky, intensely blue, immense in its depth. I merge with that sky, and I hear a voice coming from it." As this voice talks to her, stimulating her to courage and to action, she feels moved and convinced. "I experienced an expansion of my range of freedom," she says; "It is as if I have received permission to go beyond a gate. This gives me courage and joy."

As the personality ordinarily perceives it, the world is structured into *forms* (thoughts, objects, people: *anything* is a form). And forms always tend to delimit, ultimately to imprison. The world of the Self, however, is experienced as *formless* — which is why contact with it can induce a sense of freedom and expansion beyond all limitation.

Forms can be described, compared, catalogued. The Self is as unstructured as the sky envisioned by Anna. We can formulate working hypotheses and give dim indications about the Self, but we can never really pin it down. As William James put it, one of the main marks of "mystical" experience is "ineffability."[5]

It is not that forms disappear, but rather they lose their limiting aspect, so that each is seen to contain in some way all forms. For William Blake, this meant:

> To see a World in a grain of sand
> And a Heaven in a wild flower
> Hold Infinity in the palm of your hand
> And Eternity in an hour.

Or consider this haiku: "One speck of dust contains the whole earth; when one flower opens, the whole world comes into being."[5]

Likewise, Borges talks about the Aleph, the mythical place where, "without any possible confusion, all the places in the world are found, seen from every angle."[6]

The *hologram* is the technical counterpart of this intuitive kind of perception. A hologram is a picture reproduced through laser beams on a photographic plate. It differs from an ordinary image in that each point contains the whole picture. If you have a fragment of an ordinary picture — a picture of a person, for instance — that's just what you have, no more and no less: one eye, the nose, part of the lips, whatever. But if you have a fragment of a hologram, you still have the pattern of the whole picture. In our example, you still have the whole face. Each part is not only itself, but also every other part.

Some contemporary physicists (whose insights, as has been repeatedly shown, are reminiscent of those of mystics) have reached the conclusion that elementary particles are not separate building blocks standing side by side, but processes interrelated with each other in a dynamic web. This "bootstrap" hypothesis has gone so far as to state that "every particle consists of all other particles."[7] In some way they interpenetrate, involve, and contain each other, so that the whole universe is present in each one of its parts.

A parallel interpenetration of form is often mentioned by mystics from both the Eastern and the Western traditions. Meister Eckhart, for instance, claims that in spiritual realms beings are no longer separated, as in our everyday experience, but everyone is everyone else, while still mysteriously retaining his or her own identity. Likewise, to the inspired individual, each moment in life contains one's whole life, each attitude subtly comprises all the others, each person met is the universe itself. Says Milton: "Thou to me are all things under heaven, all places thou."[8]

The distinction between event and quality may further clarify these matters. In the exploration of the superconscious we may contact what can be described as a psychological *quality,* such as love, joy, strength, serenity, peace, and so on. And this quality may appear to us as it is in itself, beyond any of the specific forms imposed on it by the external world of events. A woman, for instance, writes of her meditations:

> By coming in touch with the quality of courage, I contacted the essence of courage of the Samurai and the courage of the heroes, the silent courage of everyday life manifested in countless acts and yet transcending all of them.
>
> Likewise, when tuning in to love, I got in touch with the storehouse of love energy, so to speak—the love that infuses all

the innumerable particular acts and thoughts of love that have been and ever will be.

On the other hand, insofar as one is focused in the perspective of the personality, interest will mainly be in this or that *event* taking place: winning, making money, having a career, getting married, living without preoccupations, being promoted, and so on, following the dualistic calculus of pleasure and pain, failure and success.

People who are in contact with the Self are less interested in which event is going to take place, and more in the general quality of life. They are more concerned with the *how* and less with the *what*. They are keen on playing well rather than winning; on the harmony and beauty of what they do, rather than on what they can get out of it. They live what Keyserling calls the "symbolic life"—that is, they become living symbols or expressions of love, peace or any other superconscious quality. Being firmly rooted in the realm of qualities, they tend to give no ultimate importance to the ever-changing world of events, though they operate in it with passionate competence and commitment.

Another image Anna sees in the center of the rose is reminiscent of such insights. A drop shines, resplendent because touched by a ray of light; from inside the drop Anna hears a chorus of human voices addressing her with particularly moving eloquence. From this communication Anna gets a sense of sharing participation, and of a new relationship: "I feel immersed in white light. I feel alive in a world of marvelous living creatures. I feel that I am sharing in a world of human beings from which, until now, I have been far away."

The personality in its ordinary state experiences *scarcity* everywhere. Everything it yearns for (the attention of a particular person, wealth, success, power, and so on) decreases the more it is divided; and since everybody is trying to get as much as possible, there always seems less to go around. This perception leads to a sense of urgency, of isolation and competition. The Self, instead, exists in a world where *sharing* is the norm. The more we share of love, truth, or joy, the more of them we have: it is exactly the reverse kind of mathematics.

In a subsequent exercise, Anna experiences the image of a well: "I lean out and see that it is very deep. At its bottom I see my face and behind me the iron arch of the well and the sky. The inside of the well is covered with writings of ancient wisdom. I ask the well: 'What is Life?' 'You answer me,' it says, 'because *you* are the one who can give an answer to Life, instead of expecting it from elsewhere.'"

The well reminds Anna of the central attitude of the Self—an attitude of giving and radiating. In the words of Dante, the Self is "a sure wealth that has nothing more to seek."[9] This wealth of love and joy is not, however, self-limiting but, rather, tends to overflow and propagate itself.

The basic expression of the Self is *service* — a service that is free, having nothing in common with trying to be good and seeking to help. Persons who can give without strings attached, just for the sheer delight of it, are rare, but they exist. And many of us have tested such pleasures from time to time.

On the other hand, the personality is characterized by *unfulfillment*. In it you will always find a need that cries out to be satisfied. And if that does not happen, the personality feels that its own existence is threatened. Its central and recurrent preoccupations are, therefore, physical and psychological survival.

Day after day, Anna continues practicing the rose exercise, and each time a new image emerges:

> This time it is an ocean without boundaries. It is timeless, infinite as the universe. I hear a song of peace coming from its waves. At some point a wave carries a baby to the beach. It is as if this baby were offered to me by two infinite arms, made of the two parts of the wave on my two sides. And I find myself facing this baby.
>
> Kneeling on the sand to be closer to him, I feel a sense of reverence before a being so precious and so unique.
>
> I experience a feeling of total consent, yielding to what life presents me.

At the level of the personality we try to control our life, to determine its course by what we judge favorable to us. At the level of Self, control gives way to a *surrender* to what life brings to us. There is, then, a sense of letting go, of release. As the Indian sage Ramana Maharishi once pointed out, usually we are like people on a moving train who still hang onto a suitcase. Why carry it? If we put it on the floor it will be carried by the train, and we shall be relieved of the effort of holding it.

The personality has a certain model of how it all should be and tends to be closed to any event which does not fit into the narrow circle of its expectations. The Self-realizing individual, however, is open. As the *Bhagavad Gita* put it, this person is "satisfied with whatever comes unsought,"[10] like Anna receiving her baby from the sea.

It must be stressed that this surrender implies no fatalism of any kind. It does not deny or suppress some form of wise awareness and control. It can be compared to the attitude of an orchestra conductor: nothing he or she does could be further from resignation or passivity. And yet in directing the musicians, the conductor does not follow a whim but rather the musical text, surrendering to it all efforts and personal resources.

At this point we could make the mistake of believing that the realm of the Self is *good* and the realm of the personality is *bad*. But such a judgment would prevent us from understanding that the personality and the Self can actually be seen as two aspects of the same evolution. A butterfly is not better than a caterpillar. It is a development, an unfoldment. The view we have from the valley is not worse than the one we can enjoy on top of the mountain. It is simply narrower, and that is the order of things. There would be no top without a valley, no butterfly without a caterpillar, no realization of the Self without the previous stage of personality.

We can talk of phases of the evolution from personality to Self. In the various individuals and cultures who have experienced it, transpersonal evolution has been manifested through the ages in enormously diverse ways. Typically recurrent themes, however, can be detected, and if we avoid the mistake of becoming too literal or concrete, we may succeed in throwing light on the main aspects of this great adventure.

Paradoxically, the first stage is frequently negative. It is a stage of emptiness and dissatisfaction. Before the first intimations of a spiritual awakening take place, an individual tends to blindly accept the values of personality. As we have seen, scarcity, competition, multiplicity, the struggle for survival, the limitations of form, and the terror of time constitute his daily lot. He or she may have learned to function quite efficiently in this struggle and may be enjoying some measure of social recognition for personal achievements. This person may also sense a high degree of psychological freedom.

At some point, however, the edifice starts to crack. There is a sense that something is lacking, even though the individual does not know what; or perhaps a feeling that personal endeavors have no deep meaning; or a sense of uneasiness or restlessness; or an all-encompassing guilt, even despair.

Psychological freedom does not disappear, but paradoxically becomes a nightmare — the predicament well illustrated by Sartre's famous dictum that we are condemned to be free.

In individuals at this phase, the "I" perceives itself as fundamentally isolated from all the other "I's," which appear to it as completely alien. These people have partially and temporarily transcended their normal needs. They float, so to speak, in between the world of the personality and that of the Self, yet they are unaware of the latter. The result is an existential vacuum, the state in which all possibilities are seen as equivalent and the totality of things is experienced as indifferent. In existentialist philosophy, terms for this condition have been "boredom," "nausea," and "gloom".

"True boredom," said Heidegger, "is not the one coming from a book or from a performance, but the one which invades us when 'one is just bored'; the deep boredom which, like a silent fog gathering in the abysses of our being, unites men and things, ourselves with all that is around us, in a peculiar sort of indifference."[11]

At this point all the working hypotheses on which these persons' lives have been based are obsolete. None of what they have believed in and fought for up to this time makes sense anymore. Sometimes this state emerges in an abrupt way. More often it comes and goes in waves. In still other cases, the existential vacuum is avoided by sheer dint of routine and of the continuation of the ordinary business of everyday life.

Sooner or later, gradually or abruptly, the existential vacuum is filled by the emergence of the Self. This event is of the greatest importance in the psychological life of the individual. Various symbols have been used to describe it, among them:

An *illumination* that dispels all illusions and allows one to see reality as it is

An *awakening* from a long sleep — a sleep full of dreams and unconsciousness

A *birth* into a new and wider world, full of unsuspected possibilities

There have been many other metaphors, conceptual models, and religious symbols used to describe this momentous occurrence. Similarly, there have been diverse paths, often tortuous and strange, which people have trodden to it — and as many corresponding descriptions and interpretations. But we can safely say that the event itself in its essence is universal: the understanding of new meaning, and the flow of a more intense vitality.

The personality, naturally, first understands this occurrence in its own terms. Transpersonal satisfactions are seen as being of the same nature as personal satisfactions, as their multiple. The Self is perceived as something to be reached, owned, and consumed — an object that will increase the well-being of the personality without altering its value system. The Pie in the Sky. It is at this stage that we find all these zealous and earnest people who, seeing "enlightenment" as the promise of instant happiness, are out to get it.

This phase, which immediately follows the awakening, we could call *aspiration*. It is very lively and full of joy. With relief, the individual sees that all the distress and emptiness which had previously been so painful have entirely disappeared. He or she feels strong and confident and believes that all psychological problems have been dealt with. There is often a naive belief in having reached a stable and permanent form of psychological and spiritual balance.

But soon instability threatens this confidence, and often exhilaration gives way to a sense of despair. The individual starts believing that all that has been seen and felt was an illusion. Often this person feels deceived or abandoned. Always, there is a sense of confusion. All the facile explanations, all the emotional thrills, all the enthusiastic beliefs, are gone.

Very gradually, the personality understands that a profound job of reorganization needs to take place. This work takes time and usually brings attrition because the psyche tends to resist the transmutation. There is an oscillation, a flip-flop, between old and new values, and sometimes an uneasy, unstable coexistence of the two. Confronted with new challenges, an individual may find personal limitations of which they were unaware; there may be a temporary loss of self-esteem. Metaphorically, we could say that it is as if there were more light, and this light made all the obstacles in its way pitilessly and dramatically visible.

On the other hand, this same process may be experienced as fully natural and obvious. The Self becomes the new and valuable mode of being, and the old ways are easily left behind and forgotten—as in the case of an adult who has outgrown the need of his childhood toys.

People finding themselves in the phase of transmutation often feel that they are on a path or a way to the Self. Thus it is possible to speak of the way of love or the way of illumination, the way of action or the way of beauty, the way of ritual, of devotion, of the will, of science, and so on. The various paths to the Self tend to be expressive of various types of people, thus permitting each one to utilize his or her own unique approach leading to fulfillment. As Krishna, representing the Self, says in the *Bhagavad Gita:* "As men approach me so do I accept them: men from all sides follow my path."

Transmutation culminates in the full realization of the Self. This last phase is evidenced in various degrees in the lives of the great geniuses, artists, and spiritual leaders of humankind. And it is precisely in their lives, presented in biographies and other documents, that we can best understand and study the nature of the Self and the superconscious.

Despite the great variety of ways in which this overall unfoldment occurs, it is not based on expansions of consciousness only. The superconscious realizations need to be grounded. Just as the pattern of a crystal subsists in a potential state and then, in a super-saturated solution, takes visible form, so do superconscious energies tend to materialize in the external world.

The tendency to be manifested physically is common to all contents of consciousness. A desire for escape materializes in a journey. Rage materializes in an insult; devotion, in a cathedral; desire to see, in a telescope; a defensive feeling, in barbed wire; aggression, in a gun; desire for speed, in a motorcycle.

Likewise, superconscious energies seek and need to be manifested. This is a fundamental principle of psychological health. The point, then, is not only to induce peak experiences, ecstasy, satori, and the like; but also to make the ideals of which peak experiences are an explosive demonstration a pervasive reality in our life and in the lives of others. Even without ecstasies, such inner realities as altruistic love, insight, wonder and gratefulness, the sense of beauty and justice, can constitute the themes of our life — what Maslow called "plateau experiences" — and not just passing episodes.

I will end with one simple example of grounding. We have followed the development of Anna's superconscious experiences. How did she manifest them in her life? At the end of her report, she writes: "A new event has happened in my life: my husband and I have asked to adopt a newborn baby, whose mother could not take care of him, and who would have otherwise had to go to an orphanage. This period is extraordinarily beautiful, even though it does not lack difficulties. It seems to me that I am now living practically what has happened in my inner experiences."

Chapter 13

THE BEST
THERAPIST

One day, according to an Eastern story, the gods decided to create the universe. They created the stars, the sun, the moon. They created the seas, the mountains, the flowers, and the clouds. Then they created human beings. At the end, they created Truth.

At this point, however, a problem arose: where should they hide Truth so that human beings would not find it right away? They wanted to prolong the adventure of the search.

"Let's put Truth on top of the highest mountain," said one of the gods. "Certainly it will be hard to find it there."

"Let's put it on the farthest star," said another.

"Let's hide it in the darkest and deepest of abysses."

"Let's conceal it on the secret side of the moon."

At the end, the wisest and most ancient god said, "No, we will hide Truth inside the very heart of human beings. In this way they will look for it all over the Universe, without being aware of having it inside themselves all the time."

The psychosynthetic technique of inner dialogue avails itself of the truth which lies hidden, and often forgotten, within ourselves. We imagine that we meet a person on top of a mountain, away from and above all

civilization, in a timeless realm. This person is the source of healing and
nourishing love — a love that accepts us for what we are and evokes in us
what we may become. Not myopically focused on the immediate satisfaction of personal needs, nor influenced by the capricious demands of the
environment or the passing mood, this person has great wisdom, and can
understand life as a whole, with all its contradictions and paradoxes. We
feel at ease, and, above all, there is an atmosphere of deep trust. In the
ensuing dialogue an exchange of energies takes place, ideas are clarified,
and doubts are dissipated.

In this technique much more is at work than mere fantasy. The wise
person functions as a most effective symbol of the Self and enables us to
contact its healing, vivifying, illuminating energy. Thus we can truly say
that the Self is the best therapist.

Inner dialogue is suited for all occasions, but it is particularly useful
in certain special moments, such as when:

- We are facing an important choice.
- We are in crisis.
- We think that nobody understands us.
- We want to tap our inner wisdom.
- We feel lonely.
- We are ready for a change.
- We want a free session.

But the effects of inner dialogue can go well beyond the unblocking
of an impasse. Through it there is the possibility of establishing a channel
of communication with the superconscious, setting off what Assagioli
called "vertical telepathy." We can learn how to rely on our Self rather than
following the pressures of other people or of our own subpersonalities. We
can discover how to take the whole situation into account instead of being
influenced by intense but unimportant elements. There is also the possibility of finding that the solution of a problem can always be found at a level
higher than the one where the problem itself lies. Moreover, we can avoid
all the complications that follow decisions made in a superficial, hurried,
heedless way.

INNER DIALOGUE

Imagine that it is a summer morning. You are in a valley. Gradually
become aware of your environment: the air is clean and the sky in-

tensely blue, there are flowers and grass all around you. The morning breeze gently caresses your cheeks. Feel the contact of your feet with the ground. Be aware of what clothing you are wearing. Take some time to become clearly conscious of all these perceptions.

You feel a sense of readiness and expectancy. As you look around, you see a mountain. It towers close to you, and looking at its summit gives you a sense of extraordinary elevation.

Then you decide to climb the mountain. You begin by entering a forest. You can smell the pleasant aroma of the pine trees and sense the cool, dark atmosphere.

As you leave the forest, you enter a steep path. Walking uphill, you can feel the muscular effort demanded of your legs and the energy that pleasantly animates your whole body.

The path is now ending, and all you can see is rock. As you keep climbing, the ascent becomes more arduous; you now have to use your hands.

You feel a sense of elevation; the air is getting fresher and more rarified; the surroundings are silent.

Now your climb brings you into a cloud. Everything is whitish, and you can see only the mist which envelops you. You proceed very slowly and carefully, just barely able to see your hands on the rock in front of you.

Now the cloud dissolves, and you can see the sky again. Up here, everything is very much brighter. The atmosphere is extraordinarily clean, the colors of rock and sky are vivid, and the sun is shining. You are ready to move on. Climbing is easier now; you seem to weigh less, and you feel attracted to the top and eager to reach it.

As you approach the very top of the mountain, you become filled with an increased sense of height. You pause and look around. You can see other peaks near and far, the valley in the distance, and in it a few villages.

You are now on top of the mountain, on a vast plateau. The silence here is complete. The sky is a very deep blue.

Far off, you see someone. It is a person, wise and loving, ready to listen to what you have to say and tell you what you want to know. He or she first appears as a small, luminous point in the distance.

You have noticed each other. You are walking toward each other, slowly.

> You feel the presence of this person, giving you joy and strength.
>
> You see this wise being's face and radiant smile, and feel an emanation of loving warmth.
>
> Now you are facing each other: you look into the wise person's eyes.
>
> You can talk about any problem, make any statement or ask any question you wish. Silent and attentive, you listen for the answer; and if it comes, you may want to prolong the dialogue.

Maurizio is a physically strong person. He comes from a big rural family where they all live together—not only the mother and father, but also lots of aunts and uncles and cousins—and where, also, nobody gets much attention because he is considered to be just like everybody else.

Maurizio works as a clerk and comes to see me for a few sessions: "I am 28 years old; I feel a great sense of void and isolation," he writes, "I am letting myself go, and I am almost constantly depressed." He feels tempted to give in to drugs and alcohol and to get away from everything and everybody "for some kind of self-destruction." His most important problem lies in the area of relationships: "I can't stand people and I have to avoid crowded places: dance halls, long waiting-lines, traffic jams, stadiums. I fear people and I try to stay clear of them."

This attitude recalls Kafka's short story *The Burrow,* in which a mysterious animal is continually thinking about how it can reinforce its burrow against unseen enemies and spends all its time in constructing more and more underground defenses. Maurizio writes: "I believe that my diffidence crept into me when I was very young. It is a feeling which has no reference to a person or a group or a generation. It is universal. I have done nothing else in my life but think about how to defend myself from others. I have isolated myself in my own fortress."

At the same time, Maurizio is faintly tempted to open up, because he also writes: "It is extremely difficult to learn to have faith and to love." But the main feeling at present is despair. In spontaneous imagery he visualizes himself in the middle of a marsh: "Mud, mud all the way up to the groin. I pull one foot up only to go down with the other. I have a sense of panic, and even more of weariness, or resignation. Behind me and all around there is fog. Behind the fog there is black."

After a cycle of sessions during which little seems to happen on the surface, I decide it is time for Maurizio to meet his wise person. Here is his report of how the meeting goes: "There is somebody sitting in front of the fire; I go closer. It is an old man. He is thin, with white hair. His beard is white, too. He smiles; his eyes are clear. He beckons me to come closer. A great peace pervades me as I stand before him. I feel that I know him and that he knows me. As I look at him, his smile gives me great joy."

At this point we know that Maurizio's wise person is genuine and not a fake, as sometimes happens with this technique. Joy is the surest guarantee. In performing this exercise we must beware of various inner impersonators of the wise man: the snobbish old man, the judgmental old man, the evil old man, or any other character who is not the living embodiment of love, joy, and wisdom. A woman, for instance, once said to me: "I met the wise old man, but the meeting was frustrating. Whatever I said, he kept putting me down, making hateful remarks, and speaking in such a difficult way that whatever he was saying was far above my head." That, of course, was not her wise old man at all. In talking about this experience, it turned out that he reminded her of an uncle who had acted toward her in precisely these ways. Once she understood this, she was able to perform the exercise with real satisfaction. But to return to Maurizio's experience:

"I know everything about you," says the wise man. "You can be calm, everything is all right, there is nothing to worry about."

I go away happy. He knows all about me: I am not alone anymore. I can return to him whenever I want. He will be there, knowing everything about me. I have an ally. I could fly down the mountain, I feel so light.

This feeling has been with me for several days, slowly fading. Dark thoughts again invade my field of consciousness, but because I recognize them as soon as they surface I am able to get rid of them.

After Maurizio performed this exercise he became psychologically stronger, his growth speeded up, and his relationships with other people started to improve. He found a girlfriend, and he gradually realized the value and the rewards of love. His diffidence vanished, and he was able to experience and express a wider range of emotions.

Why had all this transformation taken place? After all, the wise man just told Maurizio not to worry. How could such a simple, imaginary meeting originate such a series of changes? The answer is that inner dialogue often takes a very elementary form, but under the surface of that interaction a lot more may be going on. A door opens to superconscious energy, and, as soon as an individual is receptive, that energy flows in and starts its healing, regenerating, inspiring work. We never know the exact details of how this work unfolds. But we see the clear and undeniable results of its action.

It is not surprising, then, that meeting our wise woman may be just as important as meeting our wise man. And it is useful to practice with both—as this report, written by a woman, shows:

> I have a wise old woman as well as a wise old man. My wise woman is lovely. She is somewhat stout and has a kindly face, grey hair done in a French twist, warm brown eyes, and is dressed simply, usually in blue.
>
> I don't choose either the woman or the man—I just close my eyes and see which one emerges. Usually the man appears for explorations of a more impersonal nature. But when the discussion is more personal, the woman comes. The wise woman is much more comforting than the man, whereas the man has a strong sense of goodness and wisdom. Her kind of wisdom is different from the man's—it is a womanly wisdom, gentler and more nourishing.
>
> The wise woman makes me feel that being a woman is all right. I often criticize myself harshly, but when I meet the wise woman, I feel a strong sense of acceptance, and this deeply influences many ways in which I experience myself.

Others perceive the wise woman quite differently: as the archetype of wisdom, perhaps, much like the Greek goddess Athena, rather than as a familiar, down-to-earth individual. Both men and women find in the evocation of the wise and loving woman a positive female image, which the events of their lives may not yet have allowed them to envisage. Nearly all people find that the wise woman can give something which the wise man does not have—and vice versa.

While inner dialogue may at times cause an exceptional release of superconscious energies and a radical transformation of the personality, in the majority of situations the results are more comparable to having had a session from an extremely skillful and loving therapist—a session which we leave feeling refreshed and clarified, knowing that we have gotten there by ourselves and with no psychological dependence on another human being.

LETTER TO THE SELF

Another form of inner dialogue is that of writing a letter to the Self. Strange as it may seem, this is often an effective way of tuning in to the superconscious. You describe a situation or problem in detail, discussing the alternatives, your—and other people's—feelings about it, the advantages and disadvantages of each alternative, and so on.

The answers in inner dialogue—whether it is carried on in written or visualized form—can come in various ways and through different channels. These are the principal ones:

1. The message comes while we are doing the exercise or immediately after.

2. The answer comes in a delayed fashion. Usually our expectations of a particular solution—or our anxiety to have one—obstruct the flow of insight. But the insight may arrive later, by surprise. It may also come in a most subtle, nearly invisible way, so that after a few days we realize that our outlook has become clear, or the issue is not a problem anymore, or we now know what to do about it, even though we may not remember any particular moment when a definite shift has taken place.

3. The message reaches us through a dream.

4. The response appears as an impulse to action, as when we suddenly feel prompted to do something which we previously were not particularly inclined to do or to consider worthy of doing.

5. The answer comes through some element in the environment, such as the words of a friend, the title of a movie, a phrase read at random in a book, an event that changes our usual routine, and so on. The message is there, if we are able to read it. This is an example of what Jung and physicist Wolfgang Pauli called *synchronicity.*

Even songs can become signals. A man returning from a long trip had asked his wise person whether to go back to his old way of living or, on the contrary, face a new situation and start a wholly new course of activity. The question apparently fell in the dark. But a few days later, when the man was not thinking about the problem, he heard on the radio the song "Those were the days. . ." and these words struck him with sudden force. At that moment he *knew* that an old cycle had finished ("those *were* the days"), and it was best for him to launch into the new activity. He was struck by the sense of certainty which was suddenly engendered in him and also by the relieving quality of the humor he felt in this event—an impression that many experience. The frequency, the subjective intensity, and the liberating effects of these moments forbid us to dub them as mere coincidences. They seem to point toward some unknown interaction between what we call "inner" and "outer" reality.

How can we rest assured that the message reaching us is not a self-deceiving fantasy? We can never be one-hundred-percent certain. Some criteria, however, can help us to test the authenticity of the message. The first criterion is subjective: if the answer comes from the Self, it carries an unmistakable sense of rightness. We don't simply get a cold "yes" or "no"; rather, we are given the gifts of understanding and joy.

A second criterion derives from exercising discrimination. We look at the answer in the light of reason and soundness to see if it makes sense. We need to remember, however, that the Self can transmit messages which are non-conformist, humorous, and outside the bounds of our usual expectancies.

A third criterion is the "proof of the pudding." The results of trying out the message in life may help to tell whether it is right or not.

In any case it is important to emphasize that inner-dialogue answers come in subtle, pervasive, and even tricky ways. Often they are not direct, concrete, or given in the terms which we expect. Instead, they tend to infuse us with the psychological quality we need to modify our outlook so that the question itself is transformed. Luisa's story provides a good example.

Luisa has been married for thirteen years now. She has a highly emotional nature and has been practicing psychosynthesis exercises for quite a while. When she comes to see me she is in a period of crisis. She has a difficult relationship with her husband, who is violent at times and often prone to bizarre behavior. Everything is all right during his absences from home, but his return creates hell for Luisa. She often thinks of leaving him but is deterred from doing so by her fear of his violent reaction. At the same time she has a strong affection for him, and this relationship has taught her many things. And, deep down, she is afraid of loneliness. An essential element to remember in this story is that Luisa's life has consistently lacked a positive male image—a fact also evidenced in the exercise of meeting the wise old man, which she finds difficult to perform.

Once more we try meeting the wise old man. This time it works:

The old wise man meets me smiling and I sit down on a bench near him, for the first time on the same level as him. Right away I feel a strong emotion and I cry, because I see great peace, joy, strength in his eyes, while I feel myself to be so different, submerged by my pain, by my uncertainty in choosing. I cry and he smiles, putting a hand on my shoulder. I tell him about my problem. He doesn't speak, but makes me aware of his thoughts.

He shows me a sword that shines in the sun: "You will come out of this situation with strength." I ask how. He answers: "You will find it, but not right away. You will find it by yourself." This astonishes me, but I am also glad about it because usually I very much feel the need of other people's advice, even though I finally choose my own way. And then he adds: "But with *love*." I look at him, and he seems to be conducting music.

Dressed in luminous white, radiant in the sun and smiling, he looks younger than before.

We see here a mode of communication typical of the Self. It does not suggest a specific alternative, but rather provides access to or emphasis on the qualities needed to enable the person to choose his or her own path—for Luisa the qualities of strength and love. But Luisa is not yet satisfied:

I protest that I am not feeling the strength he is talking about. He holds out his hands, with which he then grasps mine. He raises our interlaced fingers, and I see that a stream of clean water, transparent and fresh, is flowing under them. Rapidly the water is carrying away corpses of warriors and old pieces of wood. It is sweeping away everything, and all the while our arms become longer and longer, to form an arched bridge. The wise old man shows me the landscape and smiles, and I laugh. Everything seems to have passed away, and so simply. I feel as secure as in a fortress, where there is nothing to be afraid about. Then the bridge becomes a luminous rainbow, and the wise old man and I are on two separate mountains. We are independent, but connected by the strength-giving rainbow.

Two days after the session, Luisa writes:

Yesterday, for the first time in several weeks, I slept well, and without having to take a sedative. I feel calm and confident now, and this helps me to live moment by moment without having to think about other issues and commitments. I wish I could always feel this way.

I see, as if it were in the distance, the poor creature I used to be, always in need of advice and reassurance, unhappy, alone, and immature. I hardly recognize myself in her. I am astonished to see myself acting calm, I who had a tendency to run and be in a hurry and try to do more than I could. Also, I am now apt to perceive the best in the people around me.

Finding herself in this new psychological situation, Luisa is now capable of having a much clearer perspective of her predicament. She decides to leave her husband. This decision is difficult and painful for at least two reasons. First, her husband might react violently against her. He is a sensitive and intelligent but unbalanced individual, and he might not like her decision at all. Secondly, as we have seen, Luisa is afraid of solitude. Part of her would prefer to go on living with somebody, anybody, even if it is the wrong person. But this part does not win, and at last Luisa makes her choice.

She acts then with precision and without hesitation. She prepares her suitcases, communicates her resolution to her husband, and finds a new place to live. "That evening," she says, "I experienced the strength of my Self as decisiveness, firmness, and serenity. What I thought would be the most difficult moment of my life turned out to be extremely easy."

As time goes by, Luisa's husband calls her often. And often she feels lonely. She is tempted to return to him, but she also knows that this decision would be a step backwards for her. Throughout this period she receives guidance from her wise person, whom she contacts regularly in her meditations. The wise person advises her "to leave the seashore of security and conformity and go forward into the sea," and, most important, he continually infuses her with new strength. She sticks to her decision.

Meanwhile, the quality of our relationship has changed. In the past I had felt that she was dependent on me, often asking for support and advice. Now we had succeeded in reaching the aim of any good therapeutic relationship—she could rely on her own strength and wisdom, I had made myself perfectly useless to my client.

I would now like to bring up one final point. While reading this chapter, you may have asked yourself why we imagine the wise being to be, of all places, on top of a mountain. The answer is that, along with the technique of inner dialogue, we have also used the technique of ascent or, as Assagioli called it in his essay on this subject, "psychological mountain climbing."

Mountaintops have often been said to be the abode of the gods or of holy and extraordinary beings, and they are associated with feelings and ideas more intense and desirable than ordinary ones. As we saw in Chapter 4, ascent often produces a sense of joy and liberation, and the metaphor of height has been used to describe elevated states of mind. For instance, to describe his creative moments, Bertrand Russell wrote: "My sensations resembled those one has after climbing a mountain in mist, when, on reaching a summit, the mist suddenly clears, and the country becomes visible for forty miles in every direction."[1]

The technique of ascent can be used in its own right just by imagining climbing up a mountain and, from the top, viewing the surrounding landscape. This raising of consciousness often has a vitalizing and strengthening effect, as the following report written by a woman shows: "What evoked my will very strongly was to imagine climbing a big mountain covered with snow. I often did this exercise when I felt unable to do anything, or I could not concentrate, or I wasn't able to do my accounts, or I couldn't type or even go and pick up my daughter at school.

"Then I would imagine climbing this mountain with serenity, with patience, with method. On the top I felt greater; I felt I could do what I wanted to do. Then I would be able to go and pick up my daughter and smile, or type an English translation without making any mistakes, for instance. Otherwise, I would have stayed at home in bed all day."

Chapter 14

THE PATHOLOGY
OF THE SUBLIME

S trange as it may seem, when transpersonal inspiration starts to make itself felt, the personality at times devises ways to neutralize it. The personality realm has its own laws, aims, and ways of functioning. In many cases the irruption of transpersonal energy causes an expansion and a transformation that are felt as beneficial and pleasurable. But at other times the revolutionary impact of the new energies irrupting in the preexisting framework may be felt as threateningly uncomfortable.

Even though they carry with them a strong sense of rightness, superconscious inspirations entail a necessity for the whole personality to rearrange itself in order to fit the aims and laws of the Self. In this case, old habits have to be obliterated, psychological blocks have to be courageously faced, new and vaster responsibilities have to be shouldered, and an unfamiliar rhythm has to be adopted—in other words, a series of big changes is on its way.

The changes wrought through superconscious inspiration are, of course, natural parts of a person's overall development. Sooner or later, it is right for the chrysalis to become a butterfly; but the chrysalis may feel somewhat reluctant about the process of change. Growth is understanding what we have not yet been able to conceive, feeling what we have never felt, doing what we have never done before. It is daring what we have never dared. It may not, therefore, necessarily be pleasurable. It obliges us to leave our comfort zone, to progress into the unknown, to face the tremendous impact of the Self.

Resistance to change, however, is not the only reason for the personality realm to organize defenses against the downflow of the superconscious. Another powerful cause is fear of being violently and deeply hurt where one is most vulnerable. There was once a time when each of us met life in an innocent and totally open way, without reservations or defenses. But then something went wrong—our innocence and openness were abused, our love was not returned, our spontaneity was ridiculed, our sensitivity was hurt, or our faith was betrayed. From that time was born a series of reservations and suspicions, ranging from the ordinary common sense of the mature adult all the way to an ingrained resistance, sometimes total, to surrender to the new. One just does not want to be swindled by life again.

For these two main reasons, and possibly for several others, the personality tends to restore its own laws and objectives, to defend itself against the transpersonal intruder, just so its own system can survive. It does so by using a number of skillful and nearly always unconscious strategies.*

Repression is the simplest and most common strategy. Desoille coined the phrase "repression of the sublime," pointing to the fact that it is often the cause of a "deep melancholy" and the vague sentiment of something which has been lost. He also said that this concept is similar to Baudouin's "refusal of involvement."

A foreign body, so to speak, enters our life and threatens the existing order. We push it away from our awareness, but it is too painful a presence not to make itself felt—usually in the form of dissatisfaction, boredom, feelings of inauthenticity, and a host of other disturbances.

In *The Divine Comedy* Dante looked upon the betrayal of one's spiritual destiny as the vilest form of hypocrisy, and symbolized it in the person of Caiaphas, the man who condemned Jesus. As Dorothy Sayers explains in her commentary, he illustrates the condition of the person "who sacrifices his inner truth to expediency . . . and to whom the rejected good becomes at once a heaven from which he is exiled and a rack on which he suffers."[1] In Dante's allegory, Caiaphas is crucified on the ground of Hell, and other people walk over him all the time.

---

*I am grateful to Robert Gerard for pointing out to me in a conversation the similarity between Freudian defense mechanisms and defense mechanisms in relation to the superconscious.

Projection. Instead of owning, so to speak, the transpersonal qualities which are beginning to infuse their being and therefore expressing them in their lives, some people may take a much easier though less rewarding course: they may attribute these qualities to another person—a guru, a therapist, a public figure, a friend, or the like. They then expect that person to act according to the image of the ideal they see, and they resent it if he or she does not conform to their expectations. Meanwhile, they are able to maintain the status quo in their own lives, although they are depriving themselves of precious gifts.

This strategy is accompanied by psychological laziness, low self-esteem, dependency, helplessness, and, ultimately, anger. Moreover, the qualities projected often take on a distorted and unrealistic aspect. I will never forget the disillusioned expression on the face of a client of mine when he met me at a stadium while I was watching a soccer match. The angelic image he had projected onto me—I later discovered—clashed violently in his mind with such a prosaic reality as the one he saw in me on that occasion.

Compensation consists in the personality's elaborating a new trait opposite to the quality which is prominent at the moment. Thus I have seen people compensating the inflow of feelings of love with extreme aggressiveness, or neutralizing the heights and the rarefied atmosphere of the superconscious by cultivating an extremely earthly life ("having fun," watching TV, reading trash magazines, and so on). This strategy produces strong conflicts and contradictory behaviors, unbalanced attitudes and abrupt changes of direction.

Desacralization operates by cutting down and ridiculing in a cynical way anybody or anything even reminiscent of the superconscious. It allows an individual to vent aggressive tendencies, and it is especially common in people who are quite sensitive, who have in some way been betrayed by life's events, and who have a deep fear of being ridiculed.

With *defensive pessimism,* individuals belittle themselves out of a deep, often unconscious fear that their impasses are insuperable: "I am too old," "I am not bright enough," "I am too hung up." Or they may blame the external situation: "I can't grow as long as my wife keeps nagging me," "I work too much and don't have time for anything else," and so on. People who adopt this strategy are frightened and easily discouraged and tend to indulge in self-pity. Their feelings of impotence are often accompanied by a resentment never fully and adequately expressed.

Routinization consists in formally accepting the superconscious but turning it into some form of organization, bureaucracy, or routine, from which the original creative element is gone. This is the great danger of religious and other associations which organize around an inspired leader without always succeeding in preserving the initial inspiration, sometimes even suppressing it by using the very words and forms the original leader had created but without assimilating the leader's revolutionary impact. An example of this is found in Dostoevski's novel *The Brothers Karamazov*, in which Christ returns to earth and is condemned to death by the Inquisition of the very Church he had originally founded.

This strategy also occurs in individuals, leading them to believe they have a clear explanation for just about everything—ignoring the mystery, the self-renewing, surprising power of the superconscious and its paradoxical, indescribable character. Such individuals then adopt formulas, clichés, and slogans. They hold fast to some truth, experience, teaching, or event that has meant a great deal to them in the past. They are only routinely imitating what was once a spontaneous explosion of life and has now become a crystallized fossil.

Dogmatization is a related strategy that denies by affirming. It is the means by which the superconscious becomes superego. What had originally been a vibrant experience becomes in this case a rigid norm to which one must conform, an aim it is one's duty to reach: "I *have* to be joyous" or "loving" or "enlightened." And what was once a free gift becomes a tool to please others and thus survive socially. Once more, the personality system reasserts and perpetuates its laws. In this way growth is merely added as another item to the already long list of "shoulds." This strategy is accompanied by constraint, rigidity, existential dissatisfaction and a basic lack of love for oneself.

We have now briefly seen some of the ways in which the personality tries to neutralize the Self, and some of the resulting difficulties. Troubles may also arise, however, when the personality actually opens to the inflow of the new energies. Not that these troubles are always present. On the contrary, most of them are only occasional and fleeting, and those few which are inevitable can be effectively dealt with. Contact with the superconscious is joyous, constructive, and life-giving, but it is useful to familiarize ourselves with these problems in order to better find ways to keep clear of them or ways to recognize and deal with them when and if they come.

The most common difficulty connected with expanded awareness and increased contact with the superconscious is perhaps a greater sensitivity—sensitivity to the pain of human beings in general (Wordsworth's "still, sad music of humanity"), to vulgarity, to aggression and hatred, and so on. Moreover, it is not only the horizontal direction—empathy with and understanding of others—that expands, but also the vertical one. If the peaks of consciousness within reach get higher and higher, the abysses of despair, meaninglessness, and aridity, by contrast, get deeper and deeper. In fact, a person who has awakened to the reality and livingness of the superconscious is particularly aware of cycles—cycles of ease, of insight and effortless creativity, alternating with cycles of disfunctioning and confusion.

Another common inconvenience, which occurs particularly in the beginning stages of superconscious inflow, is a sense of inadequacy. The sudden sight of unsuspected splendors may enhance awareness of our limitations. Since one of the main mental habits of the personality is comparison, we are spontaneously drawn to compare our own way of being with whatever beauty we can perceive in the superconscious. The result may well be guilt and discouragement. A client of mine, for instance, during an imagery exercise which had up to then apparently been successful, remarked—upon seeing a wonderful vision of people who were enlightened, without problems, and full of joy—that he felt himself by comparison to be "in a block of ice." "They are up and I am down," he said, "they are winning and I am losing." It was only later, when he imagined a dialogue with these people, that they helped him to understand that all separations are artificial, that they were not seeing the situation in that way at all. But up to that moment, he says, "I was feeling like someone who has been invited to a party of rich, elegant and relaxed people, where I am poorly dressed and uptight, and do not know anybody." This reaction stems from the incapacity to realize that we belong, in essence, to the world of our most beautiful visions, and that those states which we can fugitively perceive are a glimpse of what we actually can become, not an unreachable mirage.

Then there is the opposite reaction: believing that the glimpsed vision is an already manifested reality, and forgetting our present limitations. Such excessive optimism results from believing that what is true at one level is also true at another. Thus some people temporarily come to believe that all their problems are solved, that they have reached "enlightenment," and so on. The Self, indeed, seems to be living in timelessness and freedom, beyond all problems and separations. But to pretend that this is also true for our ordinary, everyday reality is a dangerous illusion. This inability to discriminate and to integrate the superconscious contact with everyday experience easily leads to inflation and exaltation.

Often this problem occurs because our emotions may be greatly stimulated by a strong inflow of superconscious energy. If one lacks a clear sense of center, he or she is lost in an ocean of overwhelming energy that cannot truly be understood or made use of. A case in point is a client of mine who called in the middle of the night to report enthusiastically that he had found the "symbol of peace," asking me to have flowers immediately sent to the great leaders of the world. In such instances the substance of what is perceived is beautiful and ultimately right, but the way in which it is understood and expressed is unbalanced and inconsistent.

Intense spiritual stimulation may bring inspirations, but it may also penetrate directly into the lower unconscious, where it throws light on and excites demons, instinctual energies, forgotten memories, and so on. These then tend to rise to consciousness, causing all sorts of trouble to the surprised conscious personality. When the demons are thus roused, the contrast between different sides of our nature is felt with particular intensity. Things may temporarily get out of hand, and individuals may experience the particularly distressing duality between what they are and what they would like to be: "Video meliora proboque," said Ovid, "deteriora sequor." ("I see the best and approve it, then I follow the worst.")

Mental overstimulation may also occur—the inflow of a great number of images, ideas, mental connections, and associations. This difficulty sometimes gives one a sense of illusory clarity, the belief of having all the solutions, and the urge to formulate a great variety of plans. This stimulation can also cause insomnia and other psychophysical disturbances.

Other forms that mental stimulation and emotional exaltation can take are absolutism, militancy, and fanaticism—what Stuart Miller, in his memorable lecture on the "Risks of Psychosynthesis," called "Stalinism of the spirit," pointing out, with Pascal, the danger of these attitudes: "Qui veut faire l'ange fait la bête." ("Whoever tries to act like an angel makes a beast of himself.")

Abstraction is another danger, especially in the case of both the scientifically and the mystically inclined. The abstraction of the genial scientist, his absorption in the realm of speculation, are proverbial.

Mystically inclined individuals may have trouble in reentering the familiar, prosaic world of everyday living, especially after a powerful meditation. The sense of floating bliss, and the amazing revelations they meet with, are for them incongruent with the extenal reality they must again come to terms with. Often in these cases there can also be a sense of condemnation, spite and repulsion for the ordinary flesh-and-blood world, a sense of being imprisoned in a reality which is experienced as foreign, a "divine homesickness" coupled with an utter incapacity to function at the practical level. An analogous situation, I believe, is exemplified by the Greek myth in which Icarus flew so high that the heat of the sun melted the wax that was holding his wings together, causing him to fall into the sea. The story aptly illustrates the attitude—and the ensuing misadventures—of all who seek to explore the higher regions of consciousness without first building dependable personal foundations. Thus we may designate an "Icarus complex," the tendency whereby spiritual ambition fails to take personality limitations into account and causes all kinds of psychological difficulties.

For others, the opposite may be the case. If they are overwhelmed by the superconscious, if they experience an abundance and an intensity which hurt, annoy, or overload, they may conclude—as one person once put it—"Enough with superbliss." Here, we have to distinguish two cases. In the one just described, we have the genuine encounter with the superconscious, and this contact is of so intense and direct a kind that it is experienced as overpowering. In other cases, instead, the contact actually occurs with caricatures and abstractions which have little to do with the superconscious, but still carry a pretense of great truth. In these cases, revulsions or a critical reaction may be the healthiest attitude.

As in just about any significant endeavor, in the path of personal evolution there can be obstacles, dangers, difficulties, and mistakes. But this fact should not deter us from proceeding, for this path is the way of our natural unfoldment. On the other hand, the fact that there is an evolutionary thrust within us does not mean that it will necessarily be manifested, just as our having a ticket for a journey does not mean that we will inevitably undertake it. Therefore, the ultimate choice of whether we want to actualize or betray our potentialities lies within us with all its questions, all its risks, all its beauty and mystery.

Fortunately, we have the means to make this adventure safe and relatively smooth and to deal effectively with the difficulties outlined in this chapter. As Assagioli used to say, if we want to climb a high mountain we first have to undergo some training in order to build physical strength and resistance. We must also have the necessary equipment and know and respect our own rhythms and possibilities. The same is true of ascending to the heights of the superconscious. We have to train and be well equipped for it.

What is called *personal psychosynthesis* represents the necessary foundation of this work. The aim is to build a personality which is efficient and relatively free from emotional blocks. This personality knows how to satisfy its own needs and is able to direct its aggressive energy constructively and use failure creatively. It has some command over all psychological functions and possesses a clear awareness of its own center. When we have developed such a personality, then we can safely and productively contact the higher regions of our being, and *transpersonal* or spiritual psychosynthesis becomes possible.

The techniques described in the first chapters of this book mainly concern personal psychosynthesis. As the book proceeds, increasing attention is given to the tools of transpersonal psychosynthesis. Naturally the two often overlap, but it is useful to make a distinction because either one can be achieved in the absence of the other. We must learn to function in both worlds, the ordinary and the extraordinary, with equal poise and know-how. As Ram Dass put it, we have to remember our ZIP code even while we are in intergalactic ecstasy.

At first, all we have is a bunch of restless, disordered, conflicting subpersonalities that refuse all guidance from a higher unifying principle, instead trapping and veiling it. Later these elements are regulated and directed by the personal Self, or "I". They are gradually brought to express their best, and as this happens their interrelationship becomes more harmonious. There is a degree of fusion and interpenetration among all, and synergy increases. At last, when the total personality is integrated, it is time for the Self to pervade it with energy and inspiration.

That is the ideal sequence. Naturally, in the life of each one of us things take on a much more varied and complex aspect. Often some form of spiritual yearning is present long before the full integration of the personality, and this can constitute an element of great value. The irruption of superconscious energy may help the integration of the personality in some cases, or it may temporarily intensify existing conflicts in other cases. There may be periods of personal psychosynthesis alternating with periods of transpersonal psychosynthesis, just as there may be individuals progressing more in one direction and less in another. It is hard to take into account the enormous variety of possibilities. It is, however, desirable for all of us to be mindful of the general, ideal unfoldment that brings us from fragmentation and disorder to personality integration and, at last, to the realization of the Self.

Chapter 15

YOUR LIFE,
YOUR MASTERPIECE

A bird pecks its way out of an egg.
A bud blossoms into a rose.
A star forms out of the condensation of interstellar gas.
Molten minerals cool into a beautiful crystal pattern.

There seems to be a way for things to happen which is intrinsically *right* for them: they become what they were meant to be. Aristotle called the end of this process "entelechy"—the full and perfect realization of what was previously in a potential state. Whether it appears in a butterfly flying out of its cocoon, in a ripe fruit falling from a tree, or in the development of an acorn into an oak, this process clearly evidences qualities of harmony and underlying intelligence.

Do human beings also tend to unfold according to such inner designs, or is our life wholly random? It seems a reasonable and useful hypothesis to believe that we are like the rest of creation. According to the Eastern doctrine of "dharma," we are each called upon to achieve a particular life-pattern. And while all patterns have equal dignity, each one of us should avail himself or herself of the possibility that is uniquely one's own and not someone else's. Each of us should try to discover the pattern and cooperate with its realization. In psychosynthesis we use the word *purpose* in a similar, though more dynamic, sense. Our entire life's purpose is already present within us, and, furthermore, at each stage of our life there are subordinate purposes—steps along the way toward the fulfillment of our ideal pattern.

Ideal: what an ambiguous and even dangerous word; but we are not talking—as is so often the case when people discuss "ideal character" or "ideal behavior"—about impractical or unreachable goals. We are not talking about a tyrannical and impersonal standard against which we must measure our actions or thoughts. Nor are we talking about some cold and abstract norm unconnected with our everyday world of flesh and blood. We mean, rather, something eminently practical and personal: fulfilling our deepest inner leanings, from moment to moment, in the most effective and desirable way. We are talking about a process of unfoldment which, to the extent that it conforms to the particular pattern within each one of us, is marked by joy.

Indeed, joy could be defined as the manifest sign that we are fulfilling our ideal purpose at any given moment. It is the sense of being on our own beam, comparable to the realization of rightness we experience in viewing certain works of art, events, or persons, a particular rose, leaf, or shell, knowing that there is nothing to be added or substracted from these entities: no sense of clutter, incompleteness, or strain, but rather a unique perfection. This adherence to an ideal norm may not be anything solemn or sensational—only what seems right for that entity. Nevertheless, whenever we see such congruence between an underlying ideal pattern and reality, it has a powerful and vitalizing effect on us.

The notion of an inner ideal form trying to manifest itself within us can help to reconceive our notions of both therapy and growth. Therapy— the exploration of the unconscious, the catharsis of pent-up emotions, the treatment of symptoms—becomes no longer an end in itself, but a series of steps in a larger process. It consists, then, in the task of becoming aware of our emerging life purpose, eliminating obstacles to it, and otherwise facilitating its realization. Growth also no longer exists for its own sake. After all, our possibilities for mere new growth at any given moment are nearly infinite: we can learn Arabic, develop our muscles, travel and meet lots of people, learn sky-diving, and so on. But, looking at such varied possibilities from the point of view of our emerging ideal pattern, we can attempt to judge which activities represent the real, the intrinsic growth of our individual beings.

But we must be very gentle in trying to conceive our inner ideal, in trying to imagine our larger purpose. This needs to be a gradual process, one subject to trial, error, and revision. To attempt to conceive our inner ideal pattern in any hasty fashion will almost always have negative results, intimidating or disheartening us or, even worse, trapping us in some artificially self-imposed form, the deadly prison of unrealistic perfectionism.

IDEAL FORMS

Let us begin, then, in a safer and more impersonal way—with an exercise that will allow us to explore the beauty of ideal shapes in general:

1. Think of some form which, in your opinion, has reached the purity and perfection of an ideal.

It may be a form belonging to the mineral world, like a crystal or a jewel.

Or to the vegetable world, like a flower in bloom or a leaf.

Or to the animal world, like a horse or a dolphin or a bird.

Or to the cosmos, such as a rainbow or a star.

It may also belong to the human world: a person in some specific function, an event you remember which just couldn't have been better—a poem, a fresco, or a sonata.

2. Consider several of these forms.

3. Experience them clearly and vividly, and enjoy the power and the beauty of the ideal.

So far so good. But when we turn our attention to people in everyday life (including, of course, ourselves), we are likely to see that ideal models are the exception rather than the rule, that the harmonious unfoldment of purpose is blocked or forgotten. What goes wrong? Perhaps the most decisive factor is an inner one: our own imagination.

What we implicitly imagine ourselves to be can either facilitate our ideal development or distort it in the most painful ways—and the latter is frequently the case. Far from being neutral, *all inner images have motor power.* And the problem is that through the falsifying veil of our subpersonalities we often form inappropriate images of what we are and can become. Consider these sadly typical examples of how people's self-images interfere with their natural process:

A woman has sexual intercourse with just about any man who asks her. Even though she is, in fact, good-looking and sensitive, she feels worthless and inferior. Terrified of loneliness, then, she gives herself up completely to any man who "deigns" to look at her. Her psychological self-image has overpowered the image she sees in the mirror.

A retired businessman, in excellent health, could and would like to visit foreign countries, take up a new sport, and enrich his social life now that he has time to do so. But he doesn't, because he thinks that he is "too old now."

A stockbroker suffers from an acute crisis of depression without knowing why. He believes that his job is the only one he is good for. When he was younger, he gave evidence of artistic interests and gifts. But these have now faded, and when he comes home from work all he does is watch television.

A young woman imagines she is a great singer and dreams of becoming a star. Her friends are hesitant to tell her that her voice is quite ordinary. She tries leaping toward fame but is mercilessly rejected by several agencies. As a consequence of this failure, she attempts suicide.

"The dream of reason generates monsters" is the title of a famous etching by Goya. We can also say that the misuse of imagination generates monsters, if by "monster" we mean whatever becomes other than what it was meant to be. When the irrational forces of the unconscious take charge of the creative power of the imagination, they give birth to distorted creatures and warped lives.

Fortunately, images do not only have such negative effects. Some of them, perhaps a majority, distort or suppress what a person potentially is. But other images, instead, stimulate and bring to life what is right, especially when they are used explicitly and systematically. One man, for example, says: "There is much joy in the very discovery that I can create constructive images and thereby mold my reactions to the world." And even when the power of imagination is activated spontaneously, it can have positive and concrete effects in the life of an individual. A six-year-old girl, for instance, having received a bicycle for Christmas, started to ride it immediately, without any difficulty, before the astonished eyes of her parents. When they asked how she had learned to do that, she answered: "I had been imagining it all the time."

Images can either imprison or liberate us. We can be their unconscious slaves and let them govern our lives, or we can deliberately put their immense power to effective use.

By clearly imagining a possibility, we automatically bring it closer to actualization. Therefore, we can intentionally use images to aid our purpose in coming into full, embodied existence. And we can do so by thinking of the next appropriate step in our personal evolution.

THE IDEAL MODEL

In this task we will adopt the same procedure the little girl spontaneously used with bicycling: we will vividly imagine the chosen goal. This is the technique of the ideal model. It is best used in terms of a quality, such as love, strength, understanding, joy, and so on. Here are the steps:

1. Choose a quality you feel will be helpful at this time in realizing your emerging life purpose.

2. Now imagine yourself as already having that quality in the highest degree of purity and intensity. Allow the image to take shape in detail. See the look in the eyes expressing the quality; the physical posture; the facial expression. (The image may not be very stable in the beginning; it may be fuzzy, or appear and disappear in flashes. Even so, it will exercise a powerful influence on your unconscious.) Hold this image in your mind for a few moments, encouraging it to increasingly express the quality you have chosen.

3. Imagine *walking into* this image and becoming one with it—something like putting on new clothes. As you merge with the image, feel its quality becoming part of you. Imagine how it feels to possess the maximum degree of this quality. Feel your body pervaded by it. Feel it penetrating each one of your cells, flowing in each vein, filling your whole body. Imagine this quality permeating your feelings, your way of thinking, and your motives.

4. Finally, imagine yourself expressing in one or several situations of your everyday life, more of this quality than you previously have. Imagine these situations dynamically and in detail.

The ideal model technique can also be used in a more extroverted fashion. Instead of focusing on a specific psychological quality, we can build for ourselves the image of a social function we want to improve: the ideal partner, the ideal teacher, the ideal friend, etc. We can then visualize the function in its essential nature, think about its value, and picture all the specific skills, traits, and abilities associated with it. Likewise, in this exercise any inner pressure, any grim determination like that associated with New Year's resolutions, or even any expectancy of success is unnecessary. The image is all that is needed.

The technique of the ideal model is based on the freedom of the individual to influence his or her destiny. Different persons approach the task in different ways. At one pole we find people who first tend to let their purpose gradually emerge, as if they were mere spectators. They become aware of the existing inner blueprint, let it unfold, and then actively stimulate its emergence with an image.

At the opposite pole we find others who, possessing a different psychological constitution, are more dynamic in trying to shape their own lives. They are more eager to search out purpose and build it. In the one case the experience tends to be characterized more by a sense of cooperation with the emerging process, in the other case by a sense of energetic activity. In both cases, however, the technique is based on human freedom and responsibility. Both types of people are craftsmen of their lives.

During the early days of the modern era, in the Italian Renaissance, the possibility of crafting our destiny was seen as the very beauty and dignity of our humanness—but also as its inherent danger. According to a story of that time, God created all beings in the universe and gave to each a particular quality and, therefore, a specific destiny. He gave cunning to the fox, fidelity to the dog, strength to the lion, and so on. When, at last, God came to the human beings, He decided to leave him with an *open destiny:*

> He welcomed him as an entity of indefinite nature, put him in the heart of the universe, and spoke to him in this way: "I created you as a being neither mortal nor immortal, neither heavenly nor earthly, so that you, as a sovereign and free artificer, could mold and forge yourself in the shape your choose. You can sink to the level of inferior beings. You can, if you so will, regenerate yourself in the likeness of superior beings."[1]

Precisely because of this freedom and this indeterminacy, it is possible to use the technique of the ideal model in a great number of constructive and also destructive ways. A common destructive mistake is to put it at the service of our frustrations. For instance, I once guided one of my clients, a short, energetic man, in an ideal-model exercise. As the visualization proceeded, I saw his face taking on a sinister grimace. So I asked him to tell me what was happening. "Yes," he said, his voice changing aggressively, "now that I am strong I can finally have my revenge. I'll be able to suffocate the people who are in my way. I have been taking a lot of abuse over the years, but now I can hit back at those who have humiliated me. I'll knock their teeth down their throats." It was obvious that he was still trapped in his resentment and could imagine his "ideal" model only from that place. It had been my mistake to ask him to use it too early. First, he needed to express the frustration and anger still seething within him; then he would need to learn to identify with his real self and make his choices for his ideal model from there. While the ideal-model technique may help us, at times, to transcend problems and undesirable traits, these generally must be worked on directly in the ways outlined in the previous chapters of this book.

Another common mistake is to confuse ideal-model work with mere daydreaming. Many people have daydreams of being extraordinary, of accomplishing astounding feats, of having their most refined desires easily satisfied, of meeting and having a wonderful time with the best people, of enjoying the greatest triumphs. These daydreams have the aim of fulfilling unsatisfied needs and compensating for the lacks of an individual. In his book of imagination, Sartre says that the act of imagination is indeed a magical one. "It is an incantation destined to produce the object of one's thoughts, the thing one desires, in such a manner that one can take possession of it."[2] But, he adds, the objects of imagination are often simply out of reach. They may be present, but at the same time they are unreal. In such cases,

> One could speak of a dance before the unreal, in the manner that a corps de ballet dances around a statue. The dancers open their arms, offer their hands, smile, offer themselves completely, approach, and take flight; but the statue is not affected by it: there is no real relationship between it and the corps de ballet. Likewise, our conduct before the object cannot really touch it or qualify it anymore than it can touch us in return; because it is in the heaven of the unreal, beyond all reach.[3]

Daydreaming, when it is excessive, tends to lead individuals astray, to make them vulnerable to the hard facts of life, to encourage withdrawal into an unreal world. It is the exact antithesis of what the technique of the ideal model is about: while daydreaming is compensatory and brings only an imaginary fulfillment, the ideal model is reality-oriented and produces satisfaction only by the progressive manifestation of the envisioned ideal; while daydreaming is unrealistic, the ideal model, when correctly used, employs images of goals within reasonable reach; while daydreams faithfully indicate the frustrations of an individual, the ideal model is the expression of one's true Self; while daydreaming is based on mere wish, the ideal model has in it a purposeful element—that same element you can find in any well-defined project.

Another potential problem in ideal model work (and, for that matter, in many types of psychosynthesis exercises) is the backlash effect. Here we have a phenomenon that can seem destructive but need not be so. At the beginning, the impact of imagining our ideals may not necessarily be pleasant. Some part of our being may react in negative ways. It may react to the ideal image as to a foreign body which disturbs the existing, even if unsatisfactory, balance. It may react with a sense of inadequacy or guilt. It may also react in a compensatory way, by expressing the opposite of the quality chosen. Frequently these consequences can be avoided by skillful, noncoercive, and timely use of the ideal model. But to some extent they may be unavoidable, even though temporary.

There is nothing unhealthy in the backlash effect, however. On the contrary, it gives us the opportunity of observing the conservative elements of our personality at work—our unwillingness to change, our fear of becoming different, and so on. We should then just take notice of these archaic and, so to speak, reactionary tendencies which are still present in ourselves and let them lose their strength, as they almost inevitably do if we do not try to interfere with them or negate them, but instead keep working along the chosen line. In any case, the backlash effect often does not even take place.

Let us finally mention an illusory danger of ideal-model work: some people feel that were they to build an ideal model, they would fashion a straitjacket which would inhibit their spontaneity. This unrealistic fear results from an inadequate understanding of the function of images. An image which stimulates a potentiality within us to come to the fore can never be a prison unless it is applied in a dictatorial way, as a self-imposed "should." We can think of our ideal model as being already present inside us, awaiting discovery and activation or the moment for the barriers to fall. By directing our attention to the ideal model within, we allow it to emerge and be manifested in somewhat the same way that Michelangelo said the sculpture "waits" inside a block of raw marble to be "discovered" by the sculptor.

A short story by Hawthorne, *The Great Stone Face,* aptly illustrates the inspiring effects an image can have, naturally and easily, without any of the deadening results that can be created by an authoritarian use of a norm. The story tells of a village lying below a big mountain whose shapes resemble the features of a man of great nobility and refinement. The inhabitants of the village call the mountain "the Great Stone Face," and believe that "thence would come a better wisdom than could be learned by books." A legend exists that someday a man will come whose face will resemble the countenance of the Great Stone Face. From his earliest childhood, one villager has been eagerly awaiting the appearance of that man, but in vain. Time passes. The villager keeps the Stone Face in his sight and thoughts. His house faces the mountain, and many are the hours he spends contemplating it, "fancying . . . that the Great Stone Face returned his gaze and looked kindly at him." At last, one day, the people in the village begin to notice that he himself has acquired a remarkable resemblance to the Great Stone Face. His physiognomy has come to reflect the same nobility and refinement.

Like the man in the story, we can allow the living presence of an ideal slowly to transfigure our life. Having chosen one quality, we can add others and, by practicing with each in turn, gradually build what we are meant and intend to become. Thus we can become the inventors of our life and make of it our masterpiece.

> Every day I am in agony, because I do not know whether spiritual love and understanding are real. I have never been able to see them, even though I have looked for them my whole life. Have I been living in illusory search for something which does not exist?

Lucia, the person who wrote these words, is thirty-nine. When she came to see me, she was suffering from deep depression and from an icy sense of void. She resented and mistrusted people, for her love—she said—had often been betrayed; and her kindness had elicited only indifference and resentment. Lucia was unmarried and childless—two facts that made her feel more alone and unrealized. She was involved in a relationship with a man who was both possessively overbearing and dependent. The relationship had no clear boundaries—emotional involvement alternated with periods of distrust and uncertainty. In her office, Lucia was competent and successful, and in general was looked upon by colleagues and friends as a strong woman. At home, however, Lucia felt oppressed and invaded by her parents, well-meaning people who had no understanding of her problems. Her emotional difficulties, according to her physician, had materialized in a dermatitis. From our very first session, I perceived in Lucia, just behind the distorting veil of despair, an overwhelming yearning to love.

We began by examining the long history of disillusionments and denials that had led her to her despair. Gradually discovering how some of her subpersonalities condition her, Lucia started changing the image she had of herself—of a useless being in a world of incapable, hostile, low people. She also began to discover her defenses. In a guided daydream, going into the depths of the ocean, Lucia found a sea urchin, which she recognized as an obvious image of herself at that moment—tender and soft inside, but needing a strong armor of quills on the outside to keep everybody away from her.

During a succeeding session, when I asked Lucia to let an image emerge representing her major obstacle in life at the moment, she visualized a narrow and stinking hut which exerted a paralyzing influence, preventing her from venturing out into the world. The hut, however, also protected her from the outside world—a world which was hostile and cold, a world that might hurt her again and again, pitilessly. At this point, I asked her to let an image appear that could help her through her impasse, and she visualized a willow: "I see it gently trembling, moved by a light breeze, which is the breath of life. There is a lot of love in those lissome branches that bend down to embrace me. We remain together in silence: words would be useless, because we are so united with each other that we feel like a single being. Silence reigns all around us, while we fully enjoy our state of effortless well-being. My body is relaxed and at the same time full of vigor. I am certain that if this state of grace could continue, I would be able to do great things."

Though still fearful and uncertain, Lucia began during this period to experience new impulses stirring within her. She began to focus on her future rather than her past. She was ripe for the technique of the ideal model. I asked Lucia what quality she wanted to work on, and she chose love. I asked her to visualize herself as being full of love, and, most important, as being able to express this love in the various moments of her everyday life. Thereafter she repeated the exercise regularly on her own.

In the course of a few weeks Lucia experienced a veritable leap in her level of consciousness. The real came to coincide, at least temporarily, with the envisioned ideal. She wrote: "The image of Lucia smiling and full of love has now become real. I experience a shining light inside and outside myself. Love, my great, hidden treasure, lives and breathes now in the light of the sun. It is marvelous to relish life in this way, having the certitude of knowing myself, knowing that I have the strength of this love and that I am able to communicate it every moment of the day."

This last fact is the most important. Lucia's love is embodied in the actual situations of her existence: "My everyday life has changed. I look at others in a different way, with more indulgence. Rather than irritating me, their limitations evoke my tenderness. It's marvelous for me to wake up in the morning and feel full of vital energy, and to know that I can distribute it as I want. I smile often now, and not only with my lips but also with my eyes. People notice it, and tell me that I have changed."

Her love was strong but not unrealistic. She has had enough of "carrying other people's suitcases," as she puts it, meaning taking responsibility for their pain. Free from any sense of guilt, she decided to sever her connection with her male friend: "I am gradually and gently bringing him to understand that it is not right for us to be together." She had not yet decided whether to leave her parents' home (many practical factors are involved in the choice), but she felt free from depending on others. "I do not ask myself continually, as I used to, whether those who are close to me love me or not."

At certain moments Lucia experienced pure ecstasy. These experiences came at the most unexpected times—when she was with friends, when leaving the hall at the end of a concert, in the office, and so on. "I often experience moments of complete rapture, moments in which I perceive the beauty and the perfection of the universe. My body seems to be disappearing, and I feel like an ethereal substance immersed in the enchantment of a perfect whole into which I feel completely integrated. I do not feel excluded anymore."

There is no self-aggrandizement in all this, and no exaggeration. Lucia still suffers like any other human being, but she is much better able to learn from her pain, instead of blindly trying to avoid it. Occasionally, old feelings of being "the victim" rise up again, but she is able to make fun of them. "I know very well that I will make thousands of mistakes in the future, but when one has the certainty of love that I have, facing life may be difficult but it will never be a hopeless task." Beyond all fleeting waves of enthusiasm, something new has emerged, and it is there to stay.

What took place for Lucia in such a short period (about two and a half months) often takes a much longer time and may not appear with such intensity. But it is no exception: it is simply the effect of fulfilling one's life purpose.

Lucia had locked inside her a strong need to love. It was precisely the thrust of this love, wanting but at the same time unable to express itself, that was causing her pain. This love was impeded by her fears and her hesitations. So we had to deal with these obstacles first. But their elimination would not have been enough by itself. They had to be replaced by another *form*—this one enabling Lucia to conceive how she was going to be if love was to manifest through her. This form was the ideal model; and as soon as Lucia was able to envision it, it inspired, stimulated and mobilized her to action. Thus Lucia was able to fulfill her purpose in that particular period.

And nothing else but love would have allowed that to happen.

Chapter 16

WHAT WE LIVE BY

An angel disobeys God—so goes a story by Tolstoy—and is punished by being precipitated, wingless and naked, into the churchyard of a small Russian village. A poor cobbler passing by, ignorant of the angel's divine origin, saves him from freezing to death; gives him clothing, food, and shelter; and keeps him on as an apprentice.

Several years pass. Then one day the fallen angel smiles in such a way that his face radiates an extraordinarily dazzling light. The cobbler begins to wonder about his guest's origins and asks him why such a radiant light shines about him. The angel then reveals himself for what he is, explaining that the only way he will be able to go back to Heaven is to learn what people live by. His understanding had begun when—having turned into a man—he was rescued from freezing in the churchyard. Now, continues the angel, he has fully realized that human beings cannot live each for himself, that they are necessary to one another, and that *love* is what they live by.

This same fundamental fact, which uncounted writers and poets (and amazingly few psychologists) have stressed in so many ways, can be seen working at different and more remote levels. A single-celled organism that lives in the water and goes by the name "paramecium" reproduces by division: one cell splits into two, these two further divide, and so on. And in that simple way several organisms are generated. At some point, however, this process comes to a stop, and some paramecia, as if they had changed their minds, fuse again with each other. This occurrence is not part of the reproductive process. On the contrary, it slows the process down considerably. Instead of continuing to reproduce, these tiny organisms regenerate each other, join their resources, and heal their tissues. Perhaps the most appropriate description of this activity is "making love."

More speculatively, we can say that the yearning for unity seems to be present even in the most elementary forms of life. It may be something analogous to that deeply rooted need, that obscure nostalgia for undifferentiated oneness, that sense of belonging and inclusiveness, which appears in innumerable forms and to which we sometimes give the name of "love." Angyal called it "the trend toward homonymy" and described it as the tendency by which "a person seeks union with larger units and wishes to share and participate in something which he regards as being greater than his individual self."[1]

Perhaps because it is a principle so intrinsic to organic life and so much embedded in our primeval roots, a harmonious unfolding of this trend seems to generate immense benefits for the mental health and well-being of a person. On the other hand, a disturbance in this area—when this need for union is warped, repressed, or frustrated—causes major difficulties to arise in the psychological life of an individual. Indeed, love is what we live by. And yet it is also what we blind ourselves by, what we suffer by, and what we torture each other by. Probably Dante was right when he said that love—its presence, its lack, its distortions—is the single cause explaining all the joys and sorrows of humanity.

What can we make out of this strange situation? One thing we must be sure to do is acknowledge the immense mystery of love. We must recognize that love is as complex, perhaps, as life itself, and no simple explanation will exhaust it. At the same time, we must have faith that we can penetrate the mystery to some extent. Without reducing love's majesty, I believe we can find ways for looking with care at some of its basic features in ourselves.

Here, again, we will start, as we often do in psychosynthesis, with an exercise that will provide an opportunity for looking at things as they are and investigating their implicit connections and meanings:

THE DIMENSIONS OF LOVE

1. Imagine a closed door. On that door is written *Love*. It opens onto the universe of love, and behind it you can find all sorts of people, beings, objects, memories, situations, and states of consciousness. Spend some time in vividly visualizing the door, its handle, and the inscription.

2. Now open the door, and let the first spontaneous impressions come up without deciding beforehand what they should be. They can come in any form—an image, a physical sensation, a feeling, a sound, a smell, and so on.

3. Gradually get accustomed to the universe behind that door. Explore it. Whatever you find, whether pleasant or unpleasant, your task is twofold:

   a. Look clearly and without judgment or interpretation at whatever you see; don't rush away, but take some time with any image that appears. Give the image the opportunity to reveal itself fully to you.

   b. Realize that this image is only one among the numberless manifestations that can be connected with love. Tell yourself, "There is also this in the universe of love." Then move on.

4. Come away and close the door. On finishing the exercise, think of the images you have found. You may want to figure out their meaning and connections with love and with your life. To further facilitate your insights, you may write about your experiences or draw what you have visualized.

An exercise such as this one, especially if it is repeated, may be quite helpful in starting to understand the vastness of the phenomenon of love, the underlying assumptions we have about it, how our past history may condition the way in which we experience it, and the future potential it holds for us.

I also suggest varying the door exercise by substituting the inscription *Sexuality* for *Love* on the door. Sexuality, even in its crudest and most primitive manifestations, may rightly be seen as a form of love—the tendency to merge with a larger unity.

Often, in exploring a person's inner sense of sexuality, one finds the most diverse implications, the deepest conditionings at work. Very few people experience sexuality in a simple, direct way. For most of us it becomes mixed with supplementary functions: the function, for instance, of erasing tension or evading solitude; the function of escaping one's own reality or attracting love or exercising control; and so on. Frequently, sexuality serves more or less neurotic needs. Moreover, in consciously exploring sexual love, a person can become more clearly aware of his or her self-image and sense of self-worth. We also find that people's attitudes toward sex actually reflect their attitudes toward life as a whole.

One further means of exploring the dimension of love consists in taking a look at how we function in relationships. How do we relate to other people? What are our strengths and limitations in this respect? What are our feelings? Any work we want to do on ourselves regarding love cannot ignore these issues. We have to find out what shape our channels of communication are in if we want to see how easily love can flow through them.

So much happens at this level that were we to be visually sensitive to relational patterns as we are to light waves, we would indeed perceive people in a surprisingly different way than we do now. Perhaps some of them would look like sea urchins, covered with quills; some would show warm bands of radiation, and others would present cold layers; some would look like tight metal compartments, while others would be shooting projectiles at any approaching thing. Still others might extend careful, sensitive, and easily retractable antennas while some would continuously display multicolored, plastic-looking, artificial signals; some would be surrounded by an atmosphere of radiant light and warmth, while others would appear as octopuses, trying to grab anything that passes by; and so on.

And all these science fiction forms would be *us:* in varying ways and proportions we are capable of manifesting aspects of diverse relational styles. Even if our particular relational style isn't pictorially visible, it certainly makes us as individually different as our fingerprints.

RELATIONSHIPS

The exercise that follows can provide fresh perspectives concerning your most important relationships.

1. Write a list of your most important relationships. Then choose five of them.

2. Take a large sheet of paper, and on it draw this simple diagram: Figure 4):
     The point in the center represents you. The points all around it represent the five people with whom you have your most important relationships.

3. In the space between the central point and each of the outer ones, make a free drawing representing the quality of your relationship to that person. You can express it in any way you like, without being concerned about technique.
     Do this for each of the five relationships.

4. When you have finished drawing, write down any considerations that come to your mind concerning the ways in which you relate to

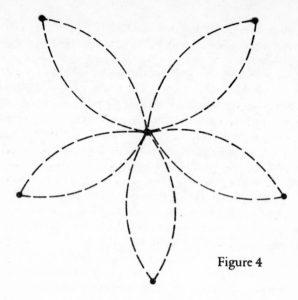

Figure 4

others, so as to have both visual and word pictures of how you are in fact relating. From such awareness can come the resolve and, eventually, concrete plans for positive changes.

We are now ready to consider love from the standpoint of our human essence — what in psychosynthesis we call the *self*. We have seen in an earlier chapter how it is possible to be situated in one's self or center. There, one's existence is characterized by clarity, mastery, and responsibility. We have also seen how we can be situated at the periphery of our being. This psychological posture is characterized by unawareness and lack of perspective. In it we are prey to illusion, and we are slave to our own ideas, emotions, and bodily states.

We can look at any dimension of human life in the light of either of these two extreme postures: there is, for example, relationship from the center and relationship from the periphery, and both have their own distinct characteristics. The same can be said about action, learning, choice, anything.

Love from the center is objective, in the sense of not being distorted by personal bias. Hence it allows us to identify with another person without being overwhelmed or manipulated. Because it does not depend on the responses from the environment or hang on the recognition and gratitude of others, it is self-generating and without fear. It is impregnated with intelligent comprehension, leading to adequate action. It frees the people it touches instead of binding them with guilt or expectation. This type of love is bountiful rather than exhausting itself on only one person, or animal, or object. It extends itself courageously to the unknown rather than restricting itself to the known.

Love springing from the silence of the self penetrates the outer shell, revealing the essence of the object loved. Therefore, it is not stopped by the possible ugliness of the surface or by the wearing away of the body, nor is it bound by boredom, by routine, by friction, or by any other event which may appear to render the object of love unattractive or less interesting.

In its higher, superconscious manifestations, centered love looks at the whole as well as the fragment. This means that it takes into account the existence, the needs, the points of view, and the creative evolution of all beings in a given situation, rather than blindly seeking to satisfy urges coming from any limited personal perspective. It also means that it is able to look back into the past and far ahead into the future, seeing any process as a whole, the problems of the present in the light of future understanding and fulfillment.

At this pitch, love becomes a synthesis of feeling, knowing, and will. Sometimes it attains great heights, seeing all beings as originating from one universal source, and therefore feels a sense of profound unity and kinship with them. Here, love is intuitively perceived as a cosmic principle—in Dante's words, "the love that moves the sun and all the stars."[2]

At the other extreme is *love from the periphery:* basically, the love of being loved. Love originating from the periphery is not necessarily experienced as negative. On the contrary, it is often quite pleasurable, and this fact makes it difficult at times to discriminate it from more centered love. But the differences are acute, if we attend to them. Peripheral love expects recognition and support and therefore lives in fear of not getting them. Needing immediate gratification, it may be capricious, dictatorial, and impermanent. It takes into account only the surface of beings rather than their core. It may imprison the person who is its object in the jail of guilt, of expectation, of imposition. It fixates itself on one restricted area to the exclusion of all others.

Because peripheral love's perception is based on needs, it produces idealizations and daydreams in order to satisfy them. This is the phenomenon which Stendhal called "crystallization" in his book *De l'Amour.* In it he presents the following example: It so happens in the Salzburg mines that if you throw a naked branch in the abandoned depths and come back to retrieve it two or three months later, you will find it completely covered, down to the last twig, with an infinity of glittering, diamond-like crystals—to the point where it is impossible to recognize the original branch. The human mind, says Stendhal, operates in a similar way. Stimulated by a material desire for enjoyment, it fictitiously attributes all kinds of shimmering qualities to the loved one, imagines him or her as having the capacity to give all the joys that no one else could ever offer, and cloaks this fabricated image with nonexistent perfections of all sorts. Soon, however, the illusion is shattered by life's events, and groundless admiration gives way to frustration and resentment.

It would be a very grave error, however, to create too sharp a duality between any one form of love and another. First, as we have implied, there are not two but rather infinite forms of love, existing along a continuum of evolution. And second, even peripheral love is not necessarily opposed to centered love, but can be considered—from a more profound point of view—as its inchoate form.

As we have seen in the chapter on subpersonalities, all psychological aspects of ourselves have the possibility of evolving. Therefore, any inner state can be seen not only statically for what it is in the frozen moment of the present, but also dynamically as a temporary stage of a potential unfoldment. Once we adopt this outlook, we soon realize that all the early manifestations of anything tend to be relatively primitive. In the world of objects, for instance, we can easily see the differences between airplanes or phonograph turntables of the early years of this century and contemporary ones. The same is true at the psychological level. Therefore, it is more realistic to look at peripheral love as love in the process of expanding and refining itself, and also to realize how it can at times be extraordinarily beautiful. Full of passion and tenderness, it may temporarily reward a person with the bliss of complete fulfillment, it may vitalize one's inner universe, it may evoke dazzling fireworks of emotion.

It's also valuable to recognize that love from the periphery may coexist, in many individuals, with more centered love, so that at certain moments one form is predominant and at other times another, or both may be present in various proportions. Moreover, for many people, just learning to love from the periphery can be a precious accomplishment. The mistake lies, then, in assuming the rudimentary stage to be the finished product. We do better to discover, to sense, in the embryonic expression the pulsating vibrancy of more profound love emerging.

Many authors have attempted to describe the different levels of love. Maslow, for instance, speaks about "deficiency-love," and "being-love."[3] Similarly, Orage talks of three kinds of love: instinctive love, which obeys the laws of biology; emotional love, which is not only short-lived, but often "evokes in its object a contrary reaction of indifference or even hate"; and conscious love, which is "the wish that the object should arrive at its own native perfection, regardless of the consequences to the lover." Conscious love appears in a primitive form in our relationship with the vegetable kingdom, as in the cultivation of flowers and fruit. It is not necessarily spontaneous, but often requires, Orage notices, "resolve, effort, self-conscious choice."[4]

In the perspective of the present work, the true mark of conscious love is that it produces synthesis. If a person is immersed in an atmosphere of authentic love, the elements of his or her being spontaneously increase their coherency. In the warmth, freedom, and support that the more essential types of love inevitably offer, our being tends to become restructured into more congruent and more inclusive patterns.

Love can provide the fertile environment in which our best psychological seeds will sprout. It can evoke the courage to step forward and the confidence necessary to plunge into the new. Love can give the space needed for insight to take place. It can protect and strengthen the most delicate elements of our being. It can nourish our intelligence and our creativity. It can help us to melt our blocks, to untie our knots, to open up our closures. Love permits us to rediscover our self and galvanize us into fulfilling our destiny. All such phenomena show how a greater synthesis takes place in our being; how we are helped to become more whole through love; and how, indeed, love is the medium which—par excellence—facilitates human synthesis.

What's more, the benefits of more conscious love are symmetrical. Not only does it have an awakening and unifying effect on the person who is loved, it has the same effect on the person who loves. Feelings and thoughts become unified as if around a magnet, and the whole personality becomes increasingly focused and harmonized. Teilhard de Chardin spoke of love in this respect as the "totalizing principle of human energy." When true love is realized, he says, it warms and animates our actions, and it brings them under one common perspective: it "binds the clouded dust of our experiences into a common lucidity."[5]

The question, then, spontaneously arises: can more conscious loving be learned? The answer is a definite "yes." Both the people who express love in its less mature forms and those who largely seem to lack it in their character can learn to love, if the task is important enough to them.

How is this done? As with any other attitude or skill, love is learned if we give it our attention, explore it, consider its various facets, experiment with it. For those who feel that their love is partly or even mainly of the uncentered kind, this will be a relatively easy task, although not immune from crisis. They already have the basic stuff to work with. Now they need to encourage its evolution.

These people are often stimulated to move forward by the circumstances of life, such as repeated and intense frustration with uncentered love, difficulty in finding a mate, loss of a loved one, and similar types of enforced solitude. People of this kind sometimes experience centered love as desirable but still see it as impersonal, cold, and abstract, while the call of peripheral love remains clear and strong. They may feel uncomfortably poised between one form of love and the other, or often oscillating between the two. Sometimes peripheral love surges and protects, relegating to oblivion their visions of greater dimension. At other times, waves of a wider love rush in with greater strength.

For those people who experience themselves as largely lacking love, the process is different. For them love is unknown territory, and often they do not even realize its importance. They may also look at it with suspicion and feel threatened by the openness and sensitivity it entails. Or they may just consider it a waste of time or nonexistent. But despite their perceptions, love is present in *all* people. We have all experienced it at some times, at some levels, and it can be cultivated anew. Consider this exercise:

THE REALIZATION OF LOVE

1. Recall a time when you were touched by love. Do not just think about it, but, in your imagination, live it again, as if it were happening *now*. Experience again all the details—sights, sounds, emotions, insights, and so on.

2. That single event is past. Realize, however, that the *quality* of love which vivified that moment is timeless.

3. Now, building on your knowledge of the quality of that love as well as on other experiences of love that pervade your being, contact—even if only for a moment, even in a vague way at first—the quality of love in its purest essence. Or at least let yourself imagine as fully as you can what that love is like.

4. Now let an image emerge which symbolizes this kind of love for you. It can be the image of absolutely anything—a landscape, a person, an abstract pattern, etc. Stay with this image and imagine that it has a subtle message, verbal or nonverbal, concerning you or love in general. Then open yourself to it.

5. Finally, write down what you have experienced in the exercise.

This exercise can teach us how we may develop a greater attunement with the quality of conscious love, as it is increasingly revealed to us by our superconscious. A few words of caution that might be reiterated in all our work: avoid such negative reactions as trying too hard and too quickly to storm the gates of higher levels. This is unwise and, indeed, unloving toward our organism as it actually exists. Love, like any quality, unfolds in us, and we are trying to cooperate with its evolution. Trying to push ourselves on the basis of a condemnatory attitude toward where we actually are in our development can only result, sooner or later, in evoking the very opposite of what we are trying to achieve. Looking for harmony with a natural process of synthesis—harmony in our own time and way—is the most productive approach.

On the other hand, love may already be intensely present in us without being expressed. It may just be lying inside us unused. Such a situation is teeming with potentialities, but, if it is not properly dealt with, it may lead to stagnation. Assagioli puts it clearly:

> Just as a screen a few millimeters thick can block the most intense solar light, which has traveled millions of miles; just as a piece of porcelain insulates an electrical current strong enough to activate hundreds of motors; just as the lack of a few degrees of heat keep inert a powder which could blow up a mountain; so a small "psychic insulator," a lack of warmth, of sympathy and love, can block the expression of immense treasures of feeling and intelligence.[6]

Any discussion of love is incomplete without attention to service. *Service is love in action,* deliberately and creatively applied and circulated. We love or serve other people by eliciting their resources, by understanding, by transmitting vision, by healing an emotional wound, by educating, and in innumerable other ways, at all levels—from the physical to the spiritual.

As with all good things, however, service has many caricatures. Many well-meaning enthusiasts produce toxic and sometimes catastrophic results. They try to serve merely by expressing their own exuberant goodwill, without any consideration of the real needs of others and without any awareness of the mess they often create. To get an idea of what I mean, just think of those times when people tried to help, improve, convert, elevate, advise, or "save" you—and just made a nuisance of themselves. On the other hand, you can probably recall a time when a person truly nourished you. Wherein lies the difference between genuine and pseudo-service?

The need for self-expression, the desire to please and to be popular, the longing for return benefits, self-complacency, and ambition, make the difference. And the remedy in this case is discrimination—simply looking into our own motives and seeing that the main propelling force for our service is genuine love.

Paradoxically, true service is a powerful tool for implementing our own growth. People report an immense variety of benefits: among others, increased efficiency, enlargement of vision, release of positive feelings, better mental functioning, stimulation of creativity, increase of self-confidence and interest in life, tapping of higher energies, and evocation of a joyous sense of interdependence with others. This whole area in itself constitutes a true mine of discoveries for anybody interested in human development.

It may be objected that service done with the motive of self-benefit is not true service, but an ego-subservient activity like any other, such as playing the stock market or eating ice cream. True enough. However, it is equally true that as people plunge into service, the demands made on them by the particular field of service and the inevitable involvement in action usually supersede egoistical motives and lead to release and expansion. I will quote here just one example, a woman:

After my husband died I felt lonely and useless. I just worked, got my money, and that was it. I felt like a zero.

So I thought: what can I give of myself? I called upon the Institute for the Blind, asking if my eyes could be of any use. Two days later they called me back, inviting me to dictate books to be written in Braille. They were schoolbooks. They wanted the blind kids to be included in the school programs with the other kids, so they needed somebody who could see to dictate.

The first impact was a shock. Two children came to get the papers. They were twins, and both were blind. They were not born blind; they became blind through being in an incubator with the wrong temperature after they were born, and this had burned their eyes. One boy was dark and the other fair. Very, very beautiful.

I hoped they wouldn't come anymore. It was too much. What struck me about these kids was their cheerfulness. All blind people there were cheerful.

I felt like a queen because I had eyes. I realized that I was lucky in spite of all that has happened to me. It was good for me to meet them. They even had a sculpture class working with clay. Once I saw them all making vases with faces on them. The teacher would say, now touch your own chin, now touch your own nose. The next day I saw the most wonderful series of vases, one better than the other, each with a different face on it. I thought, what shouldn't we who have eyes accomplish if these people can do all this without eyes?

During the first days I remained shocked. I would close my eyes for a while and imagine what it is like to be blind. Then I began to feel rich. If you do something which you know from the start will not earn you anything, you feel extraordinarily rich. I don't think I do a great deal for them, and yet what I do feels good to me in my whole being.

Thus people find that, when they serve, they cease to grasp and become able to receive. They cease to be only self-interested, and therefore they easily participate in the natural give-and-take which goes on all around them. An ancient story well illustates this fact:

A man was given permission to visit Heaven and Hell while he was still alive. He went first to Hell, and there he saw a great gathering of people seated at long tables set with rich and abundant food. Yet these people were starving and weeping. The visitor soon saw the reason: their spoons and forks were longer than their arms, so that they were unable to bring the food to their mouths. Next the man went to Heaven, where he saw the same setting: long tables richly garnished with food of every kind. Here too the people had spoons and forks longer than their arms and were likewise unable to feed themselves. Yet they were joyful and well fed. But they were not trying to feed themselves.

They were feeding each other.

Chapter 17

BEAUTY

No issue is so relevant to our inner life and at the same time so elusive as beauty. In the first place, the aesthetic experience is spontaneous, and no effort can ever succeed in triggering it if it is not meant to take place. Moreover, even in people who are sensitive to beauty in some considerable degree, its impact is unpredictable; an extreme variability in likes and dislikes prevents us from finding general criteria to orient ourselves in this dimension. And when the aesthetic experience actually takes place, nobody knows exactly what happened, and few are able to put it into words. In addition, trying to find out in what way beauty affects our personality may well breed a creeping utilitarian attitude that inevitably dispels the most intangible experience of all.

Despite all these difficulties, the task of exploring beauty and the influence it has on us is essential, for the dangers that blindness to beauty entails are great: the degradation of the urban landscape, the ruthless destruction of nature, the spreading of vulgarity, the eclipse of awe, the triumph of tactlessness, the inflation of boredom, the industry of bad taste, the apotheosis of the loud and the superficial. These are only the most glaring manifestations of a lack of aesthetic sensitivity. The deeper consequence is more difficult to pin down. It can perhaps be described as a deadly opacity affecting the whole personality like an ominous ailment.

Accordingly, talking of beauty, as we shall do here, is no mere exercise in aestheticism or babbling about the ineffable. It is a vitally compelling task, directly relevant to our possibilities for survival—or at least for decent and human survival. For this reason we can agree with Plato, who says in the *Republic* that "the aim of all education is to teach us to love beauty."

The first effect I would like to consider is beauty's *regenerative* and *healing* influence. That a natural landscape is soothing to the eye, that certain music is uplifting, that a play, poem, or picture has an exhilarating effect on us, we all know by experience, even though we may too easily forget this fact. Sometimes, however, beauty's healing influence has been used consciously and directly. One example, according to Iamblichus, was Pythagoras' use of music: "There are certain melodies devised as remedies against the passions of the soul, and also against despondency and lamentation, which Pythagoras invented as things that afford the greatest assistance in these maladies. And again, he employed other melodies against rage and anger, and against every aberration of the soul."[1]

Research has recently confirmed that Pythagoras was right. Music has a powerful effect on several bodily rhythms and functions and on psychological states. Moreover, as Anthony Trowbridge of South Africa has suggested, neural networks in the brain may be responsive to harmonic principles in general. And there is such a factor within us as an "inbuilt urge to maintain a state of intellectual and aesthetic order and harmonic balance, essential to mental health."[2]

But we do not need research to know that the magnificence of a cathedral's rose window, the design of Celtic manuscripts, a flower in full bloom, or the perfect geometry of a Greek temple does not leave us unaffected. And the moment we let ourselves be touched by beauty, that part of us which has been badly bruised or even shattered by the events of life may begin to be revitalized. At that moment a true victory takes place—a victory over discouragement, a positive affirmation against resigning ourselves to the process of crystallization and death. That victory is also a step forward in our growth in a very precise and literal sense, for the moment we fully appreciate beauty we become more than we were. *We live a moment of pure psychological health*. We effortlessly build a stronghold against the negative pressures that life inevitably brings.

But that is not all, for all stimuli—beautiful or ugly—sink into the unconscious, where their influence becomes less immediate, but more powerful and pervasive. Part of our unconscious is already impressed like a photographic plate with the innumerable stimuli which have bombarded us through the years. But another part is virgin and available to impression, and as soon as it is reached by a stimulus, it takes that stimulus much more seriously than our distracted surface mind usually does. It chews on and elaborates it. It combines it with other, preexisting stimuli. And it assimilates the psychological universe which the stimulus conveys, implicitly adopting all its limitations and distortions.

Take, for example, a picture. A picture of any kind—be it an ad or a pornographic photo, a painting by Monet or a newspaper snapshot of a riot—expresses a state of consciousness, a way of looking at life, an aesthetic standard, and a general attitude to the universe.

When stimuli of the same kind are repeated a great number of times—as in the case of the 15,000 killings the average American adolescent has seen on TV—their effects multiply and come to generate a real psychological climate in the inner world of an individual. Fortunately, however, it is especially true that stimuli with a high aesthetic value have a tremendous, all-encompassing influence, the healing power of which affects the very depths of our being.

We have a choice then. Seeking beauty becomes in great part our responsibility. We can be exposed to what Assagioli called "psychic smog"—the prevailing mass of free-floating psychological poisons—or turn instead to the healing influence of beautiful sights and sounds.

Akin to its regenerating influence is the *self-transcending effect* of beauty. An exercise that I use in my groups has particularly confirmed this fact to me. In its first phase, I just lay several dozen art reproductions on the floor and ask the participants to look at them and pick one with which they resonate. I watch them while they are doing this, and I am always amazed by the thirst they show when they plunge toward the reproductions. In fact, they usually become so absorbed as to be deaf to my subsequent instructions. In that brief moment they put their pains and problems between parentheses, so to speak, and therefore succeed in forgetting themselves.

I believe we should pay more attention to this thirst. It is a thirst for something undefinable, some promise of future, total fulfillment, or perhaps a remembrance of a lost bliss. Beauty seems to hold this promise—or to awaken this remembrance—and even though we do know that no beautiful object can bring permanent gratification, beauty often has the power of enticing us out of the stuffy world of ordinary concerns into a greater sphere of vitality and harmony.

The best favor we can do is probably that of helping people to forget themselves—not, of course, their true Selves, but the everyday minds with which they identify, the minds agitated by all kinds of preoccupations, petty grumblings, idle daydreams, and so on. Problems, Assagioli used to say, are usually not solved; they are forgotten. And they are forgotten because some other issue, with a much greater breadth and vital importance, has taken their place.

Beauty has precisely this capacity to pull a person out of his or her own individual sphere, facilitating contact with something universal which interests and touches. Without this self-transcending function—common also to other attitudes and activities such as love, reflection, and play, to name just a few—we would be suffocated by the oppressive atmosphere of a restricted life. Our personal world has to be nourished from outside its boundaries, because, if isolated, it cannot find in itself the resource to survive and the tools to solve its difficulties. Hieronymus Bosch, let us remember, depicts the damned of Hell as being enveloped by an opaque crystal ball, impeding all communication with the outside world.

Beauty's transcending effect is closely linked with its *revelatory power*. Beauty reveals unknown worlds, nameless possibilities which would escape a purely rational, matter-of-fact intelligence. The fact that beauty has the liberating, vivifying impact of truth has been noticed by a number of people along different paths. On the one hand, we have artists like Beethoven, who said that "music is a higher revelation than all wisdom and philosophy"[3] and that "music is the one incorporeal entrance into the higher world of knowledge."[4] Or like Suger, the abbot of Saint Denis and one of the fathers of the art of stained glass in twelfth-century France, who claimed that such wonderful displays of light and color as he could produce with the use of enamels, jewelry, gold, and stained glass could "enlighten people's minds,"[5] resurrect their submerged spirits, and give them the gift of higher knowledge. And then we have Keats, who wrote that he could "never feel certain of any truth but from a clear perception of its beauty."[6]

On the other hand, there are scientists who, having studied the core of physical reality, notice that the aesthetic quality of their models is itself a guideline for their validity. In a letter to Einstein, Heisenberg writes: "You may object that by speaking of simplicity and beauty I am introducing aesthetic criteria of truth, and I frankly admit that I am strongly attracted by the simplicity and beauty of the mathematical schemes which nature presents us. You must have felt this too: the almost frightening simplicity and wholeness of the relationship, which nature suddenly spreads out before us . . ."[7]

Similarly, the French mathematician Poincaré attributed a great importance to "mathematical beauty," to the "harmony of numbers and forms," and to "geometric elegance." "This harmony," he wrote, "is at once a satisfaction of our aesthetic needs and an aid to the mind, sustaining and guiding it." According to Poincaré, the mathematician's "subliminal self" blindly forms an enormous quantity of combinations, most of them false and useless. The only combinations that emerge to consciousness are the ones which are singled out by the "delicate sieve" of aesthetic sensibility and which, says Poincaré, "are at once useful and beautiful."[8]

Linked with the revealing power of beauty is its *capacity to unsettle* and even to explode the categories by means of which we habitually make sense of the universe. It is recounted that on one occasion the disciples of the Buddha were asking him all kinds of complex metaphysical questions.

He then took a flower and wordlessly put it in front of them. Only one of the disciples, Ananda, understood the inexpressible truth conveyed by the message—and smiled. As with Ananda, beauty discloses to us what is beyond thought. At times, it may even impress upon us what an ineffectual gadget our conceptual equipment can be, how limited our understanding. I have known people whose tight, ordinary mental scaffolding has been completely shattered by the sight of the stars on a clear night. In other cases it was a piece of music or the bare presence of mountain peaks that stretched a person's ideas or even forced their abandonment like a worn-out suit of clothes.

Then there is another, particular way in which beauty affects us: *it lightens our greed*. Many spiritual traditions state that we can achieve liberation or salvation only by getting rid of all attachment and greed. This teaching has often been misunderstood as an injunction to systematically and forcefully destroy all desire in ourselves. While this procedure can work for a few individuals with a vocation for asceticism, more often it generates results exactly contrary to expectation. People try to repress their desires, but only succeed in feeding them with the energy of their own denial. After a desire has been stifled for a while, it backlashes dramatically, emerges under a different guise, or merely seems to have disappeared, but, invisibly, it actually controls the individual who has tried to eliminate it.

Assagioli maintained that we can learn to enjoy the freedom of detachment in a much less painful and more practical way: by fully appreciating beauty. Usually we desire what we consider beautiful. Rather than denying that attraction, says Assagioli, we should let other ones be born beside it. By learning to expand our appreciative powers, we diffuse our attachments to the point of weakening and even dissipating them.

The mistake of the moralist, according to Assagioli, lies in confusing enjoyment with attachment. Enjoyment of any kind is in itself a profoundly positive psychological event. What complicates the situation is that soon after our enjoyment is finished—or even before, in some cases—we want to reproduce the same gratification, and thus attachment is born. But attachment is an entirely different phenomenon from enjoyment, and even if it closely follows or is mixed with it, we should be aware of the distinction between the two. Enjoyment is gratuitous and pure. Attachment is greedy and expectant. Enjoyment lives in the now. Attachment lives in the past or projects itself into the future. Enjoyment is open to experience. Attachment wants to program it.

What's more, our attachments are inversely proportional to our capacity to enjoy. As Assagioli said to me once:

The radical approach is to *enjoy more*. If you enjoy a fruit, enjoy *all* kinds of fruit. If you enjoy everything, you get attached to nothing, because you pass from one enjoyment to another. You pass from the enjoyment of a fruit to the enjoyment of a book, to the enjoyment of the starry sky . . .

If you appreciate everything, you remain free. And if you feel the desire for something which is not opportune for several reasons or because you cannot get it, turn to enjoying something else.

There is always something else that you can enjoy.[9]

The opposite is also true. If we can see beauty only in one person or object, to the exclusion of everything else, we become bewitched by it and our vision becomes calcified. We fall for the implicit and illusory belief that by grasping and possessing that being or that object we shall be able to possess beauty itself.

It is paradoxical but true that beauty may conceal a sinister side. This is illustrated in the story of Spinello, a Renaissance painter appreciated and famous in his time. During that period it was customary to represent the devil as a despicable, subhuman being, and Spinello had been working on a painting in which he had so depicted the devil. When he became seriously ill and feverish, however, the devil appeared to him, but not as the despicable creature Spinello had painted. He was, instead, an incredibly beautiful man, dressed in black, who looked at him and said: "Spinello, Spinello, how small indeed is the faith you have in your God, that you believe He would have as His greatest enemy such a lowly and unintelligent creature as the one you have portrayed. Know rather that I am so beautiful as to rival Him in splendor."

Enjoyment has often been connected with the sense of taste, as the expressions "good taste," "bad taste," and "savoring" demonstrate. Conversely, the suppression of enjoyment can also be understood in terms of eating: we often quickly swallow what we eat, perhaps even while reading or watching television, without taking time to relish the food. A gift is offered to us, and we overlook it by gulping it down mindlessly. This way of eating is parallel to the way in which we sometimes relate to the outer world in general: we quickly appropriate it, so to speak, but do not linger long enough to fully enjoy and therefore assimilate it. Very few people know how to savor a piece of music, a poem, a good book, or a landscape and then let themselves be impregnated with it, enjoying all the nuances and subtleties which a hurried, impatient awareness inevitably overlooks.

Difficulties in enjoying beauty, however, are not due only to impatience and the incapacity to assimilate. In some people they are also caused by their fear of beauty. Because these people feel ugly inside, they dread experiencing the painful discrepancy between themselves and beauty.

Others may be able to enjoy beauty with a loved one, but contact with it when they are alone evokes a poignant sense of solitude. I have seen many such people close themselves to beauty rather than enjoy it alone. At the bottom of such attitudes one usually finds a sense of inferiority, an implicit belief that one is undeserving of anything worthwhile unless the presence and approval of another person acts as an intermediary.

Still other people feel the aesthetic dimension as threateningly alien, disrupting the normal order of things. They implicitly delegate the enjoyment of beauty to others, as if it were the monopoly of one category of people only. Whoever belongs to such a category, however, is often then perceived as weird and ineffectual. "Hey, you, artist," called out a sergeant I knew in the army, when he wanted to shake up a soldier whom he perceived as being too dreamy or strange—or dangerously open to something other than the organized routine.

All of us, however, have some experience of the beautiful, and all of us can enhance our ability to contact the aesthetic dimension. We will thereby accomplish two results: first of all, we will lay solid foundations of self-appreciation; and no personality is truly well integrated unless it stands on such a foundation of deep, sincere, almost naive self-appreciation—an attitude quite different, almost opposite to narcissism or a superiority complex; secondly, this ability to perceive our own inner beauty almost automatically opens the gates to the appreciation of *outer* beauty. As Plotinus says, ". . . he that beholds must be akin to that which he beholds, and must, before he comes to this vision, be transformed into its likeness. Never could the eye have looked upon the sun had it not become sun-like, and never can the soul see Beauty unless she has become beautiful."[1]

And our true "soul," one could say, is *already* beautiful. We need only to make ourselves aware of this fundamental fact. The following exercise can help in this task:

INNER BEAUTY

1. Think of a trait, a capacity, or an attitude in yourself which you consider beautiful. It does not have to be fully manifest or active. It may be an element still partly concealed in you, something perhaps only you know about. It may even be the seed of an attitude—a pure possibility.

2. Take some time in acknowledging and enjoying this element of yourself. Then let an image appear to your inner eye that symbolizes what you have chosen—an object of art, a landscape, an animal, anything.

3. Contemplate this image, let it show you its own beauty and perhaps even transmit a message, which may be either verbal or subtly nonverbal. Any image can actually talk to you, if you allow it to do so. Take time to fully assimilate the quality of this image.

4. Pick another trait, quality, capacity, or side of yourself that you enjoy, and repeat steps 2 and 3. Then do the same with still other parts of you which you like. Repeat this same exercise on other occasions until you have come to quite a number of elements in yourself which you appreciate. You will be surprised at how many you will find—especially if you look deep enough and if you ignore inner voices of discouragement, inferiority, or skepticism.

How can we further increase our aptitude in the art of appreciating beauty? The answer is ever the same: by learning to be available to it. With an open attitude, we calmly take the time to enjoy it; we allow ourselves to absorb it, leaving aside all utilitarian orientation and all impatience. But we can also assume a more active stance and purposefully, almost systematically, look for beauty, look for it everywhere—in a face, in a piece of music, or in a tree. Stanislawski, the great Russian teacher of theater techniques, asked his pupils to look for beauty with "penetration." "Such habits," he said, "elevate their [the students'] minds and arouse feelings which will leave deep traces in their emotion memories."[11] He would also remind his pupils, however, to look for beauty in apparently ugly, distorted, or disfigured things, because any sense of beauty that does not take into account ugliness risks being sentimental. We can mention here the example of Rembrandt's painting transfiguring such an uncomely spectacle as a side of beef hanging in a butcher shop into a stupendous play of light and color. Or, in more recent times, we have the example of René Clair's statement that he could see an enchanted castle in a Parisian Metro station. Similarly, Leonardo da Vinci gave aspiring painters the following advice:

You should look at certain walls stained with damp or at stones of uneven color. If you have to invent some setting, you will be able to see in these the likeness of divine landscapes adorned with mountains, ruins, rocks, woods, great plains, hills, and valleys in great variety; and then again you will see there battles and strange figures in violent action, expressions on faces, clothes, and an infinity of things which you will be able to reduce to their complete and proper forms.[12]

Soon we will find that beauty is not to be discovered at the physical level only, as a form to be perceived, but also at subjective levels: we can appreciate beautiful attitudes in people, the purity of their motives, the refinement of their being, and so on. We can also enjoy the harmony and significance of relationships. Most important, we can, in a flash, contact the inner beauty of a person's core. Sanskrit uses the word *Namaskara* to mean "I salute the divine in you." It is a ritual recognition of the divine essence of each person one meets. Namaskara could also be translated as "I salute the inner beauty in you" or, in some cases—in a lengthier and freer rendition, which I would irreverently like to propose—as: "Independently of the fact that you irritate me, that I can't stand your presence, that I feel uneasy when I am with you, that I disagree with you, that I find myself believing you are a hopeless slob, and so on and so forth, I salute the inner beauty in you—a beauty which I may have perceived at some time or, if I never perceived it, deliberately assume is there—mysterious, immemorial, unaffected by any games we may at this moment be playing, infinite."

This sense of inner beauty in a human being is not merely an individual matter; when we contact it in one person it may well extend spontaneously to all humanity, and we may find ourselves experiencing what Kant called "the sentiment of the beauty and the dignity of human nature."[13]

And then there is the beauty of our own psychosynthesis. Harmony and rhythm in life, mastery over the psychophysical organism (comparable to the mastery of a pianist or a dancer), the extraordinary push of personal evolution into the unknown, the transformation and synthesis of the elements of our personality, the apprenticeship in the art of living, the dazzling manifestations of the Self—all these attitudes and events may carry elements of great and moving beauty, whether we perceive them in ourselves or in others.

In whatever ways it may come, however, much of the experience of beauty is too often wasted. The nourishment given to us by delight is soon submerged by the avalanche of daily cares or dissipated by the advent of countless distractions. Rarely is it assimilated—as we have seen—and, above all, treasured, like a landmark in our life, something from the past which still has the capacity to silently regenerate us, an event which brought us forward in our growth, which opened and stimulated our capacity to enjoy.

Treasuring past delights is a vital factor in enabling us to relish future beauty. The following exercise aims at stimulating and bringing back to life the treasures we once were blessed with. It starts with the recollection of ugliness, because the contrast of ugliness—not only physical ugliness, but also the ugliness of disintegration, conflict, stupidity, lovelessness—helps us to understand the nature of beauty and sometimes dramatically intensifies our yearning for it.

TREASURING BEAUTY

The following exercise will have some effect only if you vividly relive the events you are asked to contact and if you do so with all your senses, as if you were actually experiencing rather than merely evoking them intellectually.

1. Start by reliving moments of ugliness. Feel again in yourself the offending, disintegrating influence of ugliness on your psychophysical organism. And remember: it may be any kind of ugliness, not only a physical one.

2. Now recollect several moments of beauty, one by one. They may include the beauty of nature, of a relationship, of growth, of understanding, and so on. The choice is yours. Feel fully their extraordinary effects.

Take your time in relishing these moments; let them sink into you so that you can assimilate them, realize and treasure their value, reaffirm their presence in yourself.

3. Now take some time to induce in yourself a sense of openness in the totality of your being, a realization of your sensitivity and vital interest in the extraordinary presence of beauty in all dimensions.

As we explore beauty in its manifestations, we may have the exceptional experience of contacting it independently of any form. This is what Plato described as the beauty which "neither waxes nor wanes"; it is St. Augustine's "Beauty so old and so new," Shelley's "Spirit of Beauty." These are not just words, poetical metaphors, philosophical speculations. They are actual psychological experiences having a profound impact on those who happen to enjoy them. Describing precisely this kind of contact, a person writes:

I was looking at a peach tree in blossom, and then I suddenly felt that it was not just the tree that was beautiful, but *living beauty* seemed to be coming through it, and it was in touch with me. It was an intensely personal contact, and it was like some *being* was communicating with me in a wordless way. It was like meeting some very, very special person who had an extraordinary effect on me.

This entity, I felt, was seeking at all times to express itself through the activity of innumerable forms of life—through nature, as with a flower or a spider weaving a web, or through a human being creating a work of art, so that the same life could express itself through me. It was a wonderful moment: I experienced great strength in my body, and I was flooded by an overwhelming sense of harmony. In a flash countless aspects of beauty were revealed to me which I had never realized before.

Chapter 18

SYNTHESIS

A young person living in the Norwegian fjords exhibits the most astounding gifts: without having received any form of education whatsoever, he demonstrates an erudition far surpassing the knowledge of sages. He knows countless secrets concerning the inner workings of nature; he understands how plants communicate with animals, and he is able to see into the essence of things and to realize their place in the evolution of the universe. He has the capacity of looking inside strangers and reading in their eyes the most hidden motivations. His simple presence fills people with fire, and, indeed, the very thought of him is alone sufficient to purify another person. Above all, he has the mysterious power of appearing to different people in two different forms—the male and the female—and of possessing the essence and the traits traditionally ascribed to both the feminine and the masculine nature.

Seraphitus-Seraphita, the protagonist of the novel *Seraphita,* by Balzac, is an androgyne. And the androgyne is a powerful symbol of our Self, of that place within where opposites are reconciled and all possibilities coexist without mutual contradiction. As Mircea Eliade, author of a beautiful essay on the subject, put it, "the coincidence of opposites" is an extraordinary state where our usual condition—the condition of feeling like a fragment torn away from the source of life and experiencing nostalgia for the primordial unity—is exchanged for a plenitude in which all opposites fuse without conflict.[1]

200 WHAT WE MAY BE

This perfect union of opposites is a highly desirable state and one that can be approached by each of us in greater or lesser degree. But to make such an approach we first need to become aware of our common inner polarities and to see the various ways in which we can deal with them. By such a work of analysis we will then be able to approach inner synthesis.

Love and will are a common polarity in many people's lives. Love often means tenderness, softness, inclusiveness. Will implies toughness, power, and one-pointedness. Love makes one yielding. Will gives firmness and helps an individual to take straight aim and break through all obstacles in approaching the goal, even to the point, sometimes, of walking over others to get where one wants to go. Love instead makes people less interested in goals and more open to being touched by feelings, relationships, and empathy. The love-will polarity can often be seen in the dilemma facing parents and educators—choosing between being strict versus giving full freedom to the desires of the children (and sometimes even to their whims). You can find a similar dilemma in a court of law—the alternative between impersonal adherence to the law and compassionate identification with the case at hand. A similar polarity is also at work in psychotherapy—the contraposition between accepting persons as they are and giving only positive attention and empathy, or, instead, crushing through their defenses and shaking them out of their neurotic grooves.

Each side is clearly incomplete. Love entirely devoid of will may be inconclusive and weak. Many "loving" people tend to be shy, lazy, or too lenient, however nice they may be. Conversely, will without love can be ruthless. It can lead to harshness and destructiveness, to the pursuit of power for its own sake, and to isolation. I believe we can agree with Assagioli's simple statement that one of our most urgent tasks is for the loving to become stronger and for the strong to become more loving.

One way this can happen is for both to perceive the poles in their undistorted essence. At superconscious levels, love and will appear to be very much like one another. The will at its best is inclusive and works for the benefit of the whole, while love has a volitional and persistent quality to it.

Practicality and idealism are another widespread polarity. On the one hand, we have the tendency to deal with the prosaic realities of every day, giving importance to action and to visible accomplishments. On the other hand, we have the propensity to emphasize the invisible inner realities and ideals. The first tendency may lead to a gross materialism which ignores whatever cannot be seen, heard, or touched. The second may cause a person to despise action as if it were impure, to live with one's head in the clouds and be out of touch with ordinary reality—the reality of making a living, paying the bills, and emptying the garbage.

Individuals who live according to such differing tendencies will tend to misunderstand and even despise one another. But often the two traits can exist in the same person, causing perpetual contradictions. I will never forget a client of mine whose first statement when he walked into my office was: "All I am interested in is light." Everything else, he said, was irrelevant. He seemed a mystic. But one day, after a few sessions in which he had worked on his need for enlightenment and had had some quite beautiful experiences, I sensed that he was in a rather different mood. After a few minutes of conversation it became clear that his main interest in life now was making money. When I reminded him that up to a short time before the search for enlightenment had captivated his interest, he casually observed that that aim was not practical enough, that you just cannot make a living with light alone, and that he wanted something more concrete to put his hands on! His tone was full of contempt for what he had previously valued in the extreme. Naturally, the yearning for enlightenment reappeared with even stronger intensity after a few sessions.

In many ways, there was nothing unusual in this man's behavior. Both tendencies—the practical and the mystical—were present in him, as they are in many of us. They were two subpersonalities of his. But when the conflict between subpersonalities is so severe, one can see clearly how such an unresolved and even unconscious conflict leads to one's living a life divided and uncertain of its own meaning. This painful confusion occurs when each of two strong motivations tries to utterly destroy the other's very existence.

It will be clear that numerous polarities—lover/will and idealism/ practicality are examples—may partially overlap. Once again, this should caution us against trying to think that we can *wholly* understand the divisions within the psyche. Rational analysis is necessary and practically useful, but we need not pretend to have arrived at a narrow system that exhausts our inner reality. The polar forces within us are multivalent and variegated, assuming different colorations and qualities at different times.

Such a commonly found psychological polarity as that between feelings and mind, for example, can be thought of as a variant on the universal polarity of Eros and Logos. Assagioli has beautifully described Eros: "It means love in the widest sense, it is the vital, primordial impulse, the tendency at the source of the fundamental instinct to self-preservation, self-assertion, and reproduction, manifesting itself in the form of innumerable impulses and desires, becoming refined in the most delicate sentiments, and being sublimated into the highest aspirations. Eros is throbbing life, propelling power, warmth, fire."[2]

Logos, instead, is "the directing principle which regulates and coordinates life. Logos tends to gather and channel the tumultuous torrent, the turbid stream of Eros within firm and straight banks, carrying it toward a set goal. Logos always tends to model the fluid and flexible vital and psychic substance into well-defined forms. Logos is law and discipline. It is order, harmony, and beauty. It is rhythm and measure. It is intelligence and reason, understanding and light."[3]

Eros without Logos is blind and irrational. Logos without Eros is arid and cold. And, while they are never found completely separate from one another, we may partially lack one of them or house within us a conflict between the two. Many polarities—discipline and spontaneity, for instance, or reason and instinct, common sense and craziness—are other variations on the theme of Eros and Logos.

The polarity of sensuality and spirituality, though resembling some of those we have already seen, also has a story of its own. On the one hand, many people appreciate the beauty of "spirituality" in the meaning that the religious and mystical traditions have at times given it: single-minded detachment, purity, freedom from possessions, and a rigorous personal nakedness which allows the Self to shine through, without impediments.* On the other hand, many people opt for sensuality, in the broad sense of the word—the identification with all aspects of the universe, the cultivation of every kind of enjoyment, the passionate attachment to and love for the external world in all its forms.

The first tendency, by itself, may bring about a lack of sympathy with life, an aloofness and inability to participate in the dance of creation. The second tendency may lead instead to excessive attachment to forms without substance, to decadent aestheticism, to an inability to bear frustrations, and to passivity and weakness. This duality has been beautifully dramatized by Herman Hesse in his novel *Narcissus and Goldmund*. (Hesse, however, stopped short of describing in that work the full-blown synthesis of the two aspects.)

The usual division between work and play is a polarity so embedded in our culture as to pass often unnoticed. Play tends to be seen as pleasurable, but frivolous and unproductive. Work really counts to make us serious and significant members of our society—but then it seems to be just boring routine. Only a few individuals succeed in creatively working with such pleasure and interest that they no longer experience a dividing line between the two opposites. They experience all activity from the aspect of play, relishing its unpredictability, its creative vitality producing shapes forever new, its adventurous mood that does not hesitate in front of risks and doubts, its gusto, its never-ending, gratuitous inventiveness. It is these

---

*I am using the word "spirituality" here in a limited meaning which is often adopted. Spirituality in its fullest significance, of course, can be seen as the synthesis of all aspects and possibilities.

qualities that make of play, as Assagioli said, the hallmark of the spirit, and which explain why Indian tradition adopted it as a metaphor—together with dance—for describing the cosmic drama. At this level of understanding, work and play are one.

All kinds of other pairs of opposites play on the stage of our psychological life and color it in different ways: intuition and logic, prudence and adventurousness, pessimism and optimism, masculinity and femininity, conservatism and renewal, introversion and extraversion, and so on. The play of these opposites gives us the opportunity for richness of experience, action, and, eventually, synthesis. In some people, it is hard to discern any polarities at all. They appear to be completely defined by one aspect: he is only a worker, for instance, and does not know how to play; she is only mental, and her emotional life is almost absent; and so on. The result typically is *stagnation*. Contrast is usually needed for growth, and the lack of interplay can often bring about dreariness and narrowmindedness. To avoid such a danger, we can develop qualities and traits complementary to the ones we already possess. A painting is more interesting when it is not uniform. A play is more entertaining if its plot is rich in contrasts and surprises. A personality is more lively and complete when opposing tendencies are present.

Life is seldom at rest, however, and stagnation is generally impermanent. Indeed, narrowness is often only apparent: people identified with one pole may be rich in the quality of the opposite one but repress it. If they are persons with a great deal of will, for example, they may unconsciously fear, and therefore repress their capacity to be tender and to love. Consciously, they might even devalue it. Conversely, other individuals with an excess of gentleness might disown their capacity to willfully affirm themselves.

Even more common is the pattern of *oscillation*, which we have seen in the man who was alternately interested in enlightenment and financial success. Oscillations may be extremely brief—they can last only minutes—or they can be quite long, as in the case of those who adopt bourgeois values during one part of their life, but then drop out and opt for a diametrically opposite kind of existence.

Like narrowness, oscillation is often the result of repression. The moment we take sides, we build a wall between the two poles and try to stay on one side of it only. This separation does not work out, and the repressed tendency sooner or later emerges and fights back with as much energy as was employed in keeping it out of the way. Robert Louis Stevenson dramatized this process in his novel *Dr. Jekyll and Mr. Hyde,* where Dr. Jekyll is honest, well-known, and appreciated, while Mr. Hyde is evil-looking and evil-doing.

But the matter is not so clearcut. When Dr. Jekyll became Mr. Hyde, "my faculties" he wrote, "seemed sharpened to a point and my spirits more tensely elastic." And when Dr. Jekyll made the decision to reject his evil part completely, he had to say "farewell to the liberty, the comparative youth, the light step, leaping pulses and secret pleasures" that he had enjoyed in the guise of Hyde.

The "lower" side has many attractions and great vitality. When this vitality is repressed, it rebels. After a while, wrote Dr. Jekyll, "the lower side of me . . . so recently chained down, began to growl for license." Very soon he was compelled to become Mr. Hyde again, and the story ends on a note of despair as the situation, becoming increasingly uncontrollable, leads finally to his death.

A narrowly judgmental and even sectarian attitude is typical of people with a dualistic outlook. We hear them glorifying one pole and rejecting the other out of hand. We hear them extolling "spirituality" and condemning sensuality, or vice versa. We hear them praising the structured and blaming the spontaneous. Or perhaps we see them admiring the strong and despising the sensitive, or making fun of those who work and joining those who play. Naturally, because each of the qualities at either pole has great merit, those who extol it are always right: work is productive, strength is necessary, and "spirituality" is sublime.

The problem starts when we identify exclusively with one pole or quality at the expense of the other. Then we gradually become prisoners of what we have chosen and succumb to all its limitations. Our behavior becomes reactive because we blind ourselves to the richness in the opposite perspective.

As a consequence, interpersonal conflicts may also arise: between the practical father and the idealistic son, for example, or between moralists and hedonists, realists and utopians, intellectual types and emotional types, and so on.

At other times an open clash between polarities may burst within the same individual. This occurs when a person is aware of both sides but falls prey to the illusion that he or she can only embrace one of them. This frequently leads to a feeling of anguish and loss, since something very valuable has been forsaken. The individual may choose to identify with one of the poles, but this act will not really diminish a sense of inner strife and painful duality.

The solution, clearly, is to remain conscious of both poles but identify with neither: we need to achieve a creative tension, a balancing between them. The method we can use is to identify with the self, which is independent of both sides. The freedom of the self allows us to evaluate and rightly appreciate the gifts and the richness of each aspect, skillfully regulating their interplay, and deciding to express this or that side of our being according to the situation.

At some point, however, we may forget the self and fall back into identifying with one of the two poles. Caught in this trap of exclusion, we become once more a fragment, and conflict flares again. Conflict necessarily follows on partisanship and an intolerance with some aspect of ourselves. We then experience anxiety, inconsistency, and a loss of energy. The task now is to return to a state of creative tension based on clear recognition of both sides. To do so, we must realize that a part of ourselves which we may have been rejecting has a powerful contribution to offer to the rest of the personality.

Creative tension between opposites may be compared with a tennis match in which two good players exchange fast, neat, powerful shots. Their opposition enhances the talents and energy of both of them. Naturally, both players must be of approximately the same strength. And no game is possible if one of the two is missing or much weaker than the other. Similarly, in our inner life, a balanced tension between two opposite poles produces a dialectical interchange and mutual enhancement, the outcome of which is our growth.

This happens in part because tension between opposites brings about their rhythmical expression—the rhythm between introversion and extraversion, for instance, work and play, contemplation and action, and so on. In fact, we can observe that all truly integrated personalities exhibit a certain kind of musical quality in their natures: the ability to gracefully and rhythmically dance from one opposite to the other.

Although each pair of opposites is unique, we can formulate a general rule applying to all cases: the *as-well-as outlook*—actively including both at the appropriate moments.

All this does not mean that we can include all attitudes and options at all times. Choosing—with the attendant experience of exclusion and loss—is necessarily a central part of our existential situation. But realizing that so many of what appear to us as absolute dichotomies are actually artificial productions of the mind, that we do not necessarily have to cut off a part of ourselves, that both sides are valuable, can be extraordinarily relieving.

Indeed, as we examine the two poles of a dichotomy ever more carefully, we come to see that the contrast between them lessens. Like the two sides of a gothic arch, they approach each other as they mount, till they converge and fuse into a *synthesis*.

In fact, a synthesis of the opposites is both feasible and desirable. It *is* possible to be loving and strong; to have order and freedom; to be practical and utopian; to be crazy and to be reasonable; to be a dreamer and organized at the same time. And yet these words fall short of what I mean. For the fusion of opposites creates a new psychological reality which is more than the sum of its parts. Because it is new or rarely conceived, there is no word for it—no word for the synthesis of spirituality and sensuality, of work and play, of mind and feeling. And this fact underlines the extent to which our dichotomies are mirrored in the words we use, and how these words, in turn, perpetuate these same cleavages.

A synthesis occurs when a new entity is generated that is more than a mere mixture of the two original elements. Oxygen and hydrogen in combination make only a mixture. But apply a spark to it and you cause an explosion, which synthesizes the two elements into water—something more complex than either but including both. The synthesis of opposite qualities yields analogous results: a release of psychological energy; the appearance of a new quality that includes both opposites; and the realization that neither one of the original poles is truly lost, that we may get back to them if we wish, even though we usually feel no need to do so.

The following symbolic exercise is designed to deal with the specific polarity of work and play, but the same general format can easily be adapted to handle any polarity. The goal is to imagine a synthesis or at least a balanced tension between two opposites which you feel are presently active in yourself. In the process of doing the exercise, you may find yourself taking the side of the one pole and condemning the other. When this happens, gently but firmly put this prejudice aside and substitute a more neutral attitude, for instance, that of a reporter or a scientist interested in all sides of a question. It is also vital to understand that one kind of polarity cannot be brought to a synthesis; the ups and downs caused by such alternations as happiness and depression, or pleasure and pain, are themselves expressions of the cyclical life of our psychophysical organism.

THE SYNTHESIS OF OPPOSITES—I

1. Imagine that you are visiting the Country of Work. Everyone here is efficient and businesslike, and everything reflects this approach. Look at the expressions on people's faces, how they are dressed, the way they walk and talk, and so on. Look at the cars, at the shop windows, the houses. Go in and visit one or two of them.

2. Among the people living in this country you may meet someone you know—even yourself. They are human beings, not caricatures. The main qualities they possess, however, are connected with doing work. For instance, you might find some very efficient people here (look at the mail service, the firemen, etc.). They are achievement-oriented and think in terms of production. Moreover, they are ex-

ceedingly fast and accomplish a great deal. Try to see both the positive qualities and the limitations of these people.

3. Then go to the Country of Play. Everything and everyone is the polar opposite of what you saw before. The people are strolling calmly in the street, smiling, having a good time, to the point where efficiency and productivity are ignored. They are easily distracted, humorous, childlike, and jocular. They don't like serious work. Walk around and study them as you did with the people in the Country of Work. Can you see their desirable and undesirable sides?

4. Now imagine a third country. It is located in a place of outstanding beauty, where the landscape is harmonious, the climate is mild, and the buildings have been carefully integrated into nature. This country has its roots in some ancient, forgotten civilization. Over the centuries, however, the people have steadily developed a culture unknown to us but far more advanced than ours in the knowledge of psychology and its application. They have skillfully studied human beings and learned how to improve the way life is lived. One of the questions they have resolved is how to develop people in whom all variety of inner riches are blended into a single whole, thus creating synthesis where before there was fragmentation and conflict.

The particular achievement of this culture has been a synthesis of the most positive qualities of work and play. As a consequence, the inhabitants act with playfulness and commitment at the same time; they love life, and they also enjoy the work they do. They are efficient and productive but also sensitive to beauty.

5. Once more, meet some of them, talk with them, see how they are dressed, how they eat, how they work, what their way of thinking is. Visit the town, its homes, theaters, churches, museums, factories, offices, restaurants, recreational areas, etc. Write down your experiences.

Rita, a fifty-year-old woman, recognizes a split in herself: "I can see clearly," she says, "two separate worlds within myself, spirituality and sensuality. Perhaps because of my cultural heritage or because of my psychological constitution, the mere thought of experiencing one dimension hopelessly suffocates the other one." On the one hand, Rita feels that she isn't good enough or pure enough for the "spiritual" world. On the other hand, she also feels that she has missed complete sensual and sexual fulfillment.

In order to achieve communication and possibly fusion between these two opposites, I guide her in the three "towns" exercises. We start with the town of sensuality, about which Rita says, "Red appears right away; a fleshy luminosity permeates all houses, streets, sidewalks, and doors. Everything pulsates like living flesh. Naked and slow, people walk in a dense atmosphere. I see a town with no landscape, no sky, no horizon, no nature. Doors open and close thickly and densely. People in this world move all the time, but have no feelings. And I hear no sound at all." Then we pass to the town of spirituality: "It is a town which has the color of air—transparent and light. I feel a sense of joy surging in me as I look at a brook flowing down the mountain."

At this point of the session we could stop. The image is rather pleasant and soothing. But I am not satisfied; I feel that the fleshy, sensual universe is still relegated to the bitter limbo of guilt and regret. I ask Rita to imagine the third town, where the best aspects of both sides are fused. But she does not succeed: "I feel a pressure from the therapist which is respectful but disturbs me with its insistence. Emptiness and darkness are dominant. My limbs are heavy. I am tired and nauseated. I experience two lives in one, and at the same time the despair of one life divided."

I explain to Rita that often the synthesis does not emerge right away, but needs time for the unconscious elaboration to take place. Meanhile, the opposition in the polarity may temporarily be felt as even more intense than before. I ask Rita to work on her own by representing with drawings the interaction between the opposites. She works in this way for some time, but no synthesis seems to be emerging—until one day, about two weeks after our session, an important experience takes place:

I felt my heartbeat become faster and deeper, and I thought it best to stop working. The palpitations increased, I felt a great warmth all over my body, and my head was sweating. Then, suddenly, the image dropped into my mind of a very pure and luminous crystal sphere, which symbolized the joy of spiritual purity. It was made of material which I had never seen, and it was enormous, including the whole universe within itself. Immediately afterwards, I also had the image of a flame, representing sensuality—it was a wonderful flame, fleshy and warm, with many more dimensions than the ones I knew.

Then the flame moved inside the crystal.

My heartbeat slowed down and the sweating stopped as I contemplated this wonder, and I felt an immense joy, *a joy which I never felt before*. It was the relishing of happiness itself. And then I was not afraid of my palpitations anymore, I was not afraid of getting sick. Inside the crystal I could see a thousand other crystals drawn from innumerable places in the universe. It was a crystal which was the synthesis of all crystals, just as the flame was the warmth of all warmths.

After this remarkable occurrence, however, the sense of newness and excitement diminish, gradually giving way to doubt. A counter-reaction to the positive experience begins. While there is some serenity and things are generally better, a vague sense of something "not clicking" stubbornly persists in Rita. She longs for the sensuality she feels she has irreparably lost in the synthesis imagery—which clearly shows that the experience has not been complete. Every time Rita tries to visualize the crystal sphere, she can't help seeing a beautiful, naked woman desperately hanging on to it, as if she felt abandoned or excluded.

At one point Rita even has vivid images of the sphere flying far away from her and being irretrievably lost.

Days pass by and this constellation of feelings fades out, as happens sooner or later with all backlashes. Positive reactions start to emerge: "I am getting much more involved in whatever I do." Rita's sexual life also undergoes a change: "During the past nights I woke up several times, surprised to experience spontaneous orgasms at the end of dreams—something which hadn't happened for a long time." And also: "I can breathe much more easily."

Finally, the period of unconscious elaboration draws to a close and Rita is able to experience the synthesis again, this time in a more lasting way. One evening, when going to bed after turning out the lights, a vivid image flashes in front of her inner eye—the crystal sphere has come back: "The crystal strongly pulsates and then bursts into a million light crystals darting on to infinite spaces, and the fire at the heart of the sphere expands to the point of becoming pure warmth."

The next morning, when opening the window, Rita feels herself "united with the breath of nature" and experiences an intense feeling of *belonging*, which has not left her since. "Now," she writes, "I do not regret anymore a lost intimacy, the warmth of a human presence, loving arms in the darkness of the night. I belong to all this, and I feel intimate with everything." This sense of belonging and of union does not leave anything out. In it have been gathered, transformed, and fused all the elements which caused so much trouble before. We also see here that the synthesis has reached a stable state: Rita's experience, perhaps also because it needed so much time—about three months—to come to maturation, is deeply rooted and is not just a transitory feeling. It has changed her way of seeing the world and relating to others. The split is gone, and so are the concomitant feelings of guilt, loneliness, and frustration. The sense of belonging has become a permanent acquisition. This does not mean that Rita has solved all her problems. But a new dimension has come into existence, with the extraordinary sense of newness and surprise which is the hallmark of all true synthesis.

One more episode in Rita's subsequent life reveals other aspects of our subject. A few months after the events I have described, Rita went on vacation to the mountains. One day she took a walk by herself and at a certain point decided to lie down in the sun. Lying there, receiving the warmth of the sun, Rita slowly became aware that its light, perceived through closed eyelids, reminded her of the fleshy colors of the town of sensuality. Then this diffuse light shaped itself in her inner eye into the image of a magnificent golden phallus. Quickly this image drove out all other thoughts and emotions, towering powerfully in the center of Rita's inner space: "That golden phallus was good and beautiful and vitalizing; it was a source of loving life. It vibrated with infinite energy, and this energy moved freely in all directions: from my soul to my body and from body to soul; from the center to the periphery and from periphery to center."

Rita then saw the golden phallus "flaking off" into countless beautiful designs. When she went home, seized by an unrestrainable need to *create* and following the designs she saw, Rita sketched, during the following days, a great many new patterns for purses, scarves, towels, umbrellas, and other useful objects.

What can we make out of this strange occurrence? First of all, we see that the original synthesis between spirituality and sensuality has become an inner fact for Rita: "This energy could move freely in all directions." Secondly, we see that sexual energy has been sublimated, thus confirming Freud's original observation that sexual energy can be deflected from its original goal and increase a person's "psychological productivity." Finally, we can see here what distinguishes true sublimation from pseudo-sublimation:

Because it is congruent with one's unfolding personal process, true sublimation is not felt as the imposition of an outside form.

Even though it may at times be preceded by dissatisfaction and struggle, it is eventually accompanied by a subjective sense of rightness.

Because it is the result of a synthesis, it is never experienced as a loss or an amputation.

With Rita's encouraging reports in mind, let us end with another exercise for facilitating synthesis. It can be used by itself or as a complement to the first one:

THE SYNTHESIS OF OPPOSITES—II

1. Choose a polarity you want to work on.

2. Take one sheet and make a free drawing on one side representing one of the poles you have chosen. Then make a free drawing on the opposite side representing the other pole. As always in these free-drawing exercises, aesthetic standards are of no concern.

3. The two poles are facing each other. You can feel a kind of interaction going on right now between them. Now, on a new sheet, make a picture of the two poles *and* of their interaction. The interaction, like a dialogue, continues: it may be in the form of a clash, a tentative contact, distant communication or repulsion, or whatever. Keep drawing and let the interaction spontaneously take the shape it wants, making one drawing after the other. The elements may change radically.

Synthesis could be a spontaneous development: the two parts come to fuse into one single entity.

4. If and when a new entity appears, do not leave it at that, but seek to become aware of what it represents and of the inner state in you that produced that image. Then write on the back of the drawing about the whole experience and how the new synthesis could manifest itself in your life.

Chapter 19

NO FEAR TO DIE

The chair on which you are sitting at this moment is traveling through interstellar space at the speed of 18.5 miles per second—together with the planet Earth, of course, and with the whole solar system including the sun. The sun itself is a middle-aged yellow star on the periphery of our galaxy (the Milky Way), one star among the hundred billion others composing it. Astronomers tell us that there are numberless other galaxies like our Milky Way, each of them made up of myriads of stars, most of which are quite likely to have their own planets circling around them. "If only 1/10,000 of 1 percent of those planets harbors a technical civilization—and this seems to be a conservative estimate—the universe must teem with more than 100 trillion civilizations."[1]

All problems change when viewed in the context of such grandeur. If we mentally refer all our difficulties to a wider picture, they tend to lose their dramatic importance. But we usually become hypnotized by everyday events and feelings so that the small becomes big, the transient seems to be permanent, the detail is mistaken for the whole, and whatever is unimportant becomes dreadfully serious.

The realization of cosmic immensity and of the infinity of forms helps to make us more universe-centered and less ego-centered. Reminding ourselves of the grand eternity of time leads to a similar liberation. "Quod hoc ad aeternitatem?" asks a Latin saying—"What is this compared with eternity?" How heavy, indeed, are our preoccupations, irritations, and impatience when measured against eternity! Oriental traditions are rich in images aimed at deconditioning us from our habitual perception of time. One such analogy speaks of an immense mountain, bigger than any other on earth, that stands alone in the middle of a desert. Every ten thousand years a princess descends from the sky, passes by the mountain, and brushes it lightly with her robe, thus imperceptibly wearing away the rock. By the time the whole mountain is worn to nothing, the tale goes on, only one day of eternity will have gone by.

The technique of right proportions, as we call it in psychosynthesis, suggests that we take a look at ourselves, our projects, our problems, our relationships, our successes and failures, in the context of immensity. As we do that, everything takes on a different significance: all attitudes of self-importance and fanaticism disappear to leave space for that sense of liberation and joy which we invariably feel when, instead of the fragment, we perceive the whole.

A friend and colleague of mine who practices psychosynthesis has sessions with people in her office, where they are seated in such a way that they face large, magnificent photographs of stars and galaxies. Nearly always, at the beginning of the session, the people complain of the personal troubles and misfortunes in which they feel themselves immersed. But as the session goes on and work is done, the look in their eyes—my friend tells me—often changes. It is the kind of look people have when they notice something they hadn't noticed before, realize they had been worrying needlessly, or understand a joke. Not that their problems are necessarily solved—but somehow the coexistence of their difficulties with the images of the stars has induced some change in perspective. Often they end up saying that their problems are not so serious after all. Emerson beautifully expressed the value of this perspective:

> Teach me your mood, o patient stars;
> Who climb each night the ancient sky,
> Leaving on space no shade, no scars,
> No trace of age, no fear to die.

And then, if we are lucky, the most elusive of all qualities may show up: humor. True humor—as opposed to slapstick or irony—springs from a deep but amused awareness of the contrast between the immensity and mystery of the universe and the everyday, self-important, and loud hustle and bustle of unregenerated humanity—including ourselves. The gift of humor is the most delightful we can hope for. It makes our foolish defenses crumble, liberates us from the narrow prison of our ego, acts as a lubricant in relationships, and brings a general note of lightness into everything we think and do. It is the spiritual note we can catch in the smile of certain statues of the Buddha. It is, according to Assagioli, a synthesis of joy, wisdom, and compassion.

Assagioli also used to say that we are all endowed with a "capital of seriousness" which we ought to spend on really important matters—but which we squander instead on inconsequential issues deserving a more lighthearted attitude. To cure ourselves of the heavy solemnity with which we sometimes deal with everyday affairs, he recommended meditating on humor and on the contrast between the cosmic and the everyday dimension. He also advised remembering, however, that humor is to be the spice rather than the main course. The moment we give it central importance and try to grasp it, we are sadly and awkwardly left empty-handed.

RIGHT PROPORTIONS

Picture in detail the room in which you are sitting, as well as everything around you. Now, in your imagination, move up and away from the room and form a clear picture of the building that contains it.

See the building getting smaller as you rise higher and higher. From above, the whole area in which you live lies below you: houses, streets, trees, parks, skyscrapers. People and cars are just barely visible in the streets. Think how each person is the center of his own world, with his own thoughts and hopes, his own problems and projects. Watch them all moving around, living their own lives. Imagine them in their homes, too.

Continue your ascent. Your field of view expands, enabling you to see other towns in the area, green fields, mountains, and lakes.

As you rise higher and higher, you can glimpse oceans and other countries as well as banks of clouds.

Now you have the whole planet Earth before you, blue and white, slowly rotating in empty space. From this immense height, you can no longer see people or even guess their existence; but you can think of them, four and a half billion people, each one living on that same planet, breathing the same air. Four and a half billion hearts of people of many different races are beating down there. Think about this for a while, as you continue to visualize the planet Earth.

Now, as you move away from it, you see the Earth becoming smaller and smaller. Other planets enter your field of view: bright Venus, red Mars, massive Jupiter—in fact the whole solar system.

The Earth has now vanished, the sun is but a tiny point of light among innumerable stars, and you have lost all trace of it. Billions of stars are all around you, below, above, on all sides. There is no more "down," no more "up."

All these billions of stars constitute but one galaxy in the universe. It is one among an unknown number of other galaxies reaching out in every direction to infinity.

At this point, think of the infinity of time. Here there is no "tomorrow" and no "yesterday"; no haste, no pressure. Everything is scintillating peace and wonder.

10.   When you feel inclined, open your eyes again and bring back with you this sense of expansion.

A man reports: "When I perform this exercise, I sometimes have a peak experience. At this season of the year there are great expanses of yellow flowers in bloom where I live. My village is not very special—just a few scattered houses, a tower, the valley. But there comes a point in the exercise when I am able to visualize it as a *whole,* made golden by the flowers. No longer is it a village made up of little things, of events, of envy, of grudges. It is this wonderful thing which I can see through the mist and encircled by the flowers. Though this lasts only a brief moment, it leaves an almost painful joy in my chest."

An elementary schoolteacher reports: "I was sitting down in the garden with the children playing. I was looking at them running, playing soccer, or sitting near me. Then the awareness of a greater context came to my mind. I started seeing all these beings moving around. It was as if we were all like cells, parts of a greater organism. And there was this sense of fatality (not impinging on human freedom, however), as when in a microscope you see some microorganisms moving about, and you feel it all to be a part of a much wider design. It brought a great joy, a sense of liberation devoid of emotion. When I recall this state, some of my rigidity and my fear melt away, and I have a more direct contact with others."

Besides evoking a sense of wonder in us and making us a little less pompous, this larger perspective is a reminder of the immensity of the universe: by it we are prompted to reflect that we, our planet, the solar system, those distant stars with their planets orbiting around them and possibly supporting some form of life, and the most distant galaxies receding into invisibility, all are governed by the same laws, made of the same basic stuff, part of the same life. Thus we learn to see, think, and feel on a larger scale, as citizens of the universe.

Chapter 20

SILENCE

For centuries silence has been used as a way to explore the riches of the inner world. A mood of peaceful quiet—from which worries, problems, and ideas of every kind have been banished—creates a most nourishing environment for the appearance of inspiration.

Such a mood has been likened to the steady flame of a candle in still air, or to the sea when it is so calm and clear that one can see the bottom undistorted. We read all of this in books, we sit down and close our eyes in an attempt to create silence within. But we soon find that our ordinary mental activities refuse to take a vacation; the flow of thoughts continues, and the act of turning the attention inward simply makes them more active and insistent. We try to banish or quiet them, but they grow ever more intractable. Finally we become irritated and get up to do something else. Or we sit down, close our eyes, and gradually sink into a light trance, lost to the world and almost oblivious of ourselves. It is a rather pleasant and almost completely blank state. After a while, we return to normal consciousness and pass on to something else, retaining a strange sensation of sleepiness.

Neither of these two conditions is true inner silence, which is, on the contrary, a state of intense and at the same time relaxed alertness, in which we are luminously and quietly present and light. At times insights flow into this receptive space we have created. In a flash we realize, with clarity, truths previously unknown to us. New levels of consciousness are revealed. We open our eyes and carry with us a feeling of being refreshed and nourished, a lasting sense of joy.

The cultivation of silence has an immense therapeutic value. When we succeed in stilling the form-making propensity of our minds, all subjective conflict vanishes, scattering gives way to unity, we save our energy (which we otherwise disperse in countless directions), and we feel healed and purified. Part of this effect occurs because silence gives our organism a chance to harmonize itself spontaneously, without the interfering, harassing influence of the mind with all its problems. In this era of noise and hyperstimulation—of the information explosion and the action-oriented life—soothing, regenerating silence is indeed the ultimate resource. A woman reports:

> I found my inner silence, the silence that emanates from the center of the self. I felt it for the first time as something perceptible and real.
>
> I returned home without excitement, driving along the hills with a sense of calm warmth. My physical weariness had vanished and my mind had cleared up. I felt all shining like a mirror. I had the sense of eternity in space and time.
>
> I felt "washed" and clean, whole and at the same time without boundaries, as if universal life had entered me and my heart were beating in unison with its rhythm. But most of all I knew that this was more than just a state of mind. It was a way of living and being and of relating myself to others.

Real inner silence occurs only after we have first focused our attention on some chosen subject. As a result, our mental life becomes unified around a single image or thought, and, after a while, we can quietly let even this center fade out, as we remain calm and still.

The English mystic, Augustine Baker, has compared the intense activity of the mind and the subsequent inner silence to the soaring of an eagle: "The flight is continued for a good space with great swiftness, but withal with great stillness, quietness, and ease, without any waving of the wings at all, or the least force used in any member, being in as much ease and stillness as if she were reposing in her nest."[1]

Of course our inner silence does not have to be literally complete. Thoughts will keep coming, but we leave them like a river in the distant background, neither trying to stop them nor giving them our interest. And in this silence we listen for something that our mind has never conceived; we listen as if for a whisper which would be inaudible among the loud noises made by the daily striving and wants of our personality. At some point, ordinary mental activity may well fade out completely, as in Dante's description: "And so my mind, bedazzled and amazed, stood fixed in wonder, motionless, intent, and still my wonder kindled as I gazed."[2]

Though many approaches can be used to induce silence, there are two main techniques usually adopted in psychosynthesis:

1. *Receptive meditation*. We have seen in an earlier chapter how reflective meditation culminates in a state of unity of the mind. After a reflective meditation of, say, ten minutes, we can just let go of the subject and, for two or three minutes (no more at first), leave the mind without any support, silent and free. This is *receptive meditation*.

2. *Visualization of the Temple of Silence*. This exercise also evokes silence, allowing it, as Assagioli said, "to sing within us and to vivify us":

THE TEMPLE OF SILENCE

Imagine a hill covered with greenery. A path leads to the top, where you can see the Temple of Silence. Give that temple the shape of your highest consciousness: noble, harmonious, and radiant.

It is a spring morning, sunny and pleasantly warm. Notice how you are dressed. Become conscious of your body ascending the path, and feel the contact of your feet with the ground. Feel the breeze on your cheeks. Look about you at the trees and the bushes, the grass, and the wildflowers as you go up.

You are now approaching the top of the hill. Ageless stillness pervades the atmosphere of the Temple of Silence. No word has even been uttered here. You are close to its big wooden portals: see your hands on them and feel the wood. Before opening the doors, know that when you do so, you will be surrounded by silence.

You enter the temple. You feel the atmosphere of stillness and peace all around you. Now you walk forward into the silence, looking about you as you go. You see a big, luminous dome. Its luminosity not only comes from the rays of the sun, but also seems to spring from within and to be concentrated in an area of radiance just in front of you.

You enter this luminous silence and feel absorbed by it. Beams of beneficent, warm, powerful light are enveloping you. Let this luminous silence pervade you. Feel it flowing through your veins and permeating every cell in your body.

Remain in this luminous silence for two or three minutes, recollected and alert. During this time, *listen* to the silence. Silence is a living quality, not just the mere absence of sounds.

Slowly leave the area of radiance; walk back through the temple and out the portals. Outside, open yourself to the impact of the spring, feel its gentle breeze once more on your cheek, and listen to the singing of the birds.

Agostino is in his fifties and suffers from persistent severe headaches and other pains, with concomitant depression and anxiety. The following report describes a peak moment in his work with me, one in which the technique of silence partially relieved him of his physical tension and pain, also enabling him to bypass the psychological blocks that confined him to a state of despair:

The Temple of Silence has four spires and a big central dome. I open the portals and enter. Everything within is still. All mental conflicts cease, and I feel a deep inner peace.

The center of the temple is illuminated by two beams of brilliant sunlight which pour through two high windows. Then, suddenly, the end wall of the temple becomes a huge mirror. I stand before it in awe, waiting for an image to appear. After a while a sphere of golden light builds up—marvelous and vivid. From it shine innumerable rays of light, covering the entire surface of the mirror. It is a stupendous sight. Then my face becomes visible in the center of the sphere. My expression is smiling and serene. At some point I am no longer in front of the sphere: I am inside it. A voice that springs from my inner being says to me: "You can, if you will to," and I ask what. The voice replies: "You can give—give to the family, to your work, to society. You can give warmth, affection, love." I experience a desire to give and to follow the command of the voice.

We see here how silence aligns us, so to speak, with the energy impulses streaming from the Self, while allowing peripheral distractions (headaches, depression, and so on) to at least temporarily fade away.

This silence and the channel for superconscious energy that it can create may also allow for the flow of significant symbolic images, some of which are clear in their meaning. These images may on other occasions be less easy to interpret, and they may sometimes have strange or even humorous overtones. A young man reports:

During silence, the image of a stethoscope suddenly flashed into my field of inner vision. I thought at first it was one of those nonsensical images that at times come to the surface of the big cauldron of the unconscious. But the image persisted, and it carried a strong charge. I felt it wanted to tell me something. And at last I understood: the stethoscope represented an invitation to listen more to my own heart rather than follow my discursive thinking only—which is my normal, familiar, and safe ground. This advice made a lot of sense to me, and I have been applying it since with good results. It has opened up a dimension which was previously inaccessible.

This account brings us to the most important aspect of the subject of silence: the awakening of the intuition. The transcending of words and conceptual structures creates the delicate magnetic milieu to which intuitions are attracted, there to be brought to flower. Because intuitions are perhaps the most important effect of the cultivation of silence, it is appropriate to say a few words here about their nature and the means by which they can be evoked.

While the mind grasps knowledge in a mediated way (through words, concepts, mental models, memories, and so on) and analytically, intuition seizes truth in a more immediate and global manner. For this to happen, the mind must become at least temporarily silent. As the intuition is activated, the mind gradually is transformed, becoming less an organ of understanding—a function now assumed by the intuition—and more an instrument for verifying, interpreting, formulating, organizing, and communicating knowledge.

At this point we should distinguish two levels of intuition, the ordinary and the superconscious. At the ordinary level, we can have, for example, an intuition about a person. More than just a feeling of empathy or a sudden intellectual understanding, such an intuition may reveal the present life situation of a person, with its many ramifications and implications. We can also have problem-solving intuitions, as when a student sees the solution of a mathematical problem, or in general when one jumps directly to understanding rather than slowly walking to it with the aid of reasoning.

At the superconscious level, the intuition gives access to vistas usually unimaginable by our ordinary personality. Thus we can have a direct intuitive realization of a psychological quality, of a universal law, of the interconnectedness of everything with everything else, of the oneness of all reality, of eternity, and so on. The content of an intuition at this level is normally impersonal. There is often a sense of wonder; talking about the intuitive vision of the scientist, Einstein said: "His religious feeling takes the form of a rapturous amazement at the harmony of natural laws which reveal an intelligence of such superiority that, compared with it, all the systematic thinking and acting of human beings is an utterly insignificant reflection."[3]

We may also, however, have superconscious intuition concerning a person. But in this case it does not relate to the specific mood or the present situation of that person: it reveals, instead, that person's life purpose, or his or her higher possibilities or destiny—something to which the individual's ordinary appearance and lifestyle do not necessarily give any clue.

Intuition perceives *wholes*, while our everyday analytical mind is used to dealing with *parts* and therefore finds the synthesizing grasp of the intuition unfamiliar. But after an intuition does appear, it may even seem to us to have revealed something obvious; we ask, "Why haven't I seen this before?" (Often, as we have seen, this feeling of obviousness is superseded by awe.) One of my students has come up with a clarifying analogy:

> It's similar to scanning a map with the intention of finding the name of a particular place. It is an important place, and you know it just *has* to be on that map. So you look and look for it, but do not find it. You look at all the tiniest names one by one, and then you check again to make sure you didn't miss anything. Then, when you are ready to give up, you realize that the name you were looking for is made out of very large, spaced-out letters, covering almost the whole map. You were expecting to find a much smaller name and weren't open to the larger dimension, although it was under your eyes all the time.
>
> Intuitions for me are the same. They are surprisingly wider than the mental categories I would usually like to capture them with. And they are often obvious in their clarity and reality.

Let us now actually take a look at an example of full-blown superconscious intuition. A young woman reports:

> That morning I left my mother, knowing that she was going to the hospital to have what we thought was going to be a minor operation. Our understanding was that I would come and pick her up at the hospital at the end of the day. I left her happy and seemingly in good health. But when I came to the hospital, I found her unconscious. Her face was covered by an oxygen mask, and tubes ran into her body; it had been a very difficult

operation. Reluctantly the nurse told me that she was wavering between life and death.

Shocked, I felt weak and cried; it just didn't seem real. Slowly the pain sank into me: I wouldn't see my mother healthy any-more. And then, quite suddenly, this awareness changed into the absolute knowledge that—in spite of her suffering—she was fine. It was a certainty that whatever was happening was all right. It was a sense of love, but not of a sentimental kind. I knew that she was in a process and that there was this extraordi-nary impersonal love that was, so to speak, in charge of the matter. It gave me a total release from my anxiety, and I knew then that nothing could ever happen to my mother or myself that could shake that peace.

That this state is not just a compensatory discharge of feelings, but an actual cognitive experience of a fundamental principle, we can best know from this woman's remarkable words:

But the most astonishing thing was that I started seeing every-thing in a completely different way. My mother dying, the leaves falling off the trees, the people of all ages in the street, like some little baby who had just been born or some old man all wrinkled up—I saw it all as a *whole*. I didn't feel, "How sad to get old and to die." I didn't see it that way at all. Instead, there was this incredible, indescribable beauty of the entire cycle of life and death, revolving and showing all its aspects.

I was aware of a wider range. I saw the *rightness* of the whole design, and it was like different pieces of a jigsaw puzzle finally fitting together, while before I could see only the separate parts—and would react to them and judge them individually. Now I asked myself, "How could I ever judge things that way, and think this or that was ugly or bad?" Now everything ap-peared to me in a much larger dimension.

Intuitions are often registered at the level of feelings, without any involvement on the part of the mind. In this case they can trigger a sense of exhilaration, expansion, and peace. Frequently, however, when the feeling dies away the intuition often vanishes, leaving no permanent trace or sig-nificant contribution to growth.

In my work with people I have found time and again that only when intuitions are registered also at the mental level can they be fully assimilated. The right coordination of intuition and mind seems to be the best way in which the riches offered can be correctly interpreted, connected with everyday reality, and clearly communicated. In this way, intuitions of a superconscious sort can become permanent landmarks of our growth, sources of continuing inspiration, luminous points in a living, growing web of insights.

A peculiar effect of intuition, which accounts for its synthetic character, is that it has spontaneous ramification in several dimensions of an individual's life. A single intuition may often throw light on previously unrelated issues, showing the existence of the same pattern in all of them. For example, a man says:

> I had an intuition of the essence of wisdom as the capacity to correctly regulate all attitudes and actions and to find the right point of balance. The intuition in itself was abstract. But soon I found that in its light I could see the same pattern in many different areas of my life: I saw that I was giving myself away without any proper measure. It was happening in the financial area, where, perhaps for fear of being judged stingy, I just spend money without any plan or criterion. I saw it in my relationships with women, where I jump blindly into all kinds of affairs, without any thought of the consequences. I saw it in my business relationships, where I usually am just too kind and yield too easily, giving away my time and professional know-how to people who do not really need it. It was a general pattern taking many shapes—an unconsciously fearful pseudo-kindness which I could only get rid of by substituting for it the firmness that comes with wisdom.

While intuition appears in people to a greater or lesser degree, a lot can be done to awaken and stimulate it. The practice of silence is, of course, basic, quieting all the inner activities, thoughts, feelings, images, memories, etc., that may be screening out the spontaneous flow of intuition. But there are other measures we may also adopt:

1.   A first rule in cultivating any aspect of our being, as we have repeatedly seen, is to give it attention. We can increase our intuitive capacity if we will acknowledge the possibility of our receiving intuitions, recognize their value, cherish them when they come, and, finally, learn to *trust* them—when carefully interpreted—rather than relying exclusively on logical reasoning and material evidence.

2. The use of symbols also helps to awaken the intuition. Symbols are, so to speak, the alphabet of the intuition.

3. Finally, keeping an intuition workbook can be a great help. In it one freely records all insights, hunches, brilliant ideas, intimations, and so on. Intuitions often tend to come in clusters, rather than separately, and the act of writing down the first one facilitates the arrival of others connected with it. Moreover, the most original ideas do not appear full-blown, but, on the contrary, make themselves known little by little, first as vague perceptions, then in clearer outline. Later they form themselves into patterns and finally stand revealed in their full meaning. So, by recording intuitions at their outset we firmly anchor the beginning of this process of gradual revelation and give it a firm basis for unfolding.

There is, however, one higher goal—higher even than the flowering of intuition—to which the cultivation of silence can bring us. While it is rarely reached, it is of such importance that no discussion of silence can be complete without it. I refer to illumination. While intuition can be thought of as giving us a glimpse of the world in which the Self lives, illumination can best be conceived as the complete view of that world. In fact, illumination is the act of reaching the Self and contacting it fully. As we said, true illumination is a rare phenomenon. The cultivation of silence is, however, one of the well-established routes for attaining it. Assagioli, after studying the accounts of a number of illuminations, described their essence in terms of the following points:

> An inner perception of light which in certain cases is so intense as to be described as a dazzling glory and an impression of fire. It is from these characteristics that the term "illumination" has arisen, the term by which superconscious states are often designated. In many cases this illumination extends to the external world, which is perceived as transfigured and bathed in an ineffable light.
>
> A sense of release from ordinary self-consciousness and self-centeredness and an enormous expansion and elevation of conscious awareness.
>
> A sense of oneness with the whole. This inner realization has the paradoxical character that, while it is associated with the previously mentioned sense of loss or of oblivion of one's personality, there is at the same time a sense of fuller, wider, and more real life.

An impression of beauty, both of an inner formless beauty and a revelation of a hitherto unperceived beauty of the external world, even in its most common and ordinary aspects.

Feelings of joy, of peace, of love, mingled in various proportions.

A loss of the sense of time; a rising above the "flux of becoming," above past, present, and future. The realization of the Eternal Now and of the essential permanence, indestructibility, and immortality of one's own spiritual Self, of the Center of one's being.

An unshakable certainty and inner assurance of the reality of this inner experience.

An urge to express—to communicate to others—the illumination, to share this precious treasure, and a sense of compassionate love for those still wandering and suffering in darkness and illusion.[4]

EPILOGUE

I would like to end this book in a practical way, with a simple exercise that clarifies the sense of our experiments in the light of a wider context:

HUMANKIND'S POTENTIAL

1. Take a few moments of silence.

2. Now, with the help of the imagination, think about the suffering of humanity: think about the pain, the confusion, the rage, the anxiety, the loneliness, the frustration, the depression, the ignorance, the desperation of billions of people of all ages and countries—including yourself.

3. Now, instead, direct your attention to the immense resources of humanity which are still latent: intelligence, love, the desire to improve, the need for justice, the yearning for peace, the drive towards the unknown, the sense of wonder, and artistic creativity. We can consider these potentialities analogous to the enormous energy imprisoned at the core of the atom.

   Imaginatively, feel their power and beauty. Think about how these potentialities, if released, could generate an immense joy, countless beneficial effects. Imagine these resources as being present in billions of people, yourself included.

4. If you work on yourself, you are already participating in the extraordinary, ageless work of overcoming darkness and pain, and of

the evocation of latent potential. Take some time to realize that this work is not only your own private project, but the part of a wider unfoldment in which countless individuals are participating in many ways: the evolution of humankind.

REFERENCES

INTRODUCTION
1. Roberto Assagioli, "Modi e ritmi della formazione psicologica," in *L'Economia Uumana*, 7, 6, p. 2.
2. Martin Buber, *I and Thou*.
3. Christopher Lasch, "The Narcissist Society," *New York Review of Books*, 23, 15.

CHAPTER 1
1. Quoted in: Roberto Assagioli, "Concentrazione," May 17, 1934.
2. Francis Galton, *Inquiries Into Human Faculty* (London: J.M. Dent & Sons, 1883.)

CHAPTER 2
1. Charles Baudouin, *La Mobilisation de L'Énergie* (Paris: Éditions de l'Institut Pelman, 1931), p. 37.

CHAPTER 3
1. Robert Assagioli, *Psychosynthesis, a Manual of Principles and Techniques* (New York: Hobbs, Doorman & Company, 1965), pp. 17–18.
2. Carl Gustav Jung, *The Practice of Psychotherapy* (London: Routledge & Kegan Paul, 1966), p. 169.

CHAPTER 4
1. Fernando Pessoa, *Una Sola Moltitudine* (Milano: Adelphi, 1980), p. 27.
2. Roberto Assagioli, course given at the Accademia Tiberina, 1967, p. 2.
3. Robert Desoille, *Rêve Éveillé Dirigé* (Genève: Éditions du Mont-Blanc, 1961), p. 31.

CHAPTER 5
1. Rabindranath Tagore, *Fireflies* (New York: Collier, 1975), p. 99.
2. Plotinus, *Enneads*, 1, 6.

CHAPTER 6
1. This description of the evolution of the will follows the article "Neurophysiologie de la liberté," by Jacqueline Renaud, *Science et Vie,* n. 711, Dec. 1976, p. 18.
2. Elmer and Alyce Green, *Beyond Biofeedback* (San Francisco: Delacorte Press, 1977), p. 58.
3. *Time Magazine,* "Karajan: a new life," Nov. 29, 1976.

CHAPTER 7
1. Roberto Assagioli, *Per L'Armonia Della Vita — La Psicosintesi* (Firenze: Instituto di Psicosintesi, 1966), p. 152.
2. M, *The Gospel Of Ramakrishna* (New York: The Vedanta Society, 1947), p. 41.
3. Leopold Infeld, *Quest: The Evolution of a Scientist* (London, 1942), p. 208.
4. Ralph Waldo Emerson, *Journals,* 1841.
5. Quoted in: Howard Hibbard, *Michelangelo* (New York: Penguin Books, 1978), p. 282.
6. Quoted in: Howard Hibbard, *Michelangelo* (New York: Penguin Books, 1978), p. 282.
7. H.C. Robbins, *Beethoven* (London: Thames & Hudson, 1974), p. 163.
8. Ibid., p. 179.
9. Data mentioned in: Luciano Curino, "Ci stiamo abituando alla violenza," *La Stampa,* Torino, June 13, 1978, p. 3.
10. Data mentioned in: "News & Comment," *Human Nature,* August 1978, p. 15, quoting the report "World Military and Social Expenditures, 1977," prepared by the Rockefeller Foundation.
11. Data mentioned in: *Time Magazine,* April 13, 1981, p. 34.

CHAPTER 8
1. Herman Keyserling, *From Suffering to Fulfillment* (London: Selwyn & Blount, 1938), pp. 106 – 7.

CHAPTER 9
1. Marcus Aurelius, *Meditations* (Middlesex: Penguin Books, 1964), V, 16.
2. See the excellent discussion of this topic in: J.A.C. Brown, *Techniques of Persuasion* (Middlesex: Penguin Books, 1963).
3. Stephen Spender, "The Making of a Poem," reprinted in B. Ghiselin (ed.), *The Creative Process: A Symposium* (University of California Press, 1952), p. 113.
4. Quoted in: Evelyn Underhill, *Mysticism* (New York: Dutton, 1961), p. 316.
5. Ernest Dimnet, *The Art of Thinking* (New York: Fawcett, 1961), p. 316.

CHAPTER 10

1. Marcus Aurelius, *Meditations* (Middlesex: Penguin Books, 1969), II, 16.
2. Paul Reps (ed.), *Zen Flesh: Zen Bones* (New York: Doubleday Anchor, 1961), p. 32.

CHAPTER 11

1. Carl Gustav Jung, *Simboli della transformazione* (Torino: Boringhieri, 1970), p. 222.

CHAPTER 12

1. Richard Maurice Bucke, *Cosmic Consciousness* (New York: Dutton, 1969), p. 53.
2. Pierre Teilhard de Chardin, *Le Phénomène Humain* (Paris: Éditions du Seuil, 1955), p. 257.
3. Abraham H. Maslow, *The Farther Reaches of Human Nature* (New York: Viking, 1971).
4. Mircea Eliade, *Myth of the Eternal Return* (Princeton, New Jersey, Bollingen Series 46, Princeton University Press, 1954).
5. William James, *The Varieties of Religious Experience* (New York: New American Library, 1958), p. 292.
6. Jorge Luis Borges, *A Personal Anthology* (London: Jonathan Cape, 1968), p. 147.
7. Fritjof Capra, *The Tao of Physics* (London: Wildwood House, 1975), p. 313.
8. Milton, *Paradise Lost,* 12, pp. 617–18.
9. Dante Alighieri, *Divina Commedia,* "Paradiso," 27, 7, trans. John Ciardi.
10. *Bhagavad Gita,* 4, p. 11. Translation by S. Radhakrishnan (New York: Harper Torchbooks, 1973).
11. Heidegger, *Was Ist Metaphysik?,* fifth edition, 1949, p. 28.

CHAPTER 13

1. Quoted in: Maria Shrady, *Moments of Insight* (New York: Harper & Row, 1972).

CHAPTER 14

1. Notes of Dorothy Sayers in her translation of the *Divine Comedy,* "Hell" (Middlesex: Penguin Books, 1972), p. 217.

CHAPTER 15

1. Pico della Mirandola, *On the Dignity of Man.*
2. Jean-Paul Sartre, *The Psychology of Imagination* (New York: Washington Square Press, 1966), p. 159.
3. Ibid., p. 183.

232 WHAT WE MAY BE

CHAPTER 16

1. Andreas Angyal, *Foundations for a Science of Personality* (New York: Viking Compass, 1969), p. 172.
2. Dante Alighieri, *Divina Commedia,* "Paradiso," 33, 145.
3. Abraham H. Maslow, *Toward a Psychology of Being* (Princeton: Van Nostrand, 1962), p. 42.
4. A. R. Orage, *On Love* (London: Janus Press, 1966), p. 8.
5. Pierre Teilhard de Chardin, *On Love* (New York: Harper & Row, 1973), p. 59.
6. Roberto Assagioli, "Gli animali pensanti e calcolatori," in *Vita,* 4, 2, p. 5.

CHAPTER 17

1. Iamblicus, *The Life of Pythagoras.*
2. Antony V. Trowbridge, "A Psychobiological Basis for Aesthetic Perception," *Man-Environment Systems,* 7, 1977, pp. 85–94.
3. From a letter written by Bettina von Arnim to Goethe, describing a conversation with Beethoven, in: Marion M. Scott, *Beethoven* (London: Dent & Sons, 1974), p. 125.
4. Ibid.
5. Quoted in: George Duby, *The Europe of the Cathedrals* (Geneva: Skira, 1966), p. 17.
6. John Keats, letter to George and Georgiana Keats, 16 Dec. 1818.
7. Quoted in: Judith Wechsler (ed.), *On Aesthetics in Science* (Cambridge: MIT Press, 1978), p. 1.
8. Henri Poincaré, "Mathematical Creation," reprinted in: P. E. Vernon, *Creativity* (Middlesex: Penguin Books, 1970), p. 86.
9. Roberto Assagioli, personal communication, taped, Florence, 1970.
10. Plotinus, *Enneads,* 1, 6.
11. Constantin Stanislawski, *An Actor Prepares* (New York: Theatre Art Books, 1977), p. 87.
12. Quoted in: Kenneth Clark, *Leonardo Da Vinci* (Harmonsworth: Penguin Books, 1959), p. 82.
13. Immanuel Kant, *On the Sentiment of the Beautiful and of the Sublime.*

CHAPTER 18

1. Mircea Eliade, *The Two and the One* (New York: Harper Torchbooks, 1965).
2. Roberto Assagioli, *Per L'Armonia della vita —La psicosintesi* (Firenze: Instituto di Psicosintesi, 1966), p. 129.
3. Ibid., p. 130.

CHAPTER 19

1. Life Science Library, *Planets* (New York: Time/Life Books, 1966), p. 184.

CHAPTER 20

1. Augustine Baker, *Holy Wisdom*, Treatise 3, Par. 3, Chap. 7.
2. Dante Alighieri, *Divina Commedia*, "Paradiso," 33, pp. 97–99, translation by Dorothy Sayers.
3. Albert Einstein, *Ideas and Opinions* (London: Crown, 1954), p. 40.
4. Roberto Assagioli, "Immortalità; può essere provata?", unpublished article.

APPENDIX A

ADDITIONAL EXERCISES

The Potential in Subpersonalities*

Purpose: To integrate a subpersonality and encourage its evolution (see Chapter 4).

Pick a subpersonality on which you have already been working and with which you feel familiar. Then visualize it clearly and in detail.

Imagine that you are with this subpersonality in a marvelous garden full of plants and flowers. Look at the flowers, all of which are arranged in exquisite patterns. Sense their perfumes. Feel the vivifying freshness of the air. Hear the sounds of the birds.

Experience yourself and your subpersonality, and see how it looks now: it may have changed, or it may be just as before. In any case, give it space and time to absorb the atmosphere of the garden and be vivified by it.

Now you come to the center of the garden. In it you find a rose plant with a closed bud. Both you and your subpersonality watch this bud as it opens very slowly. First the sepals start to spread out and the bud itself is revealed. Then the bud starts to unfold and swell, and you can see the petals opening until the rose has fully blossomed.

Both you and your subpersonality sense the fragrance emanating from the very core of this rose. Let yourselves be pervaded by it.

*Devised by Dr. Massimo Rosselli.

Then look at your subpersonality. How does it appear now? And what is now the relationship between the two of you?

You can repeat this exercise with more than one subpersonality at a time.

Crisis and Meaning*

Purpose: To make sense out of crises (see Chapter 10).

1. Think of three crises you have encountered in the course of your life up to now. Then make a free drawing for each one of them, expressing the feelings you experienced during that crisis, the disintegration that occurred, the essence of what happened to you. Draw freely and without trying to make your drawing beautiful.

2. Now take the drawings representing the three crises and lay them in front of you according to a time sequence.

3. Look at your drawings, and see if you can sense a continuity among them. We can regard a crisis as the transition between one phase of our unfoldment and another. And as we review it in retrospect, we may be able to envisage in it a new trait trying to emerge, a new vital impulse thrusting its way into existence, a new part of ourselves being born. This possibility is enhanced by considering three crises rather than only one. Crisis means that the existing order is collapsing, and a new order, possibly more evolved, is taking its place. But the period between the two involves temporary disintegration and pain.

4. Also become aware of your own style of facing each of the three crises. Did you try to postpone or ignore them? Did you intensify the pain involved by hanging onto old patterns? Did you face them courageously? Did you deal with each crisis in a different way?

You can repeat this exercise, substituting three peak experiences for the three crises and trying to trace your unfoldment through them.

Contemplating Art

Purpose: To increase our appreciation of beauty (see Chapter 17).

1. Pick a reproduction of one of your favorite paintings. Become aware of your reaction as you first look at it.

2. Then contemplate this reproduction for a while, taking in the

*Devised by Diana Becchetti-Whitmore.

details. Observe the colors, the organization of space, the rendering of light and shade, the expressions on the people represented (if any).

3. Then look again at the whole picture, without analyzing the details, and let it sink into you, so to speak, by receptively opening yourself to it.

4. Keeping your eyes closed, stay with your inner representation of this painting. It may at times be fuzzy, disappear, or change; no matter, as long as you succeed in capturing the general atmosphere it conveys. As you open yourself totally to the beauty and meaning of the picture, become receptive to its message: it may be a silent, non-verbal message, or it may be communicated in words. In any case, it is a statement about life and the universe.

5. Now become aware of what part of you is evoked or stimulated by this painting. Letting the visualization subside, try to get a sense, even if vague, of the part of yourself which resonates with the painting. Let this part come to the foreground, bloom fully, reveal itself in all its intensity. Do not try to push this process, however. Just give it the opportunity to occur and the space it needs.

The same exercise can be adapted to other forms of art—e.g., sculpture and architecture—as well as music. (In the case of music, you first receptively listen to a passage, *then* become conscious of its message and the part of you it has evoked.)

Full Meditation Outline

Purpose: To explore the superconscious. This meditation should be used only after having practiced with the other exercises in this book, especially those in Chapters 9 and 20. In this example the quality of love has been chosen, but other psychological qualities may also be adopted.

1. **Preparation:**

   Bodily relaxation. Close your eyes. Sitting on a chair with your spine comfortably erect, relax your body for a minute or two, breathing deeply as you do so.

   Emotional calm. Let your feelings come to a point of rest, and open to the inflow of calm and serenity.

   Mental silence. Let your thoughts slow down, and seek to induce a state of relative mental stillness.

   Self-identification. Become aware of your center, or "I."

Elevation. Let your "I" return toward its source, the Self. You may help yourself with your imagination in doing this. Imagine being identified with the Self—radiant, unobstructed, timeless.

2. **Reflective meditation:**

Think about love. Reflect on all its positive, nourishing, constructive *aspects:* those you have experienced in yourself, those you have seen or heard about in other people, those you have never heard of but can conceive.

Think about the forms in which you may *distort* love in your life at present. Consider the *obstacles* and veils which may hamper your expression of love: judgment, fear of ridicule, stiffness, and so on.

Think about the *value,* the need, and the benefits of love.

Receptive meditation:

Become aware of the essence of love—its spirit, so to speak. Open yourself to its influence, to the inflow of love energy, to intuitions and flashes of the imagination.

3. **Expression**

Become aware of your own body and its contact with the chair; conscious of your physical environment, with its nearby and distant sounds; and so on. Realize that you now have the possibility of expressing and communicating to others the inner riches you have contacted.

Then open your eyes.

Inevitable Grace

Purpose: To enhance our appreciation of beauty (see Chapter 17).

1. You are in a valley near a mountain. It is a fine spring morning, with a few clouds enveloping the top of the mountain. Take a few moments to become aware of your surroundings: the vegetation, the clean air, the sounds of nature, the ground beneath your feet.

2. Now start to climb. You know that at the top of this mountain you will find the Mansion of Beauty—an extraordinary palace, inside which it will be possible for you to perceive with complete clarity your own and other people's inner beauty.

3. As you climb toward the top, you walk through fields of flowers and pass by limpid mountain lakes. At some point during the course of your ascent you enter a cloud. You keep climbing, but at a slower pace. Objects now assume elusive and mysterious shapes, as if in an

enchanted kingdom. There is an atmosphere of uncertainty, of bewilderment, perhaps, of suspense. You climb on.

4. Now the fog disperses, and as you arrive at the plateau on the top, you can suddenly see in front of you, in a clean and resplendent atmosphere, the Mansion of Beauty. Architecture, Goethe wrote, is "petrified music"; and such is the impression made upon you by this building, for the magnificence and harmony of its proportions suggest the grandeur of a symphony.

5. After contemplating this mansion for a while, you enter it and become aware of its interior. But even more striking than the visible structures is the atmosphere here, an atmosphere that enables you, as if by magic, to bypass any veil which may separate you from your own inner beauty:

The veil of skepticism
The veil of tiredness
The veil of fear
The veil of expectation
The veil of trying hard

As these veils effortlessly dissolve, you perceive directly whatever in you is unequivocally, timelessly beautiful—what Wordsworth called "inevitable grace."

As you linger in this mansion, you become conscious of this same insight extending to the perception of inner beauty in other people—both close ones and those with whom you may have some personal difficulty.

Think of them; imagine yourself to be able to perceive, even if vaguely, even if for a moment, their inner beauty. They may have their own veils or masks as well, but you can easily see through them.

The Temple of Silence in a Busy Town

In my mind's eye a Temple, like a cloud
Slowly surmounting some invidious hill,
Rose out of darkness: the bright Work stood still;
And might of its own beauty have been proud . . .

—William Wordsworth

Purpose: To realize the inner silence of the Self (see Chapters 5 and 20).

Imagine that you are in a busy town.

Realize vividly the abundance of stimuli bombarding you as you walk down the street.

You see the people and the cars and the signs; you hear the noise of the traffic and the voices; you notice the shop windows, with their varieties of merchandise. You see a newsstand teeming with pictures and titles. You see a florist displaying flowers of all kinds. You may even see people you know amidst the crowd, but they are intent on their own affairs and so pass by without noticing you. You may even see yourself.

Then, approaching the very center of this busy town, you come across a building different from the rest. It is the Temple of Silence. In the very midst of the noise and the activity, you have found an island of perfect stillness: inside the temple the silence is so complete and so real that it is almost tangible.

As soon as you enter the temple, you are immediately out of the hustle and bustle and immersed in an atmosphere of timeless quiet. The silence that greets and pervades you like a wordless caress easily and effortlessly penetrates the most hidden recesses of your being. You feel this silence soothing you, reaching deeply into the very structures of your mind, liberating you of the hold it may have on you, so that you feel free and all is still.

You remain in the silence for a while.

You listen to the silence.

You become the silence.

After a while, you decide to leave the temple and go back to the busy world outside. Finding yourself once again immersed in the traffic and the crowd, you notice how your general feeling is different from before you entered the temple.

APPENDIX B

PSYCHOSYNTHESIS CENTERS AND INSTITUTES IN THE WORLD

Various psychosynthesis centers and institutes are at present in the process of being born. Also, several individuals in various countries are doing psychosynthesis work independently of any institute or center. The following list of available psychosynthesis sources is therefore incomplete and indicates only those centers and institutes which have been in existence for some time.

Asociación Argentina de Psicosintesis
Juncal 2061 10B
Buenos Aires
ARGENTINA

Berkshire Institute of Psychosynthesis
Box 152
Monterey, MA 01245
U.S.A.

Boston Center of Psychosynthesis
Suite 400
93 Union Street
Newton Centre, MA 02159
U.S.A.

Istituto di Psicosintesi
Via San Domenico 16
50133 Firenze
ITALY

Instituto Español de Psicosintesis
Hospital Neuropsiquietrico
de la Virgen
Carretera de Andalucia
Granada
SPAIN

Instituto Mexicano de Psicosintesis, A.C.
Alfonso Reyes No 147 Depto 4
Colonia Condesa
Codigo Postal 06 140
Mexico 11, D F
MEXICO

Centre de Psychosynthèse Enr./
Psychosynthesis Center Reg.
5840 McShane
Montréal, Québec H3S 2G3
CANADA

Centre Français de
Psychosynthèse
61 Rue de la Verrerie
75004 Paris
FRANCE

Greek Center for
Psychosynthesis
Evrou 4
Athens 611
GREECE

Hill Center for
Psychosynthesis in Education
Walpole, NH 03608
U.S.A.

Kentucky Center for
Psychosynthesis
1226 Lakewood Drive
Lexington, KY 40502
U.S.A.

Institute of Psychosynthesis
Highwood Park
Nan Clark's Lane
Mill Hill, London NW7
ENGLAND

Psychosynthesis and
Education Trust
50 Guildford Road
London SW8 2BU
England

Psychosynthesis Associates
3010 Santa Monica Blvd., # 306
Santa Monica, CA 90404
U.S.A.

Psychosynthesis Center/
Highpoint Northwest
23700 Edmonds Way
Edmonds, WA 98020
U.S.A.

Psychosynthesis Institute
3352 Sacramento St.
San Francisco, CA 94117
U.S.A.

Psychosynthesis Training
Center of High Point
Foundation
647 No. Madison Ave.
Pasadena, CA 91101
U.S.A.

Stichting Psychosynthese
Nederland
Onstein 65
1052 KK Amsterdam
HOLLAND

Vermont Center for
Psychosynthesis
62 East Avenue
Burlington, VT 05401
U.S.A.

APPENDIX C

PSYCHOSYNTHESIS BIBLIOGRAPHY

BOOKS

Assagioli, Roberto, *Psychosynthesis: A Manual of Principles and Techniques*, Turnstone Press.
Assagioli, Roberto, *The Act of Will*, Turnstone Press.

BOOKLETS
(Available at psychosynthesis centers and institutes)

Alberti, Alberto, *The Will in Psychotherapy*.
Assagioli, Roberto, *Jung and Psychosynthesis*.
Assagioli, Roberto, *Life as a Game and Stage Performance (Role Playing) Cheerfulness (A Psychosynthetic Technique)*.
Assagioli, Roberto, *Meditation*.
Assagioli, Roberto, *Psychosomatic Medicine & Bio-Psychosynthesis*.
Assagioli, Roberto, *Psychosynthesis: Individual and Social*.
Assagioli, Roberto, *Symbols of Transpersonal Experience*.
Assagioli, Roberto, *The Balancing & Synthesis of the Opposites*.
Assagioli, Roberto, *The Conflict Between the Generations and Psychosynthesis of the Human Ages*.
Assagioli, Roberto, *The Education of Gifted and Super-Gifted Children*.
Assagioli, Roberto, *The Resolution of Conflicts & Spiritual Conflicts and Crises*.
Assagioli, Roberto, *The Technique of Evocative Words*.
Assagioli, Roberto, *Transpersonal Inspiration and Psychological Mountain-Climbing*.
Cirinei, Gabriello, *Psychosynthesis: A Way to Inner Freedom*.

244 WHAT WE MAY BE

Crampton, Martha, *Psychological Energy Transformation: Developing Positive Polarisation*.

Crampton, Martha, *Psychosynthesis: Some Fundamental Aspects of Theory and Practice*.

Crampton, Martha, *The Use of Mental Imagery in Psychosynthesis*.

Crampton, Martha, *Toward a Psychosynthetic Approach to the Group*.

Gerard, Robert, *Psychosynthesis: A Psychotherapy for the Whole Man*.

Haronian, Frank, *The Ethical Relevance of a Psychotherapeutic Technique*.

Haronian, Frank, *The Repression of the Sublime*.

Parks, John, *Biopsychosynthesis*.

Taylor, Graham, and Martha Crampton, *Approaches to the Self—The "Who Am I" Technique in Psychotherapy*.

Taylor, Graham, *The Essentials of Psychosynthesis*.

Vargui, James, *Global Education and Psychosynthesis*.

Several articles on psychosynthesis are also included in the journal *Synthesis* (830 Woodside Road, Redwood City, CA 94061, U.S.A.).

INDEX

Exercises are set in **bold** type

Ideal Forms, 165
Ideal models, 163–171
  and life-patterns, 164, 165
Ideal Model, The 166–167
Identification, with symbols, 118–
    119. *See also* Dis-identification;
    Self-identification
Illumination, 225–226
Imagery
  effects of, 166
  of ideal models, 165–173
  and self-exploration, 40–41
  and transformation of
    subpersonalities, 55
Images
  identification with, 119
  inner, 165
  symbolic, 118–128
Imagination, 31, 169
Inadequacy, sense of, 159
Inevitable Grace, 238–240
Inner Beauty, 193–194
Inner Dialogue, 144–146
Inner dialogue, technique of, 143–
    153
Insight, and free drawing, 39
Integration of subpersonalities, 53–
    58
Intuition, 118, 221–225

James, William, 135
Jung, Carl G., 44, 118, 149

Kafka, Franz, 146
Karajan, Herbert von, 77
Keats, John, 190
Keyserling, Herman, 30, 101, 137
Kinesthetic Evocation, 33
Krishna, 141

Letter to the Self, 148–149
Leverrier, Urbain Jean Joseph, 36
Life-patterns, 163–164, 167–173
Lighthouse, The, 119–120
Love, 175–186
  from the center, 177–178
  conscious, 179–180

levels of, 181–182
from the periphery, 180–181
realization of, 183–184
and service, 184

Maharishi, Ramana, 138
Maslow, Abraham, 132, 181
Meditation. *See also* Reflective
    meditation; Silence, inner
  receptive, 219
  reflective, 103–111, 238
Meditations (Aurelius), 114
Mental development, 108–111
Michelangelo, 92
Miller, Stuart, 160
Music, 188
Mystics, 136
Mythology, 128

Narcissism, 24
Narcissus and Goldmund (Hesse), 202
Nightingale, Florence, 91

Observation, attitude of
  and psychic distance, 65, 67
  and self-identification, 63–67
Olfactory Evocation, 32
Orage, A. R., 181–182
Overstimulation by superconscious
    energy, 159–160
Ovid, 160

Patanjali, 109
Pattern and Growth in Personality
    (Allport), 105
Patterns of behavior
  life-, 163–164, 167–173
  perpetuation of, 35–36
Pauli, Wolfgang, 149
Perseveration, 105
Personality
  and events, 137
  existence in time, 134
  and expanded awareness, 138–139,
    155–160
  integration of, 162
  reorganization of, 141

resistance to change, 155, 158
and the Self, 133–142
Personal Self. *See* Self: personal
Perspective, viewing events in, 213–216
Pessimism, defensive, 157
Pessoa, Fernando, 47
Physicists, contemporary, 136
Plato, 42, 188, 196
Poincaré, Jules Henri, 190
Potential in Subpersonalities, The, 235–236
Projection, 157
Psyche
diagram of, 44
transmutation of, 138–142
Psychic distance, 65, 67n
Psychic energy, 96, 101
Psychological function, Star diagram of, 45
Psychological mountain climbing, 152–153
Psychosomatic illness, 85–86
Psychosynthesis. *See also* Assagioli, Roberto
development of, 22
personal vs. transpersonal, 161–162
risks of, 160
techniques, (*see names of specific exercises*)
Purpose
of life, 163–164, 167–173
and the Will, 79–81
Purpose, 82–83
Pythagoras, 188

Raja yoga, 109
Ramakrishna, 89
Ram Dass, 162
Reactive attitude, 115
Realization of Love, The 183–184
Receptive meditation, 219
Recognizing Subpersonalities, 48–49
Reconstruction: The Villa, 126–127
Reflective meditation, 103–111, 135.

See also Silence, inner defined, 104, 109
and experience of timelessness, 134
and mental development, 109–111
as mental training, 109
transformative effects of, 105–107
Reflective Meditation, 104–105, 238
Relationships, 177–178
Relationships, 178–179
Repression, 156
Republic (Plato), 188
Resistance to change, 156
Reviewing the Will, 74
Review on Aggression, 86–87
Right Proportions, 215–216
Right proportions, technique of, 214
Rose, The 132–133
Roselli, M., 83n
Routinization, 157, 158
Russell, Bertrand, 152

St. Augustine, 196
Sartre, Jean-Paul, 139, 169
Sayers, Dorothy, 156
Self. *See also* Transpersonal Self
awareness of, 60
as best therapist, 144
communication with (*see* Inner Dialogue)
defined, 61, 67, 133
dis-identification of, 63, 64
evolution from personality, 139–142
formlessness of, 135
and illumination, 225
and love, 179–180
personal, 45–46, 69, 139
vs. personality, 134–141
in psychosynthesis, 61
surrender of, 138
and symbolic life, 137
timelessness of, 134
transcending, 189
as unifying center, 61, 134
and Will, 78
Self-actualization, 110–111

About the Author

Piero Ferrucci is a former student and collaborator of Roberto Assagioli. He is a staff member of the Psychosynthesis Institute of Florence, Italy and a member of the board of the Italian Society for Therapeutic Psychosynthesis. Dr. Ferrucci works with individuals and with groups, and has been teaching psychosynthesis in several European countries and the United States.

He edited *The Human Situation,* a book of Aldous Huxley's lectures, and is author of *Inevitable Grace.*

Recommended Reading . . .

PSYCHOSYNTHESIS

A MANUAL OF PRINCIPLES AND TECHNIQUES

Roberto Assagioli, M.D.

Explains a comprehensive psychology of man that predicates the notion of a self at the core of each individual that can direct the development of all personality aspects. More than a theory, it is also a practical, working method that includes many approaches to personal growth: meditation, encounter groups, inner-imagery, and others. *Contents include:* Self-realization and psychological disturbances; Technique for the training and use of imagination; Introduction to spiritual psychosynthesis; Exercise for evoking serenity; Music as a cause of disease and as a healing agent; Meditative techniques in psychotherapy.

THE ACT OF WILL

A GUIDE TO SELF-ACTUALIZATION AND SELF-REALIZATION

Roberto Assagioli, M.D.

This major work brings human will back to the centre of psychology, education and everyday life. Intensely and carefully, Roberto Assagioli traces the rise and discrediting of an older conception of human will: a 'will power' that was authoritarian, harsh and repressive. In its place he elaborates a comprehensive notion of a will which is not merely 'strong' but, more important, 'skillful'. *Contents include:* The Qualities of the Will; Practical Applications of the Skillful Will; Purpose; Evaluation, Motivation; Affirmation; Planning and Programming; The Joyous Will; Self-Identification Exercise.

Dr Assagioli goes beyond philosophizing to detail a practical understanding of will, including the means by which it may be trained and realized. Not neglecting the mere strength of will, he proposes exercises for increasing the will's basic power, and he also shows how the will can learn the skill to act with a minimum of effort and yet be effective. Exercises are given that the reader can practise at home, and these amount to a full programme for developing one's will.

The rewards of such exercises are personal harmony, right human relations and an attunement with the evolution of man and the cosmos.

THE JOY OF LEARNING

A GUIDE TO PSYCHOSYNTHESIS IN EDUCATION

Diana Whitmore

This is a practical manual for parents and teachers to enable them to address important psychological elements in children and young people that are often neglected in education. It is a complement to education, not an alternative.

The book examines the psychological and spiritual development of the young and the difficulties they may encounter along the way. It provides exercises and games for use in the classroom or at home to foster this development and to eliminate the blocks to it.

Diana Whitmore stresses the importance of a holistic, balanced process of learning and growing through the use of faculties such as the will, the intuition, feelings, imagination, creativity, and spontaneity. It addresses such issues as interpersonal relationships, emerging sexuality, communication skills, assertion, rebellion, the contradictions of adolescence, self-discipline, and young people's responses to contemporary social issues.

She also examines the role of the educator and the unconscious effects that his or her attitudes and actions may have upon the young. It shows some of the pitfalls to avoid, but also what opportunities exist for those teachers and parents who want to explore the true depth of education.

HOW TO MEDITATE

A GUIDE TO SELF-DISCOVERY

Lawrence LeShan

How to Meditate is a practical guide to meditation by a distinguished parapsychologist. Dr LeShan explains simply and clearly why we meditate, how to meditate, and what meditation does psychologically and physiologically .

Drawing on the meditational practices of Zen, Sufism, Yoga, and Jewish and Christian mysticism, Dr LeShan describes specific exercises and programmes, structured and unstructured, ranging from breath-counting and simple mantras to group movement and sensory awareness. He also explores such intriguing fields as the role of meditation in psychotherapy and the relation of meditation to the paranormal.

Through the use of meditation, LeShan shows it is possible to achieve a focusing of energies and increased concentration and confidence that can lead to efficiency in everyday life, and eventually to a higher inner peace.

THE RIGHT TO BE HUMAN

A BIOGRAPHY OF ABRAHAM MASLOW

Edward Hoffman

Abraham Maslow (1908-1970), one of the founders of humanistic psychology, stands as a great visionary of modern psychology and related social thought.

More than any other psychologist in the last half-century, Maslow has powerfully affected the way we think about ourselves. He advanced an entirely original concept of human nature—the hierarchy of inborn needs—that turn psychology on its heels. In contrast to classical approaches that studied human weakness and neurosis, Maslow focused on healthy, exceptional, high-achieving individuals. He systematically explore what he described as 'peak-experiences' and originated many concepts related to the 'self-actualized' individual that helped launch the fields of humanistic and transpersonal psychology.

The Right to be Human traces Maslow's career from his early work with primates and his study of Native American culture to his pioneering years at Brandeis and his participation in the development of the human-potential movement at the Esalen Institute and elsewhere in California. Maslow always stood at the cultural hot spots in his field, and his story is also the story of an important era in psychology.